THE SPIRITUALITY OF FRIEDRICH VON HÜGEL

Baron Friedrich von Hügel, 1903

Joseph P. Whelan, S.J.

THE SPIRITUALITY OF FRIEDRICH VON HÜGEL

With a Foreword by

Bishop B. C. Butler

COLLINS

St James's Place, London, 1971

William Collins Sons & Co. Ltd
London · Glasgow · Sydney · Auckland
Toronto · Johannesburg

De licentia Superiorum Ordinis

First published 1971

ISBN 0 00 215770 5
Set in Monotype Bembo
Made and Printed in Great Britain by
C. Tinling & Co. Ltd, London and Prescot

For my Father and my Mother

CONTENTS

FOREWORD

Theologians have assigned a dual role to the intellect in its service of religion. One is to reflect upon the given content of religion and of revelation, to seek to understand this content, and so to make our religious practice intelligent and efficient. The other is, to recommend religion and revelation to the inquiring mind and thus facilitate the act of faith. The former role was the motive-force of St Thomas Aquinas's *Summa Theologica*, the latter that of his *Summa contra Gentiles*. An interesting question arises: which of these tasks should take chronological precedence? In the ordinary manuals of theology, the task of 'proving' the truth of the Christian/Catholic claim has usually been put first. Abbot Chapman, however, argued not unreasonably that this is preposterous, since until the mind has understood what religion teaches it is absurd to ask it to decide whether what it teaches is true.

In the pages that follow Father Whelan has chosen to study von Hügel in his role of spiritual teacher. What has this role to do with that of theology? It has, in my view, everything to do with theology as an attempt to understand religion. For what is religion, considered in its vast historical extension before and after Christ, within and without the ambit of the Christian tradition? Fundamentally, according to Bernard Lonergan, it is conversion; and conversion is 'a change in one's apprehensions and one's values', accompanied by a 'change in oneself, in one's relations to other persons, and in one's relations to God'. He adds: 'Though conversion is intensely personal, utterly intimate, still it is not so private as to be solitary. It can happen to many and they can form a community to sustain one another in their self-transformation, and to help one another in working out the implications, and in fulfilling the promise of their new life. Finally, what can become communal can become historical. It can pass from generation to generation. It can spread from one cultural milieu to another. It can adapt to changing circumstances, confront new situations, survive into a different age, flourish in another period or epoch. When conversion is viewed as an ongoing process, at once personal, communal and historical, it coincides with living religion. For religion is conversion in its preparation, in its occurrence, in its development, in its consequents, and also alas in its incompleteness, its failures, its breakdown, its disintegration' ('Theology in its New Context', in *Theology of Renewal*, ed. L. K. Shook, Palm Publishers, Montreal, 1968, Vol. 1, pp. 44 f.). And since theology is reflection on religion, 'it follows that theology will be reflection on conversion' (ibid.).

Now when you have realized what Lonergan means by 'conversion in its preparation, in its occurrence, in its development, in its consequents . . .', you will see that he means just what Father Whelan means by 'spirituality'. There is no suggestion here of a body-and-soul dualism, of an indifference of religion and theology to the 'merely' natural or secular. On the contrary, religion means an orientation of the whole man, founded in his ultimate human depths, towards that Absolute which Christians call God. And it was thus that von Hügel understood religion.

Yet few Christian thinkers have emphasized so impressively as von Hügel that Christianity makes no totalitarian claim to absorb and dissolve the linked orders of created reality and natural values in a dreary, ultimately thin, uniformity of ecclesiastical dogmatism or personal piety. On the contrary, as Father Whelan makes abundantly clear, von Hügel anticipated the second Vatican Council in its respect for the autonomy of these created and natural orders, and he went further by arguing that religion, for its own health, needed the tensions thus set up between itself and its created and developing milieu. One of the most original elements in his spiritual teaching is his insistence on the 'purgative' service performed by genuine science for the religious spirit itself.

Von Hügel's name is historically linked with the Modernist Movement which was the object of a resounding condemnation by Pope St Pius X. It is therefore important to assure the reader, from the start, of the massive orthodoxy of his teaching as here set forth by Father Whelan. (One might have some reserves on the question of the imminence of the Parousia in the teaching of Jesus. The difficulties may to some extent be met by a fuller realization that the linguistic and conceptual scope of the Aramaic language and Jewish culture in Palestine in Our Lord's time limited the possibility of an exact exposition of his teaching to his own contemporaries.)

Has von Hügel's 'spirituality' any apologetic value? When, as a young Anglican somewhat shaken by my excursions into philosophy, I sought advice from Anglican sources, I was directed to the writings of von Hügel by Abbot Prideaux of Nashdom and Mr (later Professor) N. P. Williams of Exeter College. I turned to *Essays and Addresses* (First Series) and *The Mystical Element of Religion*. I can never be sufficiently grateful for the advice received and its fruits. I was quickly struck by von Hügel's vast erudition and his utter honesty. His writings helped me to remain a convinced and open-minded Christian. I hope it would not have been too much of a disappointment to my counsellors to know that their advice had also helped to prepare the way for my conversion to the Catholic Church. The fact is, of course, that Christianity, properly understood, is its own best recommendation.

There are those who see points of resemblance between our Christian experiences at the present day and the movement at the beginning of this century which was summed up under the name Modernism. The great difference between the two situations is that today, unlike that earlier period, the Church has herself officially initiated the great work of theological and spiritual renewal. The immediate result has not been altogether happy. There has been a sort of theological explosion, a centrifugal emphasis upon a vast diversity of uncoordinated topics. And this explosion has been reflected at the popular level in a lot of controversy, polemics and taking of scandal. It is a relief to turn from the contemporary scene to von Hügel who made indeed no claim to offer a scientific synthesis or system, but who was concerned to offer a presentation of Christian spirituality in its total richness and full interior tension. Despite his foreign name and partially foreign descent, he was very English in his empiricism, his docility to the facts, and his preference for fact as compared with theory. In the end, I think the reader will feel not only that von Hügel is leading him out into a world of fresh air and limitless horizons, but that his wholeness of vision enables him to be, perhaps without fully meaning it, a great apologist.

Bishop B. C. Butler

PREFACE

This is not a biographical study, though experience – both the vicarious and especially the radically personal experience of Friedrich von Hügel – is what we look to unpack here. Neither is our concern formally with the immense world of von Hügel's learning, though once again we shall not come to any useful terms with our subject – nor does von Hügel – otherwise than by that rigorous reflection on experience and that invitation to experience which is thought. In lieu of such an excursus into biography or general intellectual history, this study places a single question: What is Friedrich von Hügel's judgment as to the nature and adventure of sanctity – and of *great* sanctity too – for a fully Christian, yet also fully worldly modern man? What judgment do we get on the central issues of spirituality from this man of many parts – a married layman at once deeply read and deeply practised in classical piety, yet utterly and enthusiastically at home in the science and philosophy of his day (1852–1925)?

In the light of both published and unpublished materials, this study seeks to formulate an answer to this question. The ground traversed includes von Hügel's understanding of Christ, of God, and of ecclesial community, as these three organic realities both encounter and get appropriated by man in history through the institutional, the intellectual, and the mystical elements of religion. Our inquiry also seeks von Hügel's understanding of the other, properly non-religious activities of human life. What emerges is a view of Christian spirituality as *the production of personality through a pervasive incarnationalism that is at once profoundly theocentric in character and deeply affirmative of secularity.*

There may be a value in reflecting briefly today on such a stance as this. For it may be that our theology and our social concerns too have recently been somewhat fashion-centred, i.e. moment-canonizing if not actually promiscuous, as they move from secularity to mysticism, from death-of-God to hope, etc. Von Hügel, as will perhaps be noted in this study, is a passionate champion of liberty, a formidable critic and, within his range, a vigorous, creative reformer on the cutting edge of love as well. But he is nonetheless an inveterate enemy of the pendulum-swing and a man of rarely great impatience with the reformation of abuse through the destruction of a use. Perhaps he may do our time a service in that invitation to integrity and fidelity which underlies and governs his entire spirituality – an invitation to human life that asks for that larger whole and that fuller task which is the 'civilizing of spirituality and . . . the spiritualizing of civilization'. Our discussions about spirituality in the last decade or more have asked urgently, valuably and in detail about man – about his body, his community and his world. That discussion, I think – and largely even in the contemporary form of its questions – can profitably dialogue with Friedrich von Hügel, though in this book he shall be left to speak for himself.

Whatever further interest this present study may have perhaps especially involves: the extent to which it organizes von Hügel's considerable literary achievement precisely as a spirituality; the effort it makes to describe and locate this spirituality – and much of its detail – as a Christologically structured theocentrism; and the emphasis it places on von Hügel's striking insight into the autonomy of secularity in face of religion, and the both humanizing and sanctifying agency of this secularity within the larger whole of Christian spiritual life.

J.P.W.
All Saints' Day, 1970

CHAPTER ONE

INTRODUCING FRIEDRICH VON HÜGEL

IN this study of the spirituality of Friedrich von Hügel as found in his writings, we shall have to do with a man of many parts: who achieved an international reputation among his contemporaries in biblical exegesis, in theology, philosophy, mysticism, and in spiritual direction; who was a serious if amateur geologist; and who played – and endured – a leading role in the 'modernist' movement and crisis during the first decade of this century.

Witnesses abound to the man and the mark he made. Charles Gore, Anglican Bishop of Oxford, called von Hügel 'the most learned man living'.[1] And while he is not to be compared with Loisy and Lagrange as an exegete, he was almost their only fellow among Catholics of the time in his knowledge of biblical Hebrew and Greek and of Protestant biblical criticism.[2] William Temple said of his greatest book, *The Mystical Element of Religion*:[3] 'It is quite arguable that this is the most important theological work written in the English language during the last half-century.' The encyclopedia editor, Hastings, thought his second major work, *Eternal Life*,[4] to be 'the most thorough investigation of the subject that has ever been made',[5] while Sabatier called him the 'lay bishop' of the 'modernist' movement.[6] Finally and most importantly, there is the emphatic testimony from a vast number of his most famous contemporaries – and from humble ones too – Catholic and especially non-Catholic, 'modernist' and orthodox, about the man himself: of the depth and loyalty of his Roman Catholicism, of his splendid charity and gigantic sanctity. Evelyn Underhill wrote: 'He is the most wonderful personality I have ever known – so saintly, so truthful, sane and tolerant.' 'Under God, I owe him my whole spiritual life, and there would have been more of it than there is, if I had been more courageous and stern with myself, and followed his directions more thoroughly.' Later, she cherishes 'the memory of an immense spiritual transcendence . . . , an Alpine quality . . . , the awe and passion which were felt when the Baron uttered the name of his God . . . '[7] Following his death, Alfred Loisy wrote: 'Everyone who knew him will cherish the memory of his goodness, his loyalty, and his sanctity.'[8] And Abbot Cuthbert Butler remembered long walks on Hampstead Heath: 'And we always returned home by the little Catholic Church in Holly Place – it was his daily practice – and went in for a long visit to the Blessed Sacrament; and there I would watch him sitting, the great deep eyes on the Tabernacle, the whole being wrapt in an absorption of prayer, devotion, contemplation. Those who have not seen him so know only half the man.'[9] Finally, from a host of others, Söderblom, the Lutheran Archbishop of Uppsala: 'My first thought and act, when I understood that the Baron Friedrich von Hügel had finished his days on this earth, was to praise the Almighty on my knees, because he has given to our age that lover of mankind, that penetrator into the very mysteries of the human heart and religion, that universal teacher and that blessed saint.'[10]

All these subjects, especially the man himself, his philosophy of religion, and his role in the 'modernist' crisis, are extensive and difficult matters. None of them is the direct concern of this study. And it is important to notice this at the beginning, lest our deliberate decision here almost entirely to transmit areas so crucial to a complete understanding of von Hügel should seem to dismiss those areas as insignificant to him, or as irrelevant to our own contemporary concerns. Other writers have dealt and will deal with these other subjects. The sheer size of the man and of the material demands this division of von Hügel's problem and achievement. This study, then, confines itself to his writings, and it considers those writings under the specific rubric of spiritual doctrine, of spirituality.[11] We will, however, in the remainder of this chapter give a résumé of von Hügel's life, make a brief remark on 'modernism', and conclude with a sketch of von Hügel's quality of mind and breadth of spiritual concern.

Friedrich von Hügel, son and grandson of barons of the Holy Roman Empire, was born in Florence in 1852 and died in London in 1925.[12] His father was Austrian Minister to Tuscany until 1859 and to Brussels until 1867 when the family took up permanent residence in England. His mother, a convert from Presbyterianism, was the daughter of the Scottish general Francis Farquharson. Von Hügel had no formal schooling, but was tutored by a Lutheran pastor, by the Catholic historian Baron von Reumont, the Quaker geologist William Pengelly and the professors of Hebrew, Spira and Gustave Bickell. In later life he turned again to geology, 'my first love'.[13]

Typhus at the age of seventeen initiated the deafness which afflicted him with increasing severity throughout his life, exacerbating a generally neurasthenic constitution. The correspondence constantly refers to brain fatigue and to the resulting insomnia of many 'white nights'.[14] The deafness never finally prevented conversation, apparently, but it often made discussion difficult, and his public appearances did eventually become largely monologues. 'But what monologues! They seemed to have divined beforehand . . . *your* special need of the moment . . . , the talker seemed to exist for the sake of the listener . . .'[15] In 1873 von Hügel married Lady Mary Herbert, a convert from Anglicanism who was the daughter of a Gladstone cabinet minister and sister of the Earl of Pembroke. Three daughters were born of the marriage.

Von Hügel's central preoccupation with spirituality gives his large erudition a strongly pastoral direction and character. The massive study of Greek and scholastic philosophy, of Kant,

Hegel, Feuerbach, and his own contemporaries, seems always subordinate to early and wide reading in the Fathers, the German and Spanish mystics, and especially in French school spirituality: Bossuet, Fénelon, Grou. He speaks of fifty years' close acquaintance with Augustine's *Confessions* and of almost daily reading of the Gospels and the *Imitation of Christ*.[16] Early adult life involved a Dominican confessor and an annual retreat with the Jesuits.[17] But perhaps the watershed experience in an already intense spiritual life occurred in 1884 when von Hügel placed himself under the direction of a Parisian diocesan priest, the Abbé Huvelin, otherwise famous as confessor of Charles de Foucauld. Years later in a remark on his own prayer life, we get from von Hügel a fifty-five-year record of both fidelity and fact that is also a statement of broadening principle:

> After practising a daily three-point meditation for some twenty-five years,[18] the new helper sent me by God [Huvelin] advised me that my prayer should now be mainly informal – more of the prayer of quiet type; but that there should always remain short vocal prayers morning and night, Mass and Holy Communion twice a week [long before Pius X's famous encouragement of frequent Communion], with Confession once a week or once a fortnight; and (perhaps most characteristic point of all) one decade of the rosary every day – this especially to help prevent my interior life from losing touch with the devotion of the people.[19] After over thirty years of this mixed *régime*, I am profoundly convinced of the penetrating sagacity of this advice.[20]

Von Hügel thought Huvelin 'the greatest manifestation . . . of sheer holiness' he ever came personally to know. 'I owe more to this Frenchman than to any man I have ever known in the flesh.' '*There* sanctity stood before me in the flesh, and this as the genuine deepest effect and reason of the Catholic Church; I could now utilize the sufferings [the testing of both his integrity and his humility, as well as of his loyalty both to

Church and to friends] of these hurricane years [the 'modernist' crisis] towards growing a little less unlike this mediator of Church and Christ and God.'[21] As well as a spiritual genius, Huvelin was apparently a brilliant, very liberal – and very orthodox – theologian. In 1904, as the winds were rising quickly (five of Loisy's books were already on the Index), but before the storm had broken, Huvelin prayed for von Hügel:

> I think of you often, my deeply respected and dearly loved friend, and I pray for you from the bottom of my heart. May Our Lord enable you to do all the good that you desire to do. May he enable you to unite the holy liberty of the children of God with a childlike spirit towards the Church, and to combine a love of truth with a love of charity – two things which are indissolubly joined and which the Holy Spirit never separates.[22]

Von Hügel's concern with the Church's spiritual life channels and expresses itself in two major interests throughout his life: science (especially biblical studies) and philosophy of religion. These subjects combine with psychology, history, and a major excursion into scientific biography and textual criticism, to form von Hügel's primarily theological masterpiece: *The Mystical Element of Religion as Studied in Saint Catherine of Genoa and Her Friends.*[23] His other writings – even one imaginative work on nationalism and the morality of war – and his correspondence too, deal with these same subjects, with an almost constant stress on their implications for spiritual life.

Wide reading,[24] a vast correspondence, extensive travel, membership of one ecumenical study group, the Synthetic Society, and foundation of another, the London Society for the Study of Religion,[25] and a command of at least eight languages, brought von Hügel's tremendous capacity for learning and friendship into scholarly and often intimate personal contact with such contemporaries as Newman,[26] Tyrrell, Inge, Temple,

John Baillie, Duchesne, Laberthonnière, Blondel, Bremond, Loisy, Rudolf Eucken, Troeltsch, Heiler, Söderblom, etc., besides many Roman authorities such as Leo XIII, Merry del Val, Rampolla and the then Eugenio Pacelli (Pius XII).[27] There is the record too, however, of the education of his daughters, much like More's education of Margaret Roper, of catechism lessons to children and the spiritual direction of teenagers.[28] Söderblom once wrote to him: 'The secret is the sincere kind-heartedness which your person gives out, the personal interest for man as man, whether he is pope or cabman, English or German, professor or Sister of Charity.'[29]

While escaping censure, von Hügel played a leading role, perhaps more as catalyst than as seminal thinker or innovator, in the 'modernist' movement. We will speak of this again directly below. We may remark here, however, that his writings consistently, increasingly, and finally even polemically, show a marked insistence on two essential positions whose violation he, von Hügel himself, came to regard as 'modernism' in the heretical sense: in exegesis he argues the necessity of sheer historical 'happenedness' as basis of Catholic creed and dogma; and in philosophy and theology he grounds all possibility of religion in the 'fact' of God as ontologically absolute, distinct, prevenient Personal Spirit, and this independent of and prior to each man's, and all humanity's, experience of this fact. Our study will come back to find both these premises of perennial Catholicism as premises too of von Hügel's spirituality.

In later years von Hügel increased his dedication to spiritual direction, notably in the assistance he gave to the great Anglican writer on mysticism, Evelyn Underhill, and to his own married niece, Gwendolen Plunket Greene.[30] Von Hügel's academic work was acknowledged in 1914 and again in 1920 when St Andrews University and Oxford conferred on him the LL.D. and D.D. respectively. Edinburgh awarded him the Gifford Lectureship for 1924–26, which failing health compelled him to resign. All three honours publicly marked the massive ecumenical labours and the profound friendship and respect achieved by von Hügel among his British contemporaries, both religious and agnostic.[31] At the same time, both his own formal writings and correspondence, and the witness of the obituary notices[32] give compelling evidence of a strikingly childlike faith and simplicity, of a humility deeply involved in, and grateful to, the daily piety and devotions of simply average and traditional Roman Catholicism, as well as of an insatiably curious and adventurous mind and broad sympathy – an impulsive excitement about the latest book,[33] while probing further the Gospels' truths – vigorously bent, we shall see, on a dialogue with Darwin as well as with Augustine, with Feuerbach and Marx as well as with Plotinus, Catherine of Genoa, and John of the Cross.

As we have said, 'modernism' as a movement does not figure directly in this study of von Hügel's spiritual doctrine. Nevertheless, in order better to locate this study with regard to this large question, it may be useful to repeat here one point we have already mentioned and to make two others.

First – and here we repeat ourselves – the 'modernist' question *is* important for a complete understanding both of von Hügel as a man and of the Church of his time.[34] And indeed, much of the excitement of his spirituality arises precisely from the circumstance that the more than 800, wholly *non*-modernist pages of *The Mystical Element of Religion* are written during 1898 to 1908, the very years of the crisis and of von Hügel's major participation in its questions and affairs. The interest of this present study, therefore, remains closely if indirectly bound to this circumstance. For the facts of the matter, when viewed at large, cannot fail to pose a question hopefully of some contemporary interest: what is von Hügel's judgment as to the nature of sanctity, and of *great* sanctity too, for the fully Christian, yet also (and thereby?) fully human and worldly modern man? What judgment do we have on this from a married layman at once deeply read and deeply practised in classical piety, yet utterly and enthusiastically at home in the science and philosophy of his day; from an anti-clericalist but wholly committed churchman, who feared terribly yet frequently risked the (then powerful) censures of a Catholic Church whose evil often angered and affronted his integrity and yet which, without regret or hesitation, he loved, and loved to obey, as the special place and the chosen time – as the indefectibly holy sacrament – of God in Christ, offered to him, von Hügel, in the company of his brothers?

Secondly, von Hügel himself gives two meanings to the term 'modernism' (we have just glanced at the first, pejorative meaning he assigns it[35]), and the whole labour of his life and writings is to be 'modernist' in its second sense. Here, 'modernism' is not a movement but an attitude and style:

> A permanent, never quite finished, always sooner or later, more or less, rebeginning set of attempts to express the old faith and its permanent truths and helps – to interpret it according to what appears the best and the most abiding elements in the philosophy and the scholarship and science of the later and latest times. Such work never ceases for long, and to it I . . . try to contribute my little share . . . [36]

Thirdly, and importantly for this study, the majority of von Hügel's commentators, while stressing his deep and certain involvement in the 'modernist' crisis, consider this involvement to be, finally, episodic to von Hügel's life and peripheral to his spirituality. His involvement, both as thinker and especially as middleman and clearinghouse, is clear. And von Hügel knew this. In 1899 he hails George Tyrrell, a brilliant religious thinker and writer, and a loved friend, as 'one of those self-spending children of the dawn and of Christ's ampler day'[37] – and then rightly accepts his very real degree of responsibility for this man's difficult and tragic later history when, following

Tyrrell's early death in 1909, he writes: 'I cannot let him bear all the blame, where I did so much to stimulate his thought and knowledge.'[38] Maude Petre, a contemporary and friend of both men as well as of Loisy, and the biographer of Tyrrell, charges von Hügel with being a saint but not a martyr. She finds in his diplomacy, weakness, and in his appeal to complexity and the need for compromise, a hint of cowardice.[39] But others have thought differently. A. A. Cock, who also knew him personally, makes the judgment that 'modernism' is not fundamental to von Hügel's thought. Maurice Nédoncelle, perhaps von Hügel's best commentator, corroborates this view. And Michael de la Bedoyère, von Hügel's biographer, in direct disagreement with Miss Petre, argues that it was both 'his own deepest spiritual life' *and* 'the very studies' he shared with Tyrrell and with Loisy – and not 'diplomatic skill' or 'caution' or 'cowardice' – that led von Hügel through the 'terrible years' and their climax.[40] The Protestant Sabatier gives us an awesome picture of von Hügel at the famous 'meeting of the modernists' in the Tyrol in August 1907, midway between *Lamentabili* in July and *Pascendi* in September. Von Hügel had been silent almost throughout, but his speech at the end reminded his listeners of Paul's farewell to the Church at Ephesus. He asked for the grace of suffering and of charity, for himself and for his fellows, while staunchly defending the responsible liberty of the individual and of scholarship – and then concluded: 'In such matters it is only the whole life, faith and soul which has the right to speak. Let us pray and make ourselves ready.'[41]

Certainly von Hügel fought with all his strength against selfishness in himself and against feelings of enmity towards others. He disliked polemic and asked rather for a Catholicism of pre-Tridentine spirit, that would not be a 'negation of negations'. He loved the simple affirmation that characterized Francis of Assisi and had little heart for the splendid retorts of the yet saintly Robert Bellarmine.[42] And God was the reason why. In 1900 he tells Henri Bremond:

> It is this spirit, this constant consciousness that God and the poor best that I can offer him are not *one* thing, but *two;* that, even if and when I am objectively in the right, or at least more right than my antagonist, this opponent may be very dear to God, and blessed by him in this his opposition; it is in the conviction as to how much of touching goodness can coexist with and indeed inform density of vision and objectively unjust suspicion: it is all this that I want to cultivate without a break and without conditions.[43]

We may conclude our remarks on 'modernism' with von Hügel's own statement to Maurice Blondel on the occasion of the publication of *The Mystical Element of Religion* in 1908. René Marlé takes the statement as witness to 'those spiritual concerns which were always of still greater moment to him than the interest he took in discussion of a directly intellectual kind':

> I am strongly aware of being occupied here with questions that are far different from those which occupy the forefront of the Abbé Loisy's attention or indeed, I think, the attention of Edouard Le Roy. It was in no way whatever my intention to isolate myself these past few years from these friends of mine who are suffering so much for convictions which simply cannot be nothing but so many errors;[44] and yet I have also been much occupied with, and have come to love much, many problems which deal with matters of spiritual importance for my own soul and its religious life for thirty years now – long before I had even heard of these scholarly friends of mine, or indeed of the Abbé Laberthonnière, or of you.[45]

Many of von Hügel's best readers attest this primacy of spirituality that Marlé and von Hügel himself have just suggested. Nédoncelle believes that 'his love of God was the deepest thing in his life, and spiritual growth the aim of all his teaching. His actions were permeated by his prayer.' Douglas

Steere argues that the 'service of spiritual counseling was the central axis that . . . set the frame for his intellectual contribution'.[46] Von Hügel gives multiple witness of this predilection. He asks prayers for his own 'modest place in the great army of those who work and suffer for their own and their fellow-men's deepened spiritual life – for the deepening of this spiritual life, and the growth of its application to men's public and corporate acts'. He publicly proclaims in *The Times Literary Supplement:*

> More and more to live the spiritual life, increasingly to penetrate into the living realities it reveals, and to express my discoveries, indefinitely deepened, extended, tested, and standing by those of others, as faithfully and fearlessly as I can: this alone I can strive to do.[47]

Again and again von Hügel will stress the role of the moral will and the place of spirituality, not just as result of or contribution to, but as very *condition* of good parents, good scientists, or deeply useful philosophers of religion. And so he writes 'especially' for those who *combine* 'practice' with 'analysis' and inquiry. For reality occurs and is known principally through loving action, through what a man *is*, through personality.[48] 'Creatureliness' and 'the crying aloud after God' must impel and accompany the mind's legitimate search for him and for the world. For,

> we indeed get to know realities, in proportion as we become worthy to know them – in proportion as we become less self-occupied, less self-centred, more outward-moving, less obstinate and insistent, more gladly lost in the crowd, more rich in giving all we have, and especially all we are, our very selves.[49]

In his classic book, *Das Gebet*, von Hügel's friend, the historian-psychologist Friedrich Heiler, strongly insists that 'rational philosophical thought destroys the essential presuppositions of a simple prayer'.[50] Now prayer is the central act, surely, of von Hügel's religion, of his mysticism and his spirituality. According to Heiler's position, a man must either thoroughly compartmentalize his life, or else decide wholly to be *either* a religious man *or* a modern man. Von Hügel's spirituality, whatever its worth, is a massive refusal of this dilemma. Indeed, he views his own specific vocation as the attempt to relate mysticism both to history and to modern science, and especially, to locate the place and 'precise function' of the exact and human sciences and their activities 'within the full and spiritual life . . . ' 'More than ever the spiritual life appears now as supremely worth the having, and yet it seems to raise, or to find, the most formidable difficulties or even deadlocks.' Von Hügel hopes that his writings spring 'from the exigencies of that life itself', and that they will 'stimulate such life, its practice, love and study . . . ' He does not seek to convert, but rather to help all men 'to make the most of what they have' and, for Catholics,

> to do all I can to make the old Church as inhabitable *intellectually* as ever I can – not because the intellect is the most important thing in religion – it is not; but because the old Church already possesses in full the knowledge and the aids to *spirituality*, whilst, for various reasons which would fill a volume, it is much less strong as regards the needs, rights and duties of the mental life.[51]

We shall see, however, that the aim and effort here is not proof or demonstration, but an *exploration of commitment* in the company of 'believers' or of those who 'desire to be so' – an exploration 'of religion as constituting a realm of facts and experiences'.[52] In this one sense, as Huvelin recognized at once, von Hügel is very dogmatic, and not liberal at all.[53] Philosophy and sociology may possibly structure, but they may not dictate or limit, and they do not provide, the *facts* of faith, the simply *given* and *there* of religious experience.

> Philosophies that leave no room for prayer, adoration, sin, forgiveness, redemption, may be excellent in many other directions, and also as criticisms and stimulants of religious thought; but, as would-be adequate theories of religion, they cannot fail more or less to misconceive and to explain away *facts* of inexhaustible vitality.[54]

The position is surely the classic one: *fidens quaerens intellectum*, where faith and mystery as delivered to the Church's corporate religious experience across the ages are the point of departure for, as well as the goal of, a life and process which philosophy and anthropology serve to occasion, purify, deepen and assist.[55]

Von Hügel abhors abstraction. We shall find him veritably snooping about for the concrete, for the facts of religious and secular experience. He will attempt a good description based on observation. Only then begins the never-concluded attempt to formulate, account for and relate what experience has known and loved.[56] Von Hügel's faith convictions, therefore, do not obviate the need for arduous research and analysis. His approach to the real is radically inductive. Religion is a series of facts, *given* indeed, not constructed; but given historically; and it is an experience had, and held, and deepened, only with effort and sacrifice. It is a gift of God, but in its *received* quality, i.e. as man's fragile possession, it must be ceaselessly corrected, tested, corroborated and explored – and prayed for.[57]

In connection with this preliminary description of von Hügel's spiritual writings as essentially the probing of facts delivered in and through experience, it may be useful to recall the judgment of one of his most prestigious, non-Catholic contemporaries, Professor A. E. Taylor. It is a judgment which recognizes both the generous, ecumenical character *and* the radically non-individualist, non-subjectivist quality – the tradition and community roots – of von Hügel's yet deeply personal achievement as a theologian. Taylor finds an

> independence of 'private judgment', in the bad sense of the

> term . . . One is sure that in studying religion, with him as a guide, one is dealing not with what one individual with the peculiarities of individual temperament has found an adequate faith, but with something which has proved sufficient for the needs of countless myriads of all shades of intellectual and moral difference. . . . Writing with full conviction that his own confession presents a richer and fuller type of spiritual life than others, he is constantly on the search for the element of truth, the apprehension of a universal verity, in all the beliefs by which men have found it possible to face life and death.[58]

But if von Hügel will reject Heiler's implied demand for a choice between the modern world and the central acts of spirituality, if he will insist on the rational quality of all experience, and of mystery too, we shall also find in him a consistent and firm refusal of all Cartesian 'clarity', and a deep distrust of 'system'. T. S. Eliot in 1928 praises von Hügel for his 'emotional unity' and his fundamentally non-modernist 'sensibility'. But then Eliot continues: 'His feelings were exact, but his ideas were often vague . . . The present age seems to me much more an age of black and white, without shadows.'[59]

Hundreds of passages in von Hügel's writings, I suppose, stand witness against any such view of life and of theology. At least twice he describes his own mind as 'mystical and positive' rather than as 'scholastic and theoretical'. It

> would see all truth as a centre of intense light losing itself gradually in utter darkness; this centre would gradually extend, but the borders would ever remain fringes, they could never become clear-cut lines. Such a mind, when weary of border-work, would sink back upon its centre, its home of peace and light, and thence it would gain fresh conviction and courage to again face the twilight and the dark. Force it to commit itself absolutely to any border distinction, or force it to shift its home or to restrain its roamings,

> and you have done your best to endanger its faith and to ruin its happiness.[60]

'Life', for von Hügel, 'is not clear, but vivid'. Reality is complex; the data, the facts, are massive. Great things '*must* be dim and difficult'.[61] Life itself, therefore, and spirituality (taken here as man's reflection on experience), must *organize*, *harmonize* – and not reduce – the total real, both secular and sacred. And life and spirituality must endure, and grow, through the ensuing conflict and the creative tensions of their own historical existence. The richer the reality, the more obscure our knowledge of it will be. Knowledge (apprehension, experience) is wider and deeper than science (comprehension, reflection). Man's deepest convictions are inadequate, not primarily because unclear, but because 'not sufficiently rich'. Abundance is the goal. Simplicity must be aware of its counterfeit: simplism, the 'mangling of reality'.[62] Huvelin had warned him: 'The true means to attract a soul, is not to attenuate Christian doctrine, but to present it in its full force, because then we present it in its beauty.'[63] Von Hügel's analyses, then, will be for the sake of synthesis, not system; they will be searching more for the concrete than for its idea.

> We live in times . . . of such excess of analysis over synthesis – that it is in the air all around us to ask questions, to poke about . . . ; where to become and to be, to produce reality, to adore and to will, and to see things in the large and upon the whole, and at their best, is what we all require.[64]

Von Hügel's writings do not avoid the difficult and harsh tasks of criticism, analysis and induction, but they do constantly insist that the concrete has 'always to come first and to be reached last; the criticism, the aloofness, the negation has everywhere to remain a means, not the end, a pain, not a pleasure'.[65]

The gnostic and agnostic must play, and agonize, together

in the face of the real, for reality is, and remains, organic, *penetrable* mystery:

> a sheer conundrum is not mysterious, nor is a blank wall; but forests are mysterious, in which at first you observe but little, yet in which, with time, you see more and more, although never the whole; and the starry heavens are thus mysterious, and the spirit of man, and, above all, God, our origin and home.[66]

Von Hügel, though no agnostic, is gentle towards the problem. But towards the clarities of Hume we get something little short of contempt:

> He is the sort of person young people are taken in by . . . He knows everything. He got to the bottom of everything by the time he was sixteen: he sees everything through clear glass windows. If I were to die to-night, he would know all about me by to-morrow. These old bones would be all arranged, sorted out, explained and in his coat-pocket; but somehow he would not have got me all the same.[67]

Again, Huvelin had noticed and agreed, many years before: 'Truth is, for you, a luminous point which loses itself, little by little, in obscurity.'[68]

In concluding this introduction, it will perhaps be useful, not exactly to define our terms, but to alert the reader, even if only briefly and initially, to the distinction and differentiation of a few fundamental words in von Hügel's vocabulary.

If *religion* for von Hügel is the 'deepest of all experiences of the deepest of all facts', it is therefore, in itself, twofold: it is the *fact of God*, and it is *man's experience* of that fact.[69]

Further, within religion taken as human, *mysticism* – very broadly understood, as we shall see – both relates to and differentiates itself from *other* factors of religion, i.e. its institutional and intellectual elements.

Further again, if religion, here taken as a whole, is the *deepest* experience of the *deepest* fact, there are nevertheless *other* facts and other experiences: von Hügel's religion is not pietism: 'However much man may be supremely and finally a religious animal, he is not *only* that; but he is a physical and sexual, a fighting and an artistic, a domestic and social, a political and philosophical animal as well.'[70]

We shall find that *spirituality* concerns this *total* man, in his stance before, and as partner of, the *total* real, both finite and infinite, both secular and sacred, both historical and eternal. It is of the most extreme importance here, however, to be certain that what is distinguished in this way is not thereby separated, especially where religion is distinguished from morality.[71] On the contrary, the major impulse of von Hügel's spiritual doctrine will be to *harmonize* for life and love his basic intuition of the *organic* quality of all reality.

Von Hügel sees the spiritual life as 'essentially a dynamism'.[72] Dualisms – not dichotomies – dualisms always in arduous process of resolution, abound in his writings. Currents of worldliness and of monasticism, of paschal cross and joy, grapple at every turn. There is sympathy for the reactionary secularism of the Crusades, the Renaissance, and the French Revolution. Man 'had lost a sufficient interest in this wonderful world'.[73] And there is praise for the 'world-seeking movement' of his own time which strives for 'the social betterment of others' and the 'good things of this life'. But the question remains pressed: 'How much decency, leisure, and pay is the miner to have, till he is to be helped to love prayer and the thought of God?'[74] We shall be looking, in this study, at a proposal for spirituality that attempts to overcome such alternatives by integrating them as legitimate inner moments in the one fully *organic* life that is the person of the individual incarnate Christ and the community of his body, the Church.

Only a life sufficiently large and alive to take up and retain,

> within its own experimental range, at least some of the poignant question and conflict, as well as of the peace-bringing solution and calm: hence a life dramatic with a humble and homely heroism which, in rightful contact with and in rightful renunciation of the particular and fleeting, ever seeks and finds the omnipresent and eternal; and which again deepens and incarnates (for its own experience and apprehension and for the stimulation of other souls) this transcendence in its own thus gradually purified particular: only such a life can be largely persuasive, at least for us Westerns and in our times.[75]

A first priority in this study is to let the reader 'have' von Hügel. Direct quotation, therefore, is as frequent and lengthy as space permits. Von Hügel's style is generally agreed to be awkward and Germanic. But it is widely agreed too that it *is* a style: revelatory of an experience and a quality of life.[76] I have not tampered with it, except to reduce the old-fashioned and so, for us, excessive incidence of upper case and of italics.

Finally, this study accords with the judgment that von Hügel's central experience and thought, as they affect the structure and concerns of his spiritual doctrine, are not subject to substantive development. 'He comes into public view full-fledged, and proceeds to work out and elucidate a position already attained.'[77] There is growth, surely, but it almost always appears as the further penetration, correction, or actuation of what is there from the beginning. We will try to notice any real or apparent exceptions to this general circumstance. Our primary interest, however, will be, not to indicate the history of von Hügel's thought, but to identify and organize the governing elements of his spirituality, together with as much of its detail as space permits.

CHAPTER TWO

CHRIST

IN 1905 Friedrich von Hügel writes to Maurice Blondel: 'Christianity is essentially a religion of incarnation: it is indeed God really become flesh in time and space.'[1] And in 1928 Gwendolen Greene, the subject of what seems to have been von Hügel's lengthiest and most far-reaching spiritual direction, records: 'He "preaches Jesus."'[2] To the possible criticism 'that Christ is too little particularized in von Hügel's theology', the reply has been given that this 'is only because an all pervasive Presence cannot be particularized, and for the Baron, Christ's is a presence not to be put by'.[3] This judgment may stand, and its importance is altogether fundamental for an understanding of von Hügel's spirituality.[4] It will be the purpose of this chapter to particularize, to the extent possible, his thinking about Christ, in order that the Christological structures arising out of this material may more easily pervade – and be seen to do so – the later stages of this study of that spirituality. We will first collect materials directly touching incarnation, and then treat three areas immediately corollary to von Hügel's position on Christ: time, duration, and eternal life; the Kingdom of God and the Second Coming; monism.

In 1908, in the opening pages of *The Mystical Element of Religion*, von Hügel, in a relatively brief passage, accomplishes what it is rarely given an author to do. He synthesizes in some three hundred words, with deceptive simplicity, the substance and, when pondered, much of the detail, of his life's scholarly and devotional labour. Little that he writes, before or after, is not a commentary upon the passage.[5] It concerns being and becoming, the real and the ideal, conflict and harmony, the journey and the goal. It is a portrait of Christ, and of the following of Christ – a radical commitment to transcendence and immanence, to incarnation.

The context is Christianity as the revelation of, and the summons to, personality:

> For a person came, and lived and loved, and did and taught, and died and rose again, and lives on by his power and his Spirit for ever within us and amongst us, so unspeakably rich and yet so simple, so sublime and yet so homely, so divinely above us precisely in being so divinely near, – that his character and teaching require, for an ever fuller yet never complete understanding, the varying study, and different experiments and applications, embodiments and unrollings of all the races and civilizations, of all the individual and corporate, the simultaneous and successive experiences of the human race to the end of time. If there is nothing shifting or fitful or simply changing about him, there is everywhere energy and expansion, thought and emotion, effort and experience, joy and sorrow, loneliness and conflict, interior trial and triumph, exterior defeat and supplantation: particular affections, particular humiliations, homely labour, a homely heroism, greatness throughout in littleness. And in him, for the first and last time, we find an insight so unique, a personality so strong and supreme, as to teach us, once for all, the true attitude towards suffering.
>
> Not one of the philosophers or systems before him had effectually escaped falling either into pessimism, seeing the end of life as trouble and weariness, and seeking to escape from it into some aloofness or some nirvana; or into optimism, ignoring or explaining away that suffering and trial which, as our first experience and as our last, surround us on every side. But with him, and alone with him and those who still learn and live from and by him, there is the union of the clearest, keenest sense of all the mysterious depth and breadth

> and length and height of human sadness, suffering, and sin, *and*, in spite of this and through this and at the end of this, a note of conquest and of triumphant joy.[6]

'A person came.' Fully constituted, self-conscious Spirit, priority, prevenience – became, took flesh. And excepting sin alone, von Hügel's Christ will test the farthest reaches of the human. And be tested. The structure is vigorously Antiochene.[7] But the one person, Jesus Christ, 'is both truly God and truly Man'.[8] On at least two occasions von Hügel comments on the difficulty of applying the Chalcedonian definition in great detail.[9] But he is not disturbed by this. He does not look to Chalcedon for an explanation of a problem in theology. He considers that it states, and gives structure to, a mystery of faith, and as such, is basically successful. It enshrines for us 'an imperishable truth'.

Incarnation: 'il est bien *réellement* Dieu incarné', a real God really become flesh and history.[10] And 'the joy of religion resides, surely, in the knowledge, the love, the adoration of One *truly distinct* from, whilst *immensely penetrative* of, ourselves.'[11] Religion is thus everywhere profoundly evidential; it affirms real contacts with the world through the mediation of the senses and with a reality which, as independent and prevenient, occasions and transcends all these contacts. 'Presence, *isness*, as distinct from the *oughtness* of morals: this is the deepest characteristic of all truly religious outlooks.' All other requirements are 'primarily responses to, as effects of, previously extant realities, which thus awaken man's spirit to their existence and to his need of them as extant. The doctrine of, and the devotion to, Jesus Christ, truly present, God and man, body and soul, in the Holy Eucharist, thus forms, most characteristically, the very heart of the Catholic worship.'[12]

This passion for the reality of God as prior to and over against man's experience and thought of him is matched by an equal concern for the reality of contingent being, for facts, 'happenedness', for history. The position is simple, but profound and fundamental, if incarnation, if transcendence and immanence, are to be real. 'Christianity stands for . . . incarnation . . . [which] is not simply a doctrine . . . but . . . the real prevenience and condescension of the real God – is the penetration of spirit into sense, of the spaceless into space, of the eternal into time, of God into man.' 'It is not a simple *idea*, but a solid fact', not simply something that '*ought* to happen', but something that 'really happened'. Realism, then, and history, loom large.[13] Further, the Incarnation must be concrete. 'No doctrine of the divinity of Christ, no affirmation, even of just simply the normality of the mind of Jesus, are other than out of touch with all the real possibilities of the question, if they do not first recognize that a real incarnation of God in man can only mean incarnation in some particular human nature. Man in general is only an idea, it is not a fact, a reality.' Jesus, therefore, will be of a particular time and place and race. He will know 'imaginative and emotional peculiarities', certain 'omissions', 'stresses', 'colourings'. It will be a very *definite* man who is God.[14] Such a view, of course, does heighten the problem, but it also enriches the mystery. If taken seriously, it turns the doctrine into an adventure, and the scholar's desk, without ceasing to be such, becomes a prie-dieu, a place to struggle, and adore.

Von Hügel is clear on the primacy of descending Christology:

> People put God so far away, in a sort of mist somewhere. I pull their coat-tails. God is *near*. He is no use unless he is near. God's otherness and difference, and his nearness. You *must* get that. God's nearness is straight out of the heart of Jesus. Religion is like a cuckoo in some people's nest. They do not understand man's need. No man is satisfied in a swimming-bath; he knocks his knees and elbows against its sides; he wants the sea. So with man's soul, he hungers and

> thirsts for the ocean, for God; God infinite and other, different to man, yet working in man. God's given-ness. Love, suffering, renunciation, they are God's level; the passion and hunger *for* God comes *from* God, and God answers it with Christ. We are creatures, and we must be creaturely.[15]

And again, more directly on Christ himself:

> Christianity . . . is primarily busy with ultimates, with ends. . . . Our Lord lives and moves and has his being in those ultimates; . . . he is himself the full revelation . . . of those ultimates, as they bend down to enter into, and elevate . . . our poor little mediacies. Humanitarianism . . . has received no stimulation or awakening even approaching in fullness to that effected by Jesus Christ. And yet, in all our Lord's utterances and actions, even the love of *man*, however sincere, however pure, stands always in subordination to, is the effect and test of, the love and service of *God*. The movement is here, not from man, or even from all mankind, as the final and adequate end of man's service . . . , to a background God; but from God . . . to men, myself and others. Thus God . . . appears here [i.e. in Our Lord's utterances and actions] . . . as a personalist mind and love and power, who cares for the very birds of the air and the lilies of the field – indeed, who knows the number of the hairs upon our heads.[16]

Now such a view is decisive for spirituality. And so it is of interest that von Hügel does not regard it merely as theology, but as 'a faith' and invitation based on a living model, 'the immense force and figure of the Overlord and Master, Jesus Christ'.[17]

In 1919 von Hügel writes to Gwendolen Greene of the limits of incarnation: 'God always involves Christ, and Christ always involves the Church. – This, Dearie, is clear enough, isn't it?'[18] In 1920 he would clarify: 'The Church is not Christ – is no more Christ than it is God. We require God and Christ and Church: each in and with the other. But it ruins the whole richness, indeed the truth, of the outlook, if any one of these – especially if the Church is simply identified with either of the other two.'[19] It is due to *both* God's 'prevenience and incarnation, that we find his traces in our need and our perception of him variously everywhere'.[20] Von Hügel sees 'an unincarnate God' with 'a wider range, though a less deep message than the incarnate God'.[21] Indeed, we escape pantheism through a properly located Christ: 'A great foot, a pierced foot, prevents that door closing there.' He speaks of some theologians who 'seem to have got a kind of Christism now, not God. God is too difficult. Christ is easy. (Is he easy?) They must have everything easy. We hardly need God if we have Christ. How different all this is to Our Lord himself. Did he not come to show us the Father? Well, you can obscure Christ, but you can't shake him.'[22]

'*God is a stupendously rich reality* . . . His creation . . . is immensely rich. Still deeper and more delicate is this richness and reality in God's incarnation and redemptive action. Yet his being, his interior life, are in no wise exhausted by all this outward action, nor does this action occasion or articulate his character . . . God is God, already and apart from his occupation with us. These are the great facts which I believe to be specially revealed to us in the dogma of the Holy Trinity – facts of which we have an especial need in these our times.'[23] Negative theology, where not agnostic or pantheistic, is a right attempt to guard this richness. Prayer will lack 'the deepest and widest expansion' without it. Christian prayer and theology are not just soteriology, for even Jesus Christ does not exhaust God.[24]

These are strong words and perhaps immediately surprising and not altogether appealing. And yet von Hügel is saying something of first importance for the very structure of his spirituality, something closely connected with what he conceives to be the Gospel message of Jesus. Maurice Nédoncelle has caught the point clearly in his summary of von Hügel's criticism of this 'excessive Christocentrism' in Schleiermacher:

> Consequently, in the true sense of the word, religion can never be too theocentric, though it may be too christocentric. Schleiermacher, for instance, subsumes all human individualities in our Lord, finding through Christianity a way of escape from divine transcendence. This is a false interpretation of the Christian doctrine. By overlooking the submission of Jesus to the will of the Father, he changes the whole message. Christ is not only the Man who makes man divine, but he is also the messenger of God; he is the Mediator, who tells us of the hidden world, leading us into the mysterious presence of the Most High.[25]

Von Hügel, then, is not discounting, is not side-stepping Jesus. He is rather seeking the mind of Jesus. And if the Incarnate Logos is, in some respects, a place, yet he finds the Logos' coming was primarily as witness and as way: to mediate the Father. It is the mentality enshrined in the Latin Liturgy (much of which antedates the post-Arian reaction),[26] where the glorified Jesus raised by the Father as Lord and Christ[27] stands yet before the Father as Eucharist offered for and to and by those who live by his Spirit.[28] And it is of the greatest interest that von Hügel's attack on what he understands as 'excessive Christocentrism' directly bases itself upon the witness of the human Jesus himself.[29]

What emerges is the centrality of Christ, yet not as excluding a theocentrism.[30] There is more to God than is *revealed* in Christ (though Christ *is* God). For while the Logos is the utterly perfect image of the Father, he is, in his humanity, in Jesus of Nazareth, the perfect *human* image of the Father. And to be perfectly human does not exhaust the Godhead. This is the point von Hügel wishes to make and honour, and for man's sake. It is why Christ *needed* to pray. The task is to be perfectly human. But to be that is to recognize, submit to, reach out for, the less than human (things, science), the human (sense, history, spirit), and the more than human (God, Spirit). Von Hügel's Christ will *need* to do all this, just to be a man.[31] The journey must be made. Completed, it will find him Lord, celestial Christ, victorious grace, become for us at once the journey and its possibilities, and journey's end, the root and pattern and the goal, of faith and hope and love. And these three are that victorious grace, his Spirit, who makes the journey, ceaselessly, in us.

God alone is fully free. Therefore, he does not sin, he cannot sin, or even be tempted. 'But there exists not only God Pure, but also God Incarnate, Jesus Christ.' And the union of the divine with the human in Jesus renders sin impossible. Von Hügel is clear on this. He sees the post-Arian stress on the divinity of Christ to be not primarily out of concern for that divinity, but for the sake of the sinlessness of Jesus even as man. The doctrine of the Virgin Birth is an early, a contemporary conviction of Our Lord's sinlessness, of a fresh creation, and the foundation of the honour paid Christ's mother. All this speaks of a very beautiful, quite distinct human holiness.

But Chalcedon also proclaims the integral humanity of Jesus. And the 'limitations, obscurities, weaknesses, growths, temptations, which are interwoven with human nature as such . . . , stand on clear record in the Synoptic Gospels'. He is like us in everything but sin.[32] In 1921 von Hügel tells Evelyn Underhill that a half-way house on the way to God will not do for man, but God must come down to man, 'not half-way, but the whole way'. The apex of spirituality 'is, at bottom, the fullest self-abasement of God – Jesus Christ, in the manger, on the cross'. It is 'concrete, fullest religion'.[33] Von Hügel believes and exults in human existence as historical, and therefore as growth, conflict, as harmony through friction and tension. All human progress is a victory. Personality is an achievement.[34] He seeks the roots of this becoming, and our example for it, in the human Jesus. He loves to set out and ponder Christ's wonder and astonishment, his growth in age and grace, his Jewishness, his love of the world and of men, his fears, temptations, and his ignorance.[35]

Von Hügel's point and motive here are made clear in a passionate plea to Blondel. But in the interest of balance, let us first see his affirmation to Blondel of transcendence, of divinity, as he writes of this defect in Loisy, a defect he recognizes as early as 1903 and was increasingly to deplore: '. . . there is a great absence, in his tone and in his moral and spiritual temperament, of that noble hunger and thirst for the absolute, for the ultimate, which I love so very much in Plato and Plotinus, and in Augustine . . . You yourself possess a great deal of it too, my dear friend.' But this is preceded by a splendid and very personal appeal for a fully operative humanity in Jesus. It is worth having at length:

> As to your own position, I really do not see how your knowledge,[36] which allows for absolutely nothing of the implicit and the instinctive, remains truly human – at least human *in statu viatoris* and in a sense minimally in touch with this world and available as a model for it while penetrating it with redemptive power. And yet, I would suppose that it is precisely for this – or for this too – that we have received Emmanuel: that is, not, I do believe, to be only a vision for us . . . but in order to be a real showing-forth (that really has to do with us, even in its perfection) of the ineffably perfect exercise of all our fundamental human activities . . . Only in this way will he really be for us not only the model of *what* we must *be*, but also the model for the *way* we are to *achieve* it [*non seulement le modèle de ce qu'il faut être*; *mais encore le modèle de la manière de le devenir*]. Further, in this way we shall find in the life of him who is the master of the saints a verification rather than a denial of the view that holiness is born of contact with concrete things, that it is born of

struggles and conflicts, and that the great fullness of holiness possible to humanity is never, absolutely never, born in simple avoidance of such contact, struggles and conflicts, or just by hovering above them, even to the extent that this might be possible. For in short, my dear friend, in this matter of our *struggles*, of my painful but innocent and productive contact with things . . . , what real help, what constructive example can I get from an interior life . . . which knows *nothing at all* from experience about the shadows, the darkness, the gropings I must face; what help can I get from an example which knows nothing of my poor *human* heroisms, in so far as such heroisms directly involve such darkness and such groping? And I ask you: what heroisms of mine, small as they are, do not largely involve, and have their existence largely in terms of, just such darkness and groping?

I am well aware that theologians show the greatest repugnance for really facing up to facts of this kind . . . But is this not once again to return to an excessively *Greek conception* of human perfection – a very abstract perfection, uninvolved with, and exterior to, concrete things and situations, too static, a perfection of pure light and undisturbed harmony? Our Master is more than that, my friend. He is not that at all. Nazareth, Capharnaum, Gethsemane, Golgotha – they are more, they are other than the Academy, the Stoa Poecile . . . Indeed, real naturalism is far closer to a Christ of facile virtue than to a Christ of costly immolation. Contact, a pure and sanctifying contact with man's essential condition, and not the contrary – I beg you; and this also for him who is our model and our measure. Otherwise, he shall cease to be either.[37]

'Je vous prie.' It is a manifesto and a demand for an incarnational spirituality. Jesus Christ is truly God and truly man. Christianity is incarnation, and its specific genius lies in the 'bending down to the little in full confidence that it will turn out great', 'open . . . towards all the winds that blow in God's great heaven'. It is an invitation to humanism, Christian and devout, to a piety that 'will never be pietistic'.[38]

We are fortunate in having Evelyn Underhill's record of the effect of von Hügel's witness and spiritual direction on the question of Christ. He had told her in 1921 to visit the poor, to develop homely dispositions; he hopes this might 'distribute your blood – some of your blood – away from the brain, where too much of it is lodged at present'.[39] In 1927 Underhill writes of her conversion to Christ five years earlier:

> When I went to the Baron he said I wasn't much better than a Unitarian. Somehow by his prayers or something, he compelled me to experience Christ. He never said anything more about it – but I know humanly speaking he did it. It took about four months – it was like watching the sun rise very slowly – and then suddenly one knew what it was. . . . I seem to have to try as it were to live more and more towards him only . . . The New Testament . . . now seems full of things never noticed – all gets more and more alive and compellingly beautiful. . . . Holy Communion which at first I did simply under obedience [to von Hügel], gets more and more wonderful too. It is in that world and atmosphere one lives.[40]

Friedrich von Hügel's idea and experience of spirituality is very broad, as we have seen.[41] Man is 'incurably amphibious',[42] and von Hügel is bent on probing the total environment and resources, the better to argue and provide for the complexity and greatness of man's destiny. Few areas of thought and experience arrest his attention more consistently than the category of time, duration and eternal life. Lest the reader wonder at the relevance of such a discussion at this point, let us state the thesis at once, however briefly and incompletely: Human existence, as animal, as personal, as holy, is a gift. But it is also a task, a journey, an achievement. And – what is crucial – it is historical.

In a preface written in 1921 von Hügel hopes that 'not a line within these covers' is devoid of 'the historic sense'.[43] As a gift which is also summons and demand, human life is a call to the animal individual to grow, to deepen, to achieve personality (spirituality) and, further and more deeply, to take on the adventure of the specifically religious, the holy (Spirituality), where the element of gift stands ever more prior, yet ever more creative too of human freedom, indeed where freedom is in direct proportion to the presence of grace. These, for von Hügel, are the *facts* of spiritual life as he finds them in history and in his own experience. The movement is not deductive, therefore, but inductive and analytic, based on the search for data, the probing of facts and reflection upon them – facts of faith, indeed, but only as existentialized, as convicting experience.[44] Jesus is at once source and test for these convictions, and so it is of passionate interest that he be truly God and perfectly man. For as God, he is the presence in history of the gift itself, the absolutely valid, the holy, of what is not in process at all; while to take him seriously as man is to allow him to grow, to *become* human: spirit, and also as man, to seek the holy: Spirit. It is to let Luke stand fast: a real growth in wisdom and grace, with man and God. And so von Hügel probes into history itself, for a parallel movement and depth: time, duration, eternal life.[45] The results will be forthright, and maybe a bit unsettling, as he meditates on the results for spirituality in Jesus' teaching on the Kingdom of God. But they will have to be, if his humanism is lovingly to include, while correcting, both John of the Cross and the 'noble' Darwin.[46]

In the opening pages of *Eternal Life* von Hügel gives as part of a working definition of his subject: 'the consciousness', 'the sense . . . of non-succession, of a complete present and presence, of an utterly abiding here and now'. This experience is an ingredient of 'every specifically human life and act', and where fully operative, it is also 'specifically religious'. Von Hügel will seek, with the help of past thought and present practice, the 'difference within affinity' between 'finite, *durational* spirit', man, 'and the infinite, *eternal* Spirit, God'.[47]

Eternal life, first verified historically in Dionysiac ecstasy – and there, only in a rudimentary way – is an experience of the non-successive, the timeless, the abiding. It is distinguished from immortality, and from personal immortality, which, while closely related, is derivative.[48] The concept of endlessness, of perpetual succession, is something else again, and where believed in, is rightly productive of a doctrine like nirvana, as an authentic human cry against the pain and 'intolerable horror' of mere successiveness, of sheer flux, simply 'because it *is* sheer flux'.[49] And this applies also to evolution where conceived apart from any finalism, or where itself taken as final cause and not as instrument and method.[50] Eternal life in its perfection is the divine Now, distinct from all succession, a *totum simul*, unmoving energy, superior to motion and to change, and the basis of the distinction between function and mere process, between action and activity. Accordingly, this simultaneity is not static, nor thinly deist, but a dynamism which, in its Christian expression, is that of a rich, concrete and personalist Spirit, sociable in itself, and outgoing in function of its nature as love.[51] As participated by man, the experience is also markedly social; for St Paul, it is a present possession, though still more a future gift; while in St John we meet an all but wholly realized eschatology.[52]

Now let us pause with St Augustine, who, for von Hügel, remains 'unequalled in the delicate splendour of his insight':

> Thou, O God, precedest all past times by the height of thine ever-present eternity; and thou exceedest all future times, since these *are* future and, once they have come, will be past times. . . . Thy years neither come nor go . . . Thy years are but one day; and this thy day is not every day but *to-day*. This thy *to-day* is eternity.

'True eternity is present where there is nothing of time' – and yet, there was a moment once, at a window in Ostia. And that moment's experience of a present is due, at bottom, to his presence in our lives – the Prevenient One, rich and concrete, our cause, occasion, and our goal: 'Thou wast with me, but I was not with thee.' 'Thou hast made us for thyself, and restless is our heart . . . ' Further, there is, in Augustine, a 'keen sense of the historical element, – of the self-humiliation of the infinite in time and space'. And the organic, social quality of eternal life receives in the doctrine of the 'two cities . . . built . . . by two loves' sublime, even tragic expression: a 'great yet terribly dangerous conception' which makes von Hügel remember 'that it is Jesus Our Lord himself who alone gives us the quite full and costingly balanced statement'.[53]

And finally, eternal life, as found in man, involves things, sense, emotion, freedom and struggle: in man, eternal life has a history. This is its incarnational trend, since God, the eternal Spirit, 'here reveals himself to us and touches us' in time and through matter.[54] Such a fact rules out of court all 'superfine idealism', all '"pure" spirituality'.[55] It is also a blueprint for tension and conflict, and a mandate for the view that human personality and human holiness are not static qualities, but dynamic achievements to be pursued organically.

According to strict definition,[56] it is clear that eternal life, as fully divine, cannot be the experience of man. And yet something like it seems to accompany the birth of personality, to be ingredient to every 'specifically human life and act'.[57] And a further intensification, under grace, especially splendid in the mystics, and whose cause faith knows to be different also in kind, seems again man's experience. Von Hügel analyses this twofold phenomenon many times, generally making use of the categories of Henri Bergson. And to this analysis we now turn.

In 1900 he writes to Tyrrell of Bergson's *Essai*: 'What analysis and heart-knowledge! . . . His distinction between the soul's direct experience of duration, with its mutually inter-penetrative moments, and that artificial, bastard compromise between duration within us, and extension, space outside us, which we call clock-time, with its minutes each outside of, and simply alongside of the other, – has now got bodily into my head and heart.'[58]

This clock-time is also called 'abstract', 'conceptual', 'horizontal'.[59] It is phenomenal time, the 'equable succession of mutually exclusive, ever equally long moments'; it is 'very clear', and 'shallow'.[60] Humanly speaking it is meaningless, a dark flux where only the 'individual' exists. 'The animal man is almost pure succession, indeed all but mere change.'[61]

'The spiritual man', on the other hand, 'in proportion to his spirituality', lives in duration, which is 'real' time, 'vivid and deep, . . . never very clear'.[62] The 'distinctive' self, personality, is inverse to its 'dependence on successiveness'.[63] Duration is a thickness, 'an intensive magnitude', 'not a present thin as a knife edge, but with a certain breadth of its own'.[64] 'In proportion to its depth', as human and as holy – i.e. as spirit in the Spirit – man's personality, here under the aspect of *durée*,[65] is a steady movement into 'partial simultaneity', 'quasi-eternity'. And at the deepest, it 'apprehends, requires, and rests . . . in pure simultaneity', in 'eternity' itself, in God.[66] For while this experience of strict eternal life is never owned nor comprehended by the human subject – thus excluding all fanaticism – yet, at the deepest, it *is* fully *apprehended*, as we just saw, and is 'contrastingly experienced . . . , since it *is* owned by the divine Spirit which penetrates the human spirit'.[67]

Von Hügel concludes from all this 'how ruinous to our spiritual life would be a full triumph of the category of time'.[68] He also fights, and not just theoretically, but out of the deepest pastoral concern, any attempt to introduce successiveness or process of any kind into God, outside of his becoming in Jesus Christ.[69] The complete triumph of time or any inroad whatever into the prevenient, concrete, joyous plenitude and reality of God drastically reduces the wager and the promise which is man. For man is a journey out of animal individuality to the human significance which is personality, and on to the life of God. That journey is history.

In 1905 von Hügel writes: If God is not process at all, and man not merely that, then the mystics are right in holding that man is able, 'even here and now, vividly to conceive' – indeed man necessarily implies and to some degree experiences – the 'timeless character . . . of his own spirit', and of God, and of his experience of God who penetrates his own spirit. The best description and explanation of the foundation for this experience is Aristotle's doctrine of 'unmoving energy', where motion is imperfect and subordinate to energy, and process is subordinate to function. God is function, energy, the '*Actus Purus*' of Aquinas and the whole Christian mystical tradition. Thus 'action' is the functioning of spirit, of personality, 'in which all its potentiality is actualized, and where the very fullness, richness, and harmony of the action produces an overflowing joy and peace . . . , in contrast to "activity," which is but a restless, intermittent' fever, 'imperfect willing', and 'unactualized capabilities'. The human task is to move from activity to action, from and through process to function, from individuality to personality, ever onwards to God.[70] There is no question here of discrete states, of flight from one to the other, which would be Neoplatonist; but of a deepening, an in-through-and-with movement, which is incarnational.

'Now it is only emptiness, not action', only 'the unity of mere oneness, and not unity in diversity' which are opposed to history. For von Hügel, history is 'achieved and perceived' – indeed history exists at all – 'only if we believe and will more than mere succession, more than sheer process', while yet believing and ardently willing that succession and process. If history is concerned with becoming, it is concerned more precisely with value, with 'the worth of this becoming'.[71]

We are at the heart of the matter here. Von Hügel's history is incarnation; its structure is the God-man, Jesus of Nazareth, who *is* both being and becoming.[72] History is movement, real movement, variety and struggle, yet movement into the real which is already present. For Jesus, as Son of the Father, is both eternal life *and* the man of effort, temptation and growth, for whom von Hügel pleads so eloquently with Blondel.[73]

Man, then, is indeed amphibious, and precisely *as* historical. The implications are vast, thoroughly linked with tradition, and perhaps not altogether fashionable. But let us move further. Significant history, as an amalgam of succession and simultaneity, as duration, is a variety-in-unity:

> The worth of this variety springs from an already immanentally extant and operative scheme by which each differing constituent finds a unique meaning and happiness in developing itself in a non-interchangeable position within, and as a non-replaceable contribution to, the larger whole; . . . the work, pain, and joy required for, and following upon, the effective constitution of these 'cultural' organisms, are deeply real also, and are somehow *directly* connected with, are *already*[74] somehow represented, and will become equivalently apparent, in the ultimate non-successive reality. Thus neither any individual nor any particular age has to wait, with regard to the whole of its meaning and effectiveness, for other individuals, for other ages. For we each of us already form, at our best, one particular link in but *one great chain* from earth to heaven; yet each little link is *also*, severally, already linked to heaven itself.[75]

Now something altogether fundamental for humanism, spirituality and piety is being said here. Von Hügel is taking a very definite position which will affect everything. The concluding image is clear. Man moves, as historical, *in and through* works and pains and joys whose context is worldly, corporate, organic – and whose significance is real and *permanent* –

towards the fully human, which is, at its upper reaches, to move towards God. And man is *also* – and while in history – directly linked to, and therefore in his spirituality and piety he must directly confront, God. We have here a lapidary instance of what the famous remark about Friedrich Heiler in another context is all about: 'Indeed the Professor loves the *aut-aut* [either-or]; whilst I believe real life mostly demands the *et-et* [both-and].'[76] And there is nothing casual about it. The same position, taken here in 1905, is repeated in the posthumous and unfinished Gifford Lectures published in 1931,[77] where von Hügel goes on to add: 'Now I submit that it is simply moonshine to insist that such a view is of no practical effect. Such a view on the contrary, if it become the flesh and blood of a man's living and dying, will produce human beings as different in size and fruitfulness as it is possible to find.'[78] As spiritual director, he insists on this 'double-relatedness' in a homely and powerful letter to Gwendolen Greene, using the same image of the chain.[79] And elsewhere: 'I greatly loved seeing, actually living for a day with you, in that precise concrete time and space condition in and through which my child has to grow into eternity and God, the Ever Abiding.' 'Live all you can – as complete and full a life as you can find – do as much as you can for others. Read, work, enjoy – love and help as many souls – do all this. Yes – but remember: Be alone, be remote, be away from the world, be desolate. Then you will be near God.'[80]

Not surprisingly then, von Hügel will be found on *both* sides of almost every vital question in spirituality. As we shall see, he asks for heroic asceticism and total involvement; he will defend both marriage and celibacy, and oppose both Christian pansexualism and monastic abuses.[81] He will have no answers to some problems, and the complete answer to very few. But he will not take sides, lest he diminish the adventure and mystery, or impoverish that '*vie plus abondante*',[82] as he finds it in Jesus.

Von Hügel is as concerned to defend real process, successiveness, as he is to prevent its complete triumph. If the mystics have seized on the truth of eternal life as fully constituted present reality – and von Hügel dearly loves them for this – yet 'pure' mysticism is unincarnational, is false; indeed it is destructive of that eternal life to which it aspires *because* it is destructive of history. It denies not only clock-time, but duration too, and feeds on a simultaneity that is finally an empty blank, devoid of the richly complex and harmonious life towards which we move, in which we share. 'Harmonization . . . is our end and ideal; *therefore* has history got a true final meaning, and therefore will . . . Simultaneity in no way abolish even the least of the valuable resultants of the succession in history, or be in any sharp antagonism with what looks like mere process, but which, to be truly historical, is even now something more than such mere succession.'[83] History is indeed a permanently valuable building, by and of the corporate Christ, who is the Father's, that God may be all in all.

Von Hügel is a close and admiring student of St Catherine of Genoa on this whole question of eternal life as present here and now. He writes beautifully of her conversion experience: 'She was kneeling on . . . throughout a deep, rich age of growth, during but some minutes of poor clock-time.' He finds her orthodox, alive and valid, and yet on this question of history in its full incarnational dimensions, as in other related questions, he is severely critical, as he is of the whole mystical tradition.[84] He admires that tradition, but he also learns from it 'that it is Jesus Our Lord himself who alone gives us the quite full and costingly balanced statement'.[85] Von Hügel finds that statement in the Synoptic teaching on the Kingdom of God and the Second Coming.

The major statement on the Kingdom of God and the Parousia as proximate Second Coming is made in 1919. But this is not the parting thunder of a man preoccupied with age or with dying. Nor can it be fairly called the neo-orthodoxy of a repentant 'modernist'. The position is already fully enunciated in 1916, 1912, and as far back as 1902: 'I myself . . . had been clinging to . . . an *interior* and *present* Kingdom of Heaven', and later, to an '*external* and *future* modification', i.e. to a non-authentic and corrupt addition to Jesus' own teaching. 'That view is simply *not true*.' 'The conception of human life as, even fundamentally and permanently, not simply present and not solely spiritual and moral, cannot be simply a popular mistake and caricature of the real truth, unless the very substance of Christianity has ceased to be *normative* for us.' 'And I have so far a right to speak, since not only have I worked long and hard at these things, but because I do not think any discovery cost me, emotionally, as much to finally accept as this one.'[86]

The problem is 'delicate and far-reaching', 'difficult', yet 'bearable for the sake of the light and the power which surround the burden and the darkness'. Von Hügel sees no 'entirely clear' or 'easy' solution. But he rejoices at the 'driving forces' and spiritual fruitfulness of the mystery. In 1912 he writes that the teaching of the Synoptic Jesus on the Kingdom of God and the proximate Second Coming is 'the deepest and most operative revelation concerning the temporal and the eternal ever vouchsafed to man'.[87]

He stands, then, with those who find 'in Our Lord's life and teaching . . . two movements or elements, – a gradual, prophetic, immanental, predominantly ethical element; and this sudden, apocalyptic, transcendental, purely religious element'.[88] Again: there stands 'the reality of Jesus' with its 'immense attraction and beneficence'; yet there stands also 'the teaching concerning a very near universal cataclysm and cosmic regeneration, with Jesus himself as the centre of overwhelming power'.[89] Von Hügel does not hope to solve the problem. As for scholarship, he tells Norman Kemp Smith that he desires to encourage 'if only a few students, not to *tidy things up for God*, but just quietly to admit certain great facts'.[90] For spirituality, far from desiring to dissolve 'the tension', he seeks rather to release from it – this 'part of the mainspring, of Christianity'

– that mystery's 'abiding truth and place' in 'the deepest spiritual life'.[91]

Von Hügel will indulge no violent reaction from the more immanental, more realized eschatology of his youth. There is rather a search for the harmony-in-tension of a larger whole. Indeed, while praising the 'brilliant' and 'instructive' apocalyptic insights of Loisy and Schweitzer, he yet judges them excessive and even speaks, with unwonted harshness, of the latter's 'purely ascetical and transcendental Messiah-Christ and Saviour' as 'most rightly repulsive to the large majority of believers'.[92]

Faith in Jesus as both God and man leads von Hügel to seek in the Gospel message equivalents *both* of duration and of simultaneity or eternal life. He finds them dramatically fused at Caesarea Philippi.

'The central doctrine in the teaching' of Jesus, especially as given in Mark and Luke, 'is throughout the Kingdom of God'. The teaching 'consists of *two strongly contrasted parts*, divided by the great scene of Jesus with the apostles alone at Caesarea Philippi'.[93] Von Hügel finds this central doctrine of the Kingdom to be especially upheld, in its *pre-Caesarea* phase 'by Jesus' fundamental experience – the Fatherhood of God'. Here the Kingdom is presented 'more in the spirit of the ancient prophets', as 'predominantly ethical, as already come in its beginnings, and as subject to laws analogous to those obtaining in the natural world'.[94] It is the period of the plant parables, of gradual growth, and of rejoicing. The temper is 'balanced and sunny', 'an expansion from within outwards and from below upwards'.[95] The outlook is largely 'immanental' and 'monistic'. Indeed, in Jesus' answer to the Baptist's disciples (Matt. 11:4), the implication is strong that the very presence of Jesus *is* the Kingdom, here and now.[96] All this is the durational movement.

Von Hügel finds the central doctrine of the Kingdom *after Caesarea* to be 'especially coloured by Jesus' other great experience – of himself as the Son of Man'.[97] This is the simultaneous, the eternal life movement. The Kingdom is now presented more in the form of apocalyptic, as purely religious, intensely transcendent, and dualistic. It is not distant or gradual, but imminent and sudden, and 'not at all achieved by man, but purely given by God'.[98] The temper is not sunny now, but 'stormy' and 'abrupt', 'an irruption from without inwards and from above downwards'.[99] The parables speak now, not of growth and 'slow fruitfulness', but of 'keen watchfulness and of the proximate, sudden Second Coming'.[100]

Von Hügel is painting with a broad brush, and he knows it. But he is adamant that the distinction he is making here be acknowledged as textually demanded and as component of realities that will not suffer honest collapse of the one into the other.[101] He is also very clear that the doctrine is neither Jewish, nor apostolic, nor ecclesial, but is utterly original with Jesus.[102]

As we have seen,[103] this exegetical conclusion cost von Hügel a great deal. But he came to love the darkness and difficulty 'of this great teaching of our Lord's'. He never fully understood it: 'Our Lord sees something, I do not see clearly what. He is beyond me.'[104] But he lets the mystery have its way with him, with immense results for his spirituality. And the mystery, once again, is Jesus himself. For if the Parousia is 'the deepest and most operative revelation concerning the temporal and the eternal ever vouchsafed to man',[105] it is so because the doctrine is a massive disclosure of the person of Jesus, a profound penetration of the Messiah who, up to Caesarea, largely appears as 'lowly, radiant and with all-embracing hope'.[106] And the doctrine is a *self*-disclosure, for it is primarily revealed in the titles Jesus personally assumes at Caesarea Philippi.

Here Mark represents Jesus, 'for the first time in a manner beyond all dispute', 'as adopting the designation "Son of Man" in a messianic and eschatological sense'. Peter's conception of the Messiah is corrected by a 'repeated insistence' on both suffering and glory. For Jesus, together with the announcement of a proximate coming in power (the *simultaneous* movement), inaugurates another doctrine: the personal Messiah as Suffering Servant (which is the *durational* movement, now tragically deepened). It is in the combination that we have a 'succinct description of his specific vocation – its heavenly origin and difference from all earthly Messianism; its *combination* of the depths of human weakness, dereliction, sufferings, with the highest elevation in joy, power and glory; and its connexion of that pain with this triumph as *strictly interrelated* – only with and through the Cross, was there here the offer and the acceptance of the Crown.'[107]

The categories of the 'sudden' and the 'proximate', clear in exegesis – the 'certain great facts' of the letter to Kemp Smith – remain somewhat a dogmatic puzzle for von Hügel to the end.[108] But their uses for spirituality become clear. The Second Coming is a symbol of transcendence, of God, that leads to 'tiptoe expectations'; it is a 'pungent salt' in the mouth.[109] Both Jesus' background as a Jew – where 'divine action is, as such, conceived to be instantaneous' – and very much more importantly, von Hügel's own Bergsonian understanding of time and eternal life demand that God's termination of the present order be both 'sudden and rapid'. It is a view 'essential to all genuine spirituality'.[110]

Von Hügel immediately notices, however, that such 'nearness and suddenness . . . does not weaken but heightens the call to persistent self-purification and uninterrupted service of others'. The testing will be sharp, but it will be a testing of '*persistent* faithfulness'. The Synoptic Jesus is not to be divided, for the faithfulness to be so peremptorily tested will involve: 'respect for the human body', 'for the ties of family and of country', for the beauties of nature, for a 'forthcoming friendliness', 'even when these are transcended in a complete, heroic self-abnegation' and 'asceticism'.[111]

Von Hügel is attempting to describe a balance, a balance he found in Huvelin.[112] He sees in the transformation of Kingdom into Church the large success of the pre-Caesarea teaching of Jesus. 'This change was in its essence simply inevitable, right and beneficent.' He agrees wholeheartedly with Troeltsch that

> the historical development which succeeded in rendering the fundamental ethical convictions of Christianity fruitful for the work of the world . . . has not misunderstood the Gospel . . . [It is Christian optimism] from which springs the perception that the divine action has an end which comprises and fashions the world, and which assigns to human labour the task of constituting a community of personalities devoted to the sanctification of the ends of this world . . . The religious end [as encompassed by the doctrine of the proximate Second Coming] is indeed continuously renovated by men's concentration upon the image of that classical beginning when it stood, without a rival, with the power of the present, before men's hearts. But for the sake of God, the God of creation, from whom the world and all its good derive, the world, as soon as it becomes a lasting field for work, must also be accorded a positive value, and its ends must, as far as possible, be harmonized with the final end revealed to us by God.[113]

But such a view only heightens the adventure of living out 'the divine paradox of the life of Jesus himself'. For the doctrine of the proximate Parousia makes clear that 'Christianity is an immense warning' as well, and the task always remains to achieve the combination found in 'Our Lord himself – to have caught up a few drops of that genial rain, that royally generous west wind, that gently drops and brightly blows through the virile sunshine of his love'.[114] In 1913 he writes:

> It is clear that we can either concentrate upon the relatively immanent, ethical, continuous, out-going, joyous movement, or upon the exclusively transcendent, religious, abrupt, incoming, heroic movement, or upon both . . . Only

> the last . . . gives us the complete Jesus, the true genius of Christianity. And thus we get . . . the continuous sense that the very things we, men, are to love and seek are also the same things which we are to be detached from, and from which we are to flee. Attachment and cultivation, and detachment and renouncement . . . There will be no fanaticism, but a profound earnestness; there will be no worldliness, but an immense variety of interest and expansion toward all things in their specific . . . goodness, truth and beauty.[115]

Given the richly social understanding of eternal life which we have already seen, it is not surprising to find von Hügel adopting a similarly social emphasis within the context of this double movement resulting from a strictly interpreted doctrine of the proximate Parousia. 'The Kingdom of God, whether insisted upon apocalyptically or prophetically, is throughout conceived by Our Lord as a social organism.'[116] For the perfection of the earthly kingdom 'consists in the greatest within it being he who is the servant of all'.[117] And the same is true of the future life. Von Hügel finds no trace of the Plotinian *solus cum solo* 'in Our Lord's conception of . . . ultimate life'. The imagery of the banquet and the thrones rather insists 'on the great fact and truth that the inner spiritual life, to be deep and genuine, permanently requires a rich variety and organization within a strongly social life'. 'The Soul's perfection is thus practised and proclaimed by Jesus as its complete self-donation to the service of man for God and of God in man.'[118]

At this point we are given one of von Hügel's finest portraits of Jesus, where 'detachment . . . is planted . . . , not outside of, but right within, even the purest attachment . . . '; where 'a wise and noble . . . asceticism is . . . the instrument, concomitant and guardian, though *never the first motive or last end*':[119]

> And this self-donation is effected in utter dependence upon God's aid, and yet with the fullest actuation of all the feelings,

> motives, and passions of chaste fear, tender pity, manly wrath, childlike simplicity and humility, homely heroism, joy in God, love of our very enemies, sense of and contrition for sin, and trust in God's fatherly care even in deep desolation and an agonizing death. The expansive happiness of his early ministry, the loving observation of flower and bird, sky, wind, and wave; the lonely night-watches on the mountain-side; the delight in children; the mercifulness to publicans and sinners; the standing in the midst of the disciples as a servant . . . ; the emphatic anger in purifying the temple; the sadness of the Last Supper; the craving for the disciples' sympathy and the terror of death in Gethsemane; the lofty silence before Caiaphas and Pilate; the cry of desolation on the Cross:

all this is eternal life as proclaimed in Jesus: 'self-donation to the service of man for God and of God in man.'[120]

Von Hügel, then, seeks to keep 'the suffering of the Messiah, and the return of the same Messiah in power and majesty . . . in a close interconnection . . . as but two constituents of one great fact and law'. For only in this way does the latter lose 'every vestige of . . . inflation' and the former avoid 'ultimate . . . pessimism'.[121] Suffering and evil are 'most real' and are also, 'if taken in simple self-abandonment to God', the way to 'an otherwise uncapturable regal beatitude and peace'.[122] Jesus is joyful power, and he is suffering. And

> both the passion and the power are all, in the first instance, borne for God, borne through God, crowned by God. A virile and wholesome humanitarianism flows indeed necessarily from the heart of Jesus and from men's love of his Spirit; but they do so, thus wholesomely, because grounded continuously in the primary motive, not of man, but of God.[123]

This emphasis on the priority of God leads von Hügel to some stern judgments on millenarianism, judgments which both imply and reflect the structure of his spirituality. He is content that as with 'the change from Kingdom to Church, so with that from a renovated earth [millenarianism] to heaven', the spirit of Jesus has been maintained.[124] The original millenarian doctrine, like its parallel and presupposition, the proximate Parousia, had its religious power and retains its perennial truth for spiritual life in its peremptory summons to human watchfulness and preparedness: the expectation of the Messianic gift which is both judgment and salvation and which, however present, is always 'coming soon': Jesus, and the Spirit of Jesus. The whole notion and experience is caught in the ages-long cry of the Church: maranatha!

In von Hügel's judgment, modern millenarianism 'shows badly'. The biblical sources give consistent witness to millenarian outlooks which 'are full of God; which there stand, not for man's work, but for God's gift; which indeed in precisely this their proximity, suddenness and completeness of transforming power, express this lightning illapse from without and from above into human life and human nature, and not a slow, gradual growth upwards and from within'.[125] 'With Jesus the proximity and suddenness meant Gift of God, meant God.' With non-religious millenarianism, 'on the other hand, God, gift, test, preparation – all have gone; man and man's work – even pure, unaided human work – have succeeded'. Von Hügel sees this as 'harebrained, inflating, sterilising'.[126]

He goes on to condemn even 'religiously intended' millenarianism. 'Here God is fully acknowledged', but the Kingdom in its proximate suddenness is interpreted as 'the coalescence of devoted, heroic human wills to which God has promised millenarian results'. This is gravely to misunderstand Jesus; it makes 'human nature and human progress . . . , and not God and his perfect simultaneity, the centre of man's care and striving'. Such a view of human earthly perfectibility 'is not a cause or an effect of theism . . . , but always its substitute. You can have as your centre God; or you can have as your centre such sudden and complete human progress and perfection: you cannot have both.'[127]

Nevertheless, von Hügel is clear that 'theism remains fully compatible with man's indefinite . . . improvement', and is fully equipped to meet any legitimate secularist pressure. But we have seen this point made already in his repeated insistence on the permanent value of the human, striving Jesus.[128] And it is present in his trenchant criticism of religion as the whole of life and spirituality.

In 1919 von Hügel writes feelingly to Norman Kemp Smith on the whole question. He had been to a meeting of the 'Army and Religion' committee where, out of twenty-two members, there were only three or four

> who held that preliminary pessimism, that conviction as to the abiding costliness of our little earthly life. [The large majority were] definitely hostile to all such abiding limitations and difficulties . . . Any and every doctrine of original sin was sensitively traced and scouted in even the most moderate positions and forms. Nothing but the strongly accentuated possibility of our being able, by our best conjointed efforts, to bring about, *hic et nunc*, perfection . . . upon this our earth . . . was congenial . . . And it greatly interested me to find for myself, gradually, how the one religious argument which at first appeared to me to be strong in their case . . . really crumbled away, upon closer consideration. I mean the Parousia conviction, as it underlies the earliest utterance and documents of the Christian outlook. It was this suddenness, this proximateness . . . which these friends thought themselves to be simply reaffirming. Yet this their thinking is demonstrably mistaken – they do *not* reproduce that primitive Christian mentality at all . . . [The *main* point of the ancient doctrine was that] this new order of things was not the work of men, whether slow or gradual, or quick and *hic et nunc*; but that it was the pure work, the sheer gift of

> God. Men could not produce it, work they ever so hard . . . Men could only prepare themselves to be awake and not unworthy of it . . . Thus it is a profound travesty of the Parousia doctrine and temper to take the element of proximity and suddenness, and to use this element as part of the scheme of human effort and productivity, in lieu of the original scheme of divine activity and human passivity. The original scheme is profoundly pessimistic in its manward side. This other scheme is enthusiastically optimistic (i.e. shallow) in its manward side. The original scheme is deeply religious. The new scheme is a sort of fanatical moralism.[129]

Martin Green has written that 'von Hügel probably could be convicted of telling us not of a risen and triumphant Christ, but of a suffering and dying one'.[130] There is, I think, no question but that von Hügel tells us of the latter. The 'preliminary pessimism' we have just seen in the letter to Kemp Smith may seem to lend support to Green's view that von Hügel fails to tell us of the former. The following text may also seem to give this view particularly strong statement, and within the context of our present discussion of the twofold movement in Jesus' doctrine of the Kingdom. What is in question, of course, is whether there *is* any such twofold movement for those who follow Christ. Is there Christian joy and victory *now*, as well as struggle? Of *what* is baptism effective sign: of suffering and dying only? or also of eternal life proleptically shared as fruit of Christ's resurrection? What is the basis of von Hügel's hope?

> I do not believe we shall ever have the Kingdom of Heaven here, not in this world. The Sermon on the Mount cannot be here . . . The kingdom cannot be here. That is God's level. Utopias are no use . . . ; nothing but God himself . . . is any use.[131]

Green's judgment, if correct, obviously weakens the fully Christian character of von Hügel's spirituality. It is a judgment which it is well to place just here, since it suggests: that a wholly futurist eschatology is at work, that eternal life as a partial but present ingredient of man's durational spirit, and that the precisely Christological basis of eternal life, resurrection, together with joy as the main fruit of victorious grace, are not operative in von Hügel's spiritual doctrine. Any positive Christian value of duration is thereby put in doubt. The economy, if it ever was incarnational, is in danger of ceasing to be so, for a view of history as enduringly incarnational demands the presence either of Jesus or of the Spirit of Jesus: giver and gift of life, abroad in history through the *Easter* declaration of Jesus as Lord and Christ. I believe the texts and doctrine we have examined thus far make such a view untenable. The original doctrine of the proximate Parousia as employed by von Hügel, together with his strongly seized Christian notion of Kingdom-Church as apocalyptic-prophetic, and as summons to joyously confident action and suffering as well as to earnestly watchful passivity, seems finally unintelligible apart from resurrection. But it is a matter for the reader to judge, now, and as we proceed.[132]

It is particularly important at this point to remember that we are engaged here in a construction of the spirituality of Friedrich von Hügel as found in his writings. We are not examining von Hügel's life, either as source or as test of that doctrine. His personal achievement and his personal limitations are therefore not at issue here. It may well be true, as Gwendolen Greene tells us, that while von Hügel 'was a great laugher', he lacked 'zest and happiness', and that while 'he loved life and people' and 'natural beauty', 'sheer beauty always left him cold'.[133] And von Hügel's biographer clearly pictures for us a man of notably sickly, worrisome and diffident temperament.[134]

In 1886 von Hügel's spiritual director, Huvelin, tells him: '. . . sanctity and suffering are the same thing . . . Our Lord won the world, not by . . . the Sermon on the Mount, but by his blood, by his agony on the cross.' But Huvelin also says to him: 'You will never save yourself by mutilation.' 'The proper spirit for you is one of blessing for every creature.' And finally: ' . . . do not be afraid: act, love.'[135]

As we noted before, and like Huvelin here, von Hügel will generally be found on both sides of the vital questions of spirituality. Where he approaches a balanced literary statement of any central spiritual experience he will also be close to paradox. And the famous doctrine of tension and the struggle for harmony will appear. For von Hügel, this is inevitable, if we are to speak and to live in the light of the full, non-attenuated mystery of Christ as von Hügel himself understands that mystery and Christ's own living of it. Harmony-in-tension has already appeared everywhere in this study and will continue to do so. But it is so central to von Hügel's understanding of all spiritual life that we will consider it directly now. But before doing so, let us look briefly at some few further texts which capture von Hügel's massive sense of joy and which point to the basis of his hope, the Resurrection. It will be characteristic of von Hügel's quest for wholeness that these texts are usually also statements about suffering.

> Religion has never made me happy; it's no use shutting your eyes to the fact that the deeper you go, the more alone you will find yourself . . . . Religion has never made me comfy. I have been in the desert ten years. All deepened life is deepened suffering, deepened dreariness, deepened joy. Suffering and joy. The final note of religion is joy.[136]

And the joy is not merely the 'Crown' that *follows* the '*Cross*', as many texts suggest. The eschaton is inaugurated, if not realized, and the joy of God is a necessary element of Christian life in a Kingdom already under way. Several times he writes of

> the fine rule by which the Roman Church tribunals require, for canonization as distinct from beatification, that the Servant of God concerned should be proved to have possessed and to have transmitted a deep spiritual joy.

This makes him wonder at the gloomy, if much tried, Newman and marvel at the radiant Huvelin.[137] He exults with Tyrrell in 1902:

> The world is wide and rich, complex and difficult, my masters. The battle in it, the struggle upwards and inwards of life and light is slow, varied, often checked and thrown back. Those that try and push matters on must be prepared for more or less of martyrdom. But, oh joy! – things move, things grow, light comes, and souls are helped, for all that, and all that.[138]

And finally, to Gwendolen Greene, about twenty years later:

> If we are Christians there are always two notes, suffering and joy. Gethsemane is awful, but it does not end with Gethsemane; there is the Resurrection. We want the *whole* of religion; renunciation and joy, the Cross and the Crown. I don't like Christians who have concentrated only on the Cross: Christianity is the *whole* life of Christ.[139]

Later, Gwendolen Greene writes of her visit to her uncle four days before his death: 'He was very tired and weak, and everything was a great effort. But he spoke of nearly everyone – he seemed to be recalling them one by one. He spoke, too, of the Resurrection.'[140]

In 1921 von Hügel dedicates his first series of *Essays and Addresses* to Dante, in gratitude 'for inspiration and support throughout some sixty years of spiritual stress'.[141] Stress. He is not complaining. Finite reality is a multiplicity, not static, but dynamic, an organism on the way. Harmony is the goal, to be sure, the harmony of God's own Trinitarian love life. But the journey to personality and holiness is accomplished, not by travelling light, not by short-cuts; it is a march through, a penetration into, the total real – both finite and infinite – involving struggle, conflict, tension. Thus all progress, as we have seen, 'est une victoire'.[142] For von Hügel, this is the human condition and the stuff of Christian experience. It is why he asks Blondel so fiercely for a fully human, concrete and striving Jesus who is not only the model of what a man should be, 'mais encore le modèle de la manière de le devenir'.[143]

And so he writes in 1923: 'religion has no subtler, and yet also no deadlier enemy in the region of the mind, than every and all monism.'[144] Indeed as early as 1912, the charge is already broadened to a wide range of spirituality:

> Effective love for our enemies, real pardon . . . , true, profound humility, a sense of sin, the experience of conversion, a deep belief in the given [*du Donné*] and in grace, that noble thirst for the non-contingent and the non-successive, for perfect, simultaneous reality: all this . . . rapidly loses its native colour and its virile, liberating poignancy under the influence of monism of whatever kind.[145]

The unfinished Gifford Lectures have as part of their fuller title: 'Concerning the Reality of Finites and the Reality of God.'[146] They constitute von Hügel's final witness against subjectivism and idealism, both as to God and as to the finite objects of experience.[147] But the lectures are also a ringing affirmation of subjectivity, of man's involvement with a reality that is *organic*, of the 'interaction of any one thing with everything else'.[148] Evelyn Underhill sees that the reality of finites, as distinct from and as prior to man's experience of those finites and as 'the scene within which alone our capacity for the infinite can expand', is for von Hügel the invitation to 'creatureliness', 'the first term of all genuine spirituality'. She also finds the *organic* quality of this reality to be von Hügel's 'ruling intuition'.[149] But this is only to formulate the Incarnation, for von Hügel's vision of the real is a Christian metaphysic both presupposed by and revealed in the constitution of Christ:

> The incarnation and self-imparting of the ultimate through persons and things requires the reality of the incarnating

> medium, as well as that of the absolute thus revealed. It involves the deep significance of every level of creation; yet also the fact that this significance is deep and real, just because the significance of God is still more real and deep, and his relation to his world is not a relation of sheer immanence but free, distinct, many-graded, sacramental.[150]

Such a view is utterly repugnant to monism.

Monism takes many forms for von Hügel. It is always a short-cut, a simplism. It reduces everything to the human, or even the animal.[151] Or it levels everything up to God.[152] Or it makes religion the whole of spirituality, the whole of life. He finds in it the result and the mirror of that flight from mystery he abhorred: 'the distinctively modern passion for utter logical clearness and consistency – the hunger of the mind which seeks its satisfaction in the mathematical and physical sciences.'[153] Von Hügel is especially harsh on the *technique* of 'pure immanentism, all evolution taken as final cause and not merely as instrument and method':

> The favourite method of . . . all monists, has always been the insistence upon immense ranges of time and space, and upon the appearance, little by little, within substances vulgarly dubbed 'material', of what are as vulgarly dubbed 'spiritual' characteristics. If only you thus manoeuvre with little by little, you can delude yourself and others into holding that this exquisite quantification solves the problem of utterly different qualities. It is at this point that Jesus calls a most impressive halt. He points, in the expectation of the Proximate Second Coming, to something not slow of growth, but sudden; not small and imperceptible, but huge and public; not produced by the sheer evolution from below of the already extant, but by the descent from without and above, of a newly given, a sheer illapse of quite another quality. Perhaps all the points of this stupendous picture require permanent softening by us his followers, if we would

> be equally faithful to his earlier, sunnier outlook. . . . Yet the magnificent massiveness of the anti-pantheism here, is a permanent service to religion of the very first magnitude.[154]

And yet, if such a 'materialism readily appears as the arch-enemy of the spirit . . . it very certainly is not the most dangerous of the spirit's enemies'.[155] Von Hügel fears the pride of Hegelian 'spirit' more than all other reductions of the real. It is the death of the creaturely mind, and ruinous to incarnation and the whole meaning of Jesus. 'There is no room' here 'for humility, for contrition, for adoration, because no room for sin or for God'.[156]

Von Hügel is nevertheless deeply sympathetic to the specifically religious temper, 'the appeal to boundless simplification', the simplicity of Christ himself. And God *is* One 'with a unity which all our best thinking can only distantly and analogously represent'. Religion will rightly 'long to be one and to give itself to the One – to follow naked the naked Jesus'.[157] But just what *is* the simplicity of the oneness of God? What *is* the content of Jesus' nakedness? For von Hügel, in both we have a rich, concrete multiplicity-in-unity; not an emptiness, but a harmony. And a harmony that, outside of God, is fought for and maintained in tension. Unity is everywhere Ignatius Loyola's peace: 'the simplicity of *order*.'[158]

The very unity of God is triune. But it is Our Lord himself who is of central interest. He is a 'duality of natures, God and Man', and the subject of a 'trinity of offices, the kingly, the prophetic and the priestly . . . , corresponding roughly to the external, the intellectual, and the mystical element of the human soul'. In his humanity, we

> come continually upon a rich multiplicity, variety, and play of different exterior and interior apprehensions and activities, emotions and sufferings, all profoundly permeated by one great end and aim, yet each differing from the other, and contributing a different share to the one great result. The

> astonishment at the disciples' slowness of comprehension, the flash of anger at Peter, the sad reproachfulness towards Judas, the love of the children . . . are all *different* emotions. The perception of the beauty of the flowers of the field, of the habits of plants and of birds, of the varieties of the day's early and late cloud and sunshine . . . ; and again of the psychology of various classes of character, age, temperament . . . are all *different* observations. The lonely recollection in the desert, the nights spent in prayer upon the mountains . . . , the long foot-journeyings, the many flights . . . are all *different* activities.[159]

This is the true nakedness of Jesus, the incarnational simplicity which is our goal, and the model of that goal's becoming. And so von Hügel will inveigh against contemplation conceived as an empty oneness. 'Inattention to more than one thing at a time' *within* contemplation is a defect.[160] And any notion, whether of a God preoccupied wholly with himself, or of a human contemplation of him which does not move *beyond* him to active love and concern for our fellow-men, has 'no place in an incarnational religion'. 'Indeed all Our Lord's Synoptic teachings, as to man's ultimate standard and destiny, belong to this God-in-man and man-in-God type of doctrine: for there the two great commandments are strictly inseparable; God's interest in the world is direct and detailed . . . ; and man, in the Kingdom of God, will sit down at a banquet, the unmistakable type of social joys.' 'Our Lord's whole life and message become unintelligible, and the Church loses its deepest roots, unless the Kingdom of God is, for us human souls, as truly a part of our ultimate destiny as is God himself.' Variety-in-unity is the permanent condition of Christian man in his very God-likeness.[161]

An important letter to Maude Petre presses our subject-matter further. The context is creation and incarnation. When we say we believe in creation, we affirm the mystery of God's self-alienation of part of his own power. He has given creation a 'relative independence of its own'. He has 'set up (relative but still real) obstacles, limits, friction as it were against himself':

> And thus we may well wonder at this mysteriously thin barrier between our poor finite relativity, and the engulfing infinite Absolute, a barrier which is absolutely necessary for us, for though God was and could ever be without us, God is no more God for us, if we cease to be relatively distinct from him. . . . And note further that this poor little shelter of reeds, with the Absolute ever burning down upon it; this poor little paper boat, on the sea of the infinite, – God took pity on them, quite apart from sin and the Fall, – God wanted to give their relative independence a quite absolute worth, he took as it were sides with his own handiwork against himself and gave us the rampart of his tender strong humanity. . . . we cannot, I am persuaded through and through, show our apprehension of the secret of his law of spiritual life for us all . . . better than in ever remembering . . . , ever practising, ever suffering the . . . *true and real independence* which God has chosen to give creation, by the very fact of creating it, and still more by incarnating himself in its head and centre, man. Never, as truly as creation will never be absorbed in the Creator, nor man, even the God-man, become . . . simply and purely God, will or can science and art, morals and politics be without each their own inside, their own true law of growth and existence *other than, in no wise a department or simple dependency of, religion*. The creature is not the Creator . . . , it is not a little god . . . Even so are science and all the other departments of life not religion.[162]

Multiplicity: finite and infinite, incarnation – and now: religion and 'all the other departments of life'. These are the *facts*, the materials, of spiritual life. The goal is harmony. And the way is friction. Religion is declared very really, if inadequately, distinct from spirituality. The sacred is acclaimed, together with the rejection of pansacralism. And a broad secularity is the situation, the stuff of, and the opportunity for, a profoundly *religious* Christianity. 'The Professor loves the *aut-aut*; whilst I believe real life mostly demands the *et-et*.'

Von Hügel's specifically *spiritual* direction of Gwendolen Greene shows this whole doctrine pastorally at work: the reading and advice he gives her is heavily weighted on the non-religious side. He desires to establish a 'double current' in her, and warns against the 'elimination of . . . divinely intended tensions'. 'I want to *organize* you for life . . . and death.'[163] Underhill records that he could be severe: 'You should see my old man dusting me down!'[164] Any religious vehemence 'was likely to be met by a humiliating request to "try a little gardening" or . . . " some quiet needlework".'[165] Or more importantly: 'I believe you ought to get yourself . . . interested *in the poor*.'[166]

Von Hügel's most powerful condemnation of monism and his contrastingly strong affirmation of harmony-in-tension receive statement in his discussion of religious and worldly morality. Here he largely follows Ernst Troeltsch. But the citation of Troeltsch, *on just this question*, is so massive, frequent and approving, is over such a large span of years, and is in such agreement with von Hügel's own writing in related areas, that the reader must conclude that we have here in Troeltsch von Hügel's own spiritual doctrine.[167]

> The chief problem of Christian ethics [is not] the relation between certain subjective means . . . but with the relation between certain objective ends, which have . . . to be brought . . . to the greatest possible unity. And the difficulty here lies in the fact, that the sublunar among these ends are none the less moral ends . . . , that they are ends-in-themselves, and necessary for their own sakes . . . ; whilst the super-worldly end cannot share its rule with any other end.

> [Modern civilization is characterized precisely by] a simultaneous insistence upon the inner-worldly ends, as possessing the nature of ends-in-themselves, and upon the religious, super-worldly end: it is indeed from just this combination that this civilization derives its peculiar richness, power, and freedom, but also its painful, interior tension.
>
> [Clearly,] ethical life is not, in its beginnings, a unity but a multiplicity: man grows up amidst a number of moral ends, whose unification is not his starting-point, but his problem....
>
> The tension present in this multiplicity of elements ... is of an importance equal to that of the multiplicity itself; indeed in this tension resides the main driving-force of religion. ...
>
> [Christianity is a] polarity ..., and its formula must be dualistic; it resembles, not a circle with one centre, but an ellipse with two focuses [calling at once for detachment and attachment]. For Christianity is unchangeably an ethics of redemption, with a conception of the world both optimistic and pessimistic, both transcendental and immanental, and an apprehension both of a severe antagonism and of a close interior union between the world and God. It is, in principle, a dualism, and yet a dualism which is ever in process of abolition by faith and action. ... [As religious ethic, it concentrates] with abrupt exclusiveness [upon God; as humane ethic, it is] busy with the moulding and transforming of nature, and through love bringing about an eventual reconciliation with it. ... [The poles may alternate in prominence;] but neither of them may be completely absent, if the Christian outlook is to be maintained.

Von Hügel sees the problem 'as one of spiritual dynamics and not of intellectual statics', requiring three kinds of action. First, the recognition of 'centres of human energy and duty of a primarily this-world character', each with its automomy and laws. Second, 'the attempt at organizing ... and ... harmonizing, (whilst never emasculating or eliminating), these various [elements] . . . into an ever larger ultimate unity. And lastly, there is as strong a turning away from all this occupation with the contingent and finite, to the sense and apprehension of the infinite and abiding.'

A dynamism so rich will require alternation *within the individual* Christian and also *between various groups* of men within the corporate body of Christ. But such 'subdivision of labour' will avoid damage and fanaticism 'only on condition that it is felt and worked *as* such a subdivision'. 'The undeniable abuses' of the ascetic and contemplative life have been due mainly to the plausible error that since religion, God, *is* man's primary and highest concern, everything else may be dispensed with. 'This is not so.' Such a unity is 'empty and mechanical'. It makes men narrow. Conversely, 'humane ethics', though 'ends in themselves, do not contain the ultimate'. Where conceived and acted on as ultimate, they 'make men superficial'.

> From first to last, God, the final and finally alone necessary end, should be placed and be kept before the soul; yet a certain liberty and range should be left for both ends and forms, so that continually, and with as great ease as possible, there may result the deepening of the humane ends by Christian ethics, and the humanising of the Christian end – so that life, within the humane ends, may, simultaneously, be a service of God; and that the service of God may, simultaneously, transfigure the world.

Now this last is but an ethical formulation of the major theme with which our study is concerned: the civilizing of spirituality, and the spiritualizing of civilization.[168]

Von Hügel, nevertheless, sets definite limits to dualism. And just here lies the perennial truth of the mystics' witness. For life also is, and therefore experience ought to be, ingredient of 'synthesis' and 'organizing unity', as well as of 'contrast and tension'.[169] On the classical question of the body, von Hügel is clear that any final 'antagonism between body and spirit cannot be accepted'. It is 'unsound in psychology . . . , narrow in cosmology . . . , and ruinous for ethics . . . It is directly contradictory of the central truth and temper of Christianity', where incarnation and resurrection demand 'God's condescension to man's whole physico-spiritual organism' and the permanent value and survival 'of all that is essential to man's true personality across and after death'.[170] Indeed – leaving aside good and evil – any dualism that is absolutized, at any level of von Hügel's vast, graded reality, and any friction that is viewed as end and not as means and medium of a richer harmony, is self-destructive and destructive of spirituality itself: the birth of personality and its growth in holiness.[171]

A letter of 1911 gives us one of von Hügel's finest spiritual testaments on this whole subject:

> God is an immense concretion, not an abstraction. He is a multiplicity (for our apprehension) in unity. He has 'gone out of himself' by love, and shows his nature supremely in his attention and care for every sparrow; he has come down to man . . . He has made my body and its senses, he has made my love of the historical, social, institutional, even the legal; *I am to incarnate, in my turn, the incarnate God;* I am not only to express spirit in and through matter, I am also to awaken, and cause to grow, and to purify (by the painful contraction and friction involved) by my contacts with, by my give and take, this my spirit from and to matter. No floating, no drifting, no dreaming above the body, the family, society, history, institutions, but a penetrating into them, and a returning out of them, again to return, Antaeus-like, to earth.[172]

Christianity is indeed 'essentiellement religion d'incarnation', whose 'flower and strength' is Christ: 'transcendence in the immanence', 'the eternal in the temporal', 'this tension and duality in harmony and union'. [173] The perennial danger for spirituality is the sterilizing short-cut: 'the premature unity . . .

The struggle . . . , the war must be accepted . . . , man has to be crucified . . . Victory . . . means a unity that is organic, and this is achieved by slow harmonization alone.'[174] We are summoned to a 'variety up to the verge of dissipation' and to a 'recollection up to the verge of emptiness'; to an ecumenism that combines 'a deep fervour without fanaticism, and a generous sympathy without indifference'. We must take seriously the body of an action, as well as its spirit, and value heat and passion, together with and for the sake of, light and repose. It is a 'creaturely' spirituality, 'which plants the Cross everywhere', 'but like all crosses bringing with it the joy of life'.[175]

Von Hügel's eye is steadily on Jesus. This means direct preoccupation with and love of God in his being, and equally direct love and concern for both man and the world, in their becoming. Teilhard wrote similarly:

> I have always offered myself to Our Lord as a sort of field of experience where the fusion between the two great loves of God and the world would take place in a small way.[176]

Incarnation, of itself, affirms infinite plenitude, simultaneity, eternity, God, together with striving, durational, human spirit. In von Hügel's view, then, to be preoccupied with Christ is to be preoccupied with God, and with the essence of religion, adoration. Christ, both as God and as man, is the image and revelation of the Father. Indeed, we have seen that von Hügel regards the fatherhood of God as Jesus' fundamental pre-Caesarea experience.[177] 'Did he not come to show us the Father?'[178] He writes in 1912: 'The joy of religion resides . . . in adoration.' And in 1922, to Norman Kemp Smith: 'We both believe in, adore, love God! What a gift of his *that* is!'[179] He puts it plainly to Loisy: how shall '*les rayons du soleil*' ('the rays of the sun') – which are the Christian message – survive, if the sun itself, Christ's divinity, be extinguished? And further: ' . . . I believe that this (the divinity of Jesus) shall have or fail to have an acceptable meaning for modern man, depending on whether we maintain or abandon our faith in the transcendent, in the ontological, in God.'[180]

The von Hügel literature on God is extensive. We turn to that material now. Assuming the incarnational framework described in this chapter – a description which ought to have located, in a general way, God, man and world – our aim will be to state more precisely the place and influence of God in von Hügel's spirituality.

CHAPTER THREE

GOD

Friedrich von Hügel's spirituality bases itself upon a view of man as an organic movement, a complex journey into the real. And this movement, while it effects and is effected by man as an individual, equally pertains to him as social and as historical. For man is essentially constituted by the interconnection and the interaction which is his sociality. And still further – this man is a being in a world which makes the journey with him.

Religion, a part of this complex situation we have just reviewed, is itself a thing of parts, of elements. Religion is historical, 'a sacred torch race across the centuries',[1] and it is institutional, wherever man 'incarnates [for himself] . . . the incarnate God'.[2] Religion has also a speculative element and is therefore perennially bent upon that ceaseless criticism and synthesis which aids its own self-understanding. But religion, taken even as a whole, is not the whole truth about man. Religion is not the only 'given', but remains to the end a *part* of man's organic situation. It is not the only value, but is '*a* factor of life'.[3] There remain, and importantly, art, politics, science, social amelioration, the building of the world.

> Man's personality, the instrument of all his fuller and deeper apprehensions, is constituted by the presence and harmonization of a whole mass of energies and intimations belonging to different levels and values; and not one of these can (in the long run and for mankind at large) be left aside or left unchecked by the others, without grave drawback to that personality. Religion is indeed the deepest of energisings and

> intimations within man's entirety, but it is not the only one; and . . . those other energies and intimations are also willed by God and come from him, and (in the long run and for mankind at large) are necessary to man's health and balance even in religion itself.[4]

Yet it is in the midst of just this passage that von Hügel enunciates the subject-matter and much of the burden of this chapter: 'Through religion alone God becomes definitely revealed to man as self-conscious Spirit, as an object, as *the* Object, of direct, explicit adoration . . . ' And in the closing pages of *The Mystical Element of Religion*, after a long summary and synthesis of the 'whole movement', both religious and non-religious, which is man and his world in their becoming and their destiny, von Hügel asserts the centrality of that mystical element, its centrality both for religion *and* for human existence as such. To repeat then, he is identifying here what is for him not only the heart of that narrower complex, man's specifically religious life, but also the heart of the whole broad reach of human living. 'Life, and life's centre, religion, are flat and dreary, vain and philistine', unless there penetrate 'every part, as salt and yeast'

> the vivid, continuous sense that God, the Spirit upholding our poor little spirits, is the true originator and the true end of the whole movement, in all it may have of spiritual beauty, truth, goodness and vitality; that all the various levels and kinds of reality and action are, in whatever they have of worth, already immanently fitted to stimulate, supplement and purify each other by him who, an infinite spiritual interiority himself, gives thus to each one of us indefinite opportunities for actualizing our own degree and kind of spiritual possibility and ideal; and that he it is who, however dimly yet directly, touches our souls and awakens them, in and through all those minor stimulations and apprehensions, to that noblest, incurable discontent with our own

petty self and to that sense of and thirst for the infinite and abiding, which articulates *man's deepest requirement and characteristic*...[5]

This conviction about the centrality of God and of the action of God as the very condition of man's fully operative humanity is an old faith with von Hügel. Nevertheless, in later years he chides himself for not having always stressed this truth that was always with him and for not having sufficiently attended to the philosophical basis required – indeed latent and given – in such a faith. The 1923 Preface to the second edition of *The Mystical Element* suggests for the book a single change, which would be 'no more than a full development into a quite conscious decision of what, in 1908, was already predominant but not yet persistently articulate and comfortably final':

> By now I perceive with entire clarity that, though religion cannot even be conceived as extant at all without a human subject humanly apprehending the Object of religion, the reality of the Object (in itself the Subject of all subjects) and its presence independently of all our apprehension of it – that its givenness is the central characteristic of all religion worthy of the name. The otherness, the prevenience of God, the one-sided relation between God and man, these constitute the deepest measure and touchstone of all religion. . . . The central and final philosophic system and temper of mind which is alone genuinely appropriate to the subject-matter of religion is, I cannot doubt, some kind of realism.[6]

But this change is one of emphasis and not of direction, for the note for the second impression of the same book, as far back as 1909, already speaks of the 'pre-existence, the super-eminence, the independence of the august object of religion . . . God, the divine Spirit, is indeed before, within, and after all our truest dignity and deepest disquiet'.[7] As an old man von Hügel remembers that

> at five and six years of age, I possessed a sense, not only of God in the external, especially the organic, world, but of a mysterious divine Presence in the churches of Florence. Thus historical religion was with me, together with metaphysical (and natural) religion, from the first.
>
> . . . The religion which was already so strong was of the mystical type, in so far, at least, that its thirst and support were not drawn from ethics . . . , but from existence, and the sense of existence, in the sense of various realities penetrated and supported by the Supreme Reality, God. Such an outlook is necessarily out after *what is*, rather than *what ought to be*.

But this is not remembered as pantheism, for 'my delight was precisely in the fact that, beautiful as the external nature was, God did not consist even in its full totality, but was a life, an intelligence, a love distinct from it all, in spite of his close penetration of it all. Thus otherness was as part of the outlook as was reality.'[8]

In another major work, *Eternal Life*, published in 1912, von Hügel announces that the book will give 'vigilant attention . . . to the ontological character and witness of religion – the central position occupied, in the fullest experiences and articulations of religion, by the reality, the difference, and yet the likeness, of God. A critical realism – a realism not of categories and ideas but of organisms and spirits, of *the* Spirit, a purified but firm anthropomorphism are here maintained throughout as essential to the full vigor and clear articulation of religion.' And he complains there of the copious subjectivist literature 'proceeding from thinkers of distinction and technical competence, which attempts to find or make a world worthy of man's deepest, ever costly and difficult, requirements and ideals, within avowedly mere projections of himself'.[9] In his last years this view of God as man's self-projection of what man himself is, or may through progress hope to be, evokes a reaction close to anger: 'Try and prove, if you will, that religion is untrue;

but do not mislead yourself and others as to what constitutes its power and its worth.'[10]

He tells Gwendolen Greene:

> Some people are so fond of ideas. A new idea is a kind of magic to them! I don't care about ideas, I want facts. God is not an idea. He is a fact. 'I find God outside of myself. He is an illapse from outside.' There, that is right, that does away with all this miserable subjectivism. . . . We are becoming creatures – becoming in order to be – God *is*. We are getting to being. Religion is not man-made: it is immense: it comes from outside.[11]

And the strictures grow as he speaks of the truth that is fundamental for his whole life's work: 'We are so fond of men, we can't keep God. The most subtle enemy of religion is humanitarianism.' 'You can't have religion without adoration.' We want *more* love, more adoration: 'more God, more Christ.'[12] And *thus* the importance of the Real: 'it is clear, moreover, that if prayer, and especially adoration, are the soul of religion, then the firm ontological stance which forms the basis for such prayer and adoration must likewise pertain to the very soul of religion.'[13]

Adoration, then, is 'man's deepest requirement and characteristic', just simply as man, and 'if ontology is an illusion, so is religion', so is adoration.[14] But if adoration has ontology as its presupposition in von Hügel's spiritual doctrine, philosophy and theology distinctly do not enjoy any such privileged position. Quite the other way around. For as we shall see, adoration, as the act and stance most constitutive of man's very humanity, is not an hypothesis born of, much less a conclusion deduced from, von Hügel's philosophy or theology. Adoration is an immediate datum and demand of man's experience of the real. Out of this experience, and not otherwise, philosophy and theology take their origin, and upon it they reflect. And while this experience will indeed be modified by the successive character of the history which it is and in which it comes to be, it will also, across the centuries and within each individual's lifetime, know and witness to a continuity and a weighty permanence of its own. Indeed the durational constituent of history itself has its roots in the prayer of adoration.

It is important to be clear, before proceeding further, on the restricted and very intense meaning assigned to the term religion in this central theme of God in von Hügel's spirituality. Thought and emotion are involved in this understanding of religion, but being and doing are the first concern. Religion is defined primarily in terms of its truly first subject and its final object: God, God is. And the secondary reference of religion here is man's adoration of God, *simply because he is*. While the institutional and intellectual elements are indeed elements of religion and are seen to be utterly necessary for the fullest actuation of that heart of religion which is man's adoration of God, they are not that heart. They are, along with the non-religious factors of life, its means, its occasion, its incarnation. They remain, at the first and the last, as does man himself, at the service of the adoration of God.

Religion, then, in its most essential note, is identified with its own mystical element. As such, it 'is never a means, is always an end, *the* end'. Von Hügel is clear about this. Religion is an affirmation of 'Reality, *the* Reality distinct from ourselves, the self-subsistent Spirit, God. . . . It is . . . ontological, metaphysical: it is this, or it is nothing.' 'Religion, at least among the mystics (and I believe that, on this point at least, the mystics merely dive deeper into and bring out more explicitly the sap or the central core of the religious passion), consists centrally in the sense of Presence – the sense of an overflowing Existence distinct from our own and in the adoration of the same.'[15]

Von Hügel also gives frequent and prolonged attention throughout his writings to the phenomenon of mysticism. And again, it is important that his meaning and concern here be correctly understood. His interest is not the esoteric. The preternatural and even the miraculous, most certainly the odd and the extraordinary, hold no appeal for him personally and receive very little of his attention and time. Where the latter phenomena do occur, their importance and validity are judged by one only criterion: do they help the mystic and those he serves 'to become more humble, true, and loving'.[16]

Von Hügel gives at least two definitions of mysticism which clearly indicate the meaning he wishes the term to have. In both definitions, mysticism is located well within what he considers to be centrally human. The mystical is *what man is*, what he may expect to do and to have happen, *because God is*. It is man's 'deepest requirement and characteristic', in the sense we have been discussing above.

> Mysticism . . . is an experience (more or less clear and vivid) of God as distinct, self-conscious Spirit.[17]
>
> [Mysticism is] the intuitive and emotional apprehension of the most specifically religious of all truths, viz., the already full operative existence of eternal beauty, truth, goodness, of infinite Personality and Spirit, independently of our action.[18]

For our present purposes these definitions are, I believe, sufficiently clear in themselves. The present chapter ought to prove their adequate commentary.

The spirituality of Friedrich von Hügel is a Christologically structured theocentrism. 'The centre of the picture has thus to be God and not ourselves . . . '[19] Von Hügel finds in the Old Testament that 'the emphasis and the detail of the religious experience and teaching are ever upon God, not upon man, and, nevertheless, upon this life, not upon the next'.[20] He cites 'the glorious self-commitment' of Psalm 73: 'I was as a beast before thee. Nevertheless I am continually with thee. Whom have I in heaven but thee? and there is none upon earth that I desire beside thee', and he calls it a 'deathless articulation . . . of the reality, prevenience, presence . . . of God'.[21]

In the New Testament, von Hügel sees 'Christianity . . . primarily busy with ultimates, with ends', with God, like Jesus Christ her Lord who 'lives and moves and has his being in those ultimates'. 'God is indeed the beginning, the middle and the end, the ceaseless presupposition of Jesus' teaching.'[22] The Sermon on the Mount is the ethical equivalent of Jesus' teaching on the proximate Second Coming.[23] When pressed 'to its metaphysical foundations', this teaching 'indicates the presence and the pressure, within our profoundest life, of a, of *the*, contrasting Other, of the non-contingent reality, of God'. Within man 'lie intimations . . . of more than just merely human, or sub-human, realities. And this instinct primarily wants God, not man; and, in man, it wants his union with God and his union with other men through God. . . . Thus it is that Our Lord's temper and teaching precisely meet, after they themselves have more fully awakened and articulated, this metaphysical apprehension and thirst.'[24] And the *persistent devotedness*[25] called for by this doctrine of the sudden Second Coming is the exact ethical expression of that durational, that incarnational 'junction between the simultaneity of God and the successiveness . . . of man. Thus the two points essential to every real mysticism are secured.'[26]

In St Paul, von Hügel finds that that brotherhood of men which is the Church is initiated, 'effected and maintained' by 'Christ, the Spirit, God', and that the entire Pauline movement is 'steeped in a manly humility and deepest *creatureliness*, and in a sense of the prevenience, the omnipresent holiness and love, of God'.[27] Finally, turning to St John, he sees pulsing through the Fourth Gospel 'the sense and the effect of the two great concrete realities – God, the already fully extant and operative eternal beauty, truth, love and goodness, infinite Personality and Spirit, who is all this independently of our apprehension and action; and Jesus, who actually lived in the flesh here below amongst us, the lowly servant . . . '[28]

In addition to his frequent citations of the biblical Revelation, von Hügel often speaks as philosopher or theologian when assessing what he believes to be the root facts of spirituality. Nevertheless, he is emphatic on what the priorities are. Spirituality deals with realities, with facts. And facts remain, unshaken and vital, whether we manage to speak well or badly about them. Neither God nor our certitudes about our basic experience of him depend upon the ingenuity or even the existence of theology. 'Religion . . . begins and proceeds and ends with the given.'

> The sense of *awe*, derived by the religious soul from its vivid apprehension of the greatness of the Reality, a Reality experienced as so much deeper and richer than the soul can ever express, is specifically different from any sense of *uncertainty* as to the existence and the superhuman nature of the Reality underlying and occasioning this apprehension. Healthy mysticism and genuine scepticism are thus intrinsically opposites.[29]

Religion 'is essentially affirmation of fact, of what *is*'. Von Hügel writes to Gwendolen Greene: 'I am always so glad when you can and do articulate some perplexity about one or other of the huge, rich, many-sided – not questions, but facts . . . ' He persistently argues for the 'full autonomy of religion, of religion as constituting a realm of facts and experiences'. Philosophy and theology are not religion:[30]

> Philosophy no more makes religion than botany makes plants or astronomy suns and moons; and criticism of all sorts is – in these matters especially – worse than useless unless it is inspired by a genuine experience and love of religion. Hence we must here always have our nails before we pare them; we . . . pare them, not in order to make them or to have them . . . Love – love of religion and love of the other kinds, levels, ranges of life – is here the fundamental need – a standing within these living complexes and necessi-

> ties. The concrete has here always to come first, and to be reached last.[31]

The important point just here – and it is a fundamental stand – is that the experience – love and concrete living – must come *first*, and that fruitful philosophy of religion perhaps may not, but certainly may only, occur from *within* a life of adoration of a God who is loved. When von Hügel gives his niece his great book on God, *Eternal Life*, he writes to her: 'I wrote the thing praying; read it as written, Child!'[32] And he concludes the introduction to his last, unfinished book, *The Reality of God*, with a similar point:

> The thirst after, the longing for, the reaching out and the crying aloud for God, for the Reality which underlies, environs, protects, and perfects all the lesser realities and all our apprehensions of them – this will have to impel and sustain our long search after a more explicit grasp of what we already dimly hold, of what, in strictness, already holds us from without and from within.

It is only because God is with us, prevenient and incarnate, that we find him at all.[33]

One of von Hügel's editors, Bernard Holland, records a relevant conversation for us: '"What is religion, then?" . . . "Religion is adoration," answered the Baron. . . . "It is very awful to think of the unbelieving soul" – the soul void of God-consciousness and adoration.'[34] And this all-importance of the first thing necessary is even pressed upon a very young girl to whom von Hügel is giving spiritual direction: '*You . . . can never be happy without religion*. And by religion I mean not some vague sentiment, or some beautiful thought, not even . . . moral striving as apart from faith in . . . God, in whose presence, and as whose will, we thus strive to grow and be: but by and in self-donation, such self-commitment to a, to *the* Reality other than, yet immensely near to, ourselves.'[35]

Nevertheless, von Hügel is keenly aware that many men do lack this religious sense, this felt need and desire to adore God which is the foundation of his spirituality. 'It is curious, but it seems to me that some people are quite deficient in the religious sense. I don't understand it at all.' He is aware of the 'great' and 'humble' Darwin, and he will not judge John Stuart Mill. 'God must allow it, it is somehow his will. Religion to them is a purely this-world affair.'[36] But he is frankly put off when he meets this deficiency in a cleric:

> He has established himself permanently in my mind as a living example of how greatly ethical a soul can be with little of the specifically religious sense. And this strong impression prevented me from feeling quite at ease in his company or even in his books; for, after all, he was a Christian cleric, who had deliberately chosen to be one, so that, quite spontaneously, I would renew my expectation of what was hardly there.[37]

Von Hügel does not judge. And he is well aware 'that belief in the superhuman reality of the Infinite' has often been the reason for turning away from 'other great and necessary human activities . . . , from science and philosophy, from art and politics, even from society . . . And again, has not precisely that belief, when it has turned attention to these other sides of life, attempted to dominate, to mould or to break them . . . ?' Von Hügel loathes this abuse, this clericalism which often leads to 'angry hatred of the very words metaphysic, transcendence, ontology'.[38] Many an upright man will repudiate this emasculation or perversion by religion of the other genuinely and autonomously valuable elements of human existence and will instead and at best – whether theoretically or practically – collapse religion into ethics. God, and Christ too perhaps, become the world and its destiny, they become especially one's fellow-men. Where the substitution is humanity in its ideal state, a quasi- (and for von Hügel religiously bogus) transcendence is thus maintained. Adoration is no longer the ground for, or the accompaniment of, it is not expressed by and in – rather it is displaced by – the service of one's brothers.[39]

Von Hügel does not judge. But he asks, and frequently, about humility, about creatureliness, 'the first term of all genuine spirituality'.[40] 'We are creatures, and we must be creaturely . . . I have always tried to teach my children humility.' It is especially difficult for the young: 'They have not enough experience, they need humility; that will come.' 'So many people are too clever for religion: we want less brains, more heart. Brains are no use, we want the child. I always try to get the child to come up in people.'[41]

Von Hügel asks too, and rather more sternly, about philosophical humility. He fears above all the pride of Hegelian spirit, where thinking is identified with reality and logic is transformed into metaphysic.[42] He praises Hegel for his 'magnificent sense of the fundamental importance of history for man . . . , and of the presence, within this *durational* history, of a Concrete Reality, giving to this history its full worth and an abiding, indeed eternal, meaning'. However, von Hügel is of the opinion that what had started out as completed self-consciousness, the *prius* and cause of historical process, becomes in Hegel the *posterius* and effect. God comes to his own self-consciousness in and through the development of man. 'What appalling chauvinism!' For what and before whom shall man have contrition? Where is 'the homeliness alone truly appropriate to man . . . ? Gethsemane and Calvary, are they truly, fully here?' Is this what impels us 'to our divine unrest? We take it, decidedly *not*.' There is nothing to be humble about, and no Other left for man's adoration of love.[43]

The evidence for the reality of God 'is what it is: no good will can increase or change it; no evil inclination can suppress or diminish it.' What about guilt, then?

The answer is, that certain dispositions of the will very

> certainly enter into all deep and delicate apprehensions . . . A certain rare disoccupation with the petty self is here a *sine qua non* condition of any success . . . It can do but good if, whilst practising the greatest reserve in our judgment of individuals, we keep alive within us this sense that a certain pang accompanies, in the meanness and jealousy of the human heart, (and any one human heart is liable to more or less of such meanness and jealousy), the full, persistent recognition of a perfection entirely not of our own making, a perfection we can never equal, and yet a perfection, the recognition of our utter dependence upon which constitutes the very centre, the inevitable condition, of our own (even then essentially finite) perfection. I believe that not to be aware of the costliness, to unspiritualised man, of the change from his self-centredness, from *anthropocentrism* to *theocentrism*, means not only a want of awakeness to the central demand of religion, but an ignorance or oblivion of the poorer, the perverse, tendencies of the human heart.[44]

We turn now to von Hügel's discussion of religious experience itself, and then to a closer indication of that experience as a panentheism; and finally, to von Hügel's understanding of God as joy. Before we do so, however, we are well reminded once more, here by Douglas Steere, that von Hügel's 'philosophical scaffolding' is 'but a description of a kind of stance by which the soul is poised and directed toward the Object of adoration . . . The goal of his philosophical thought is always identical. It is to give a clue to the breathing space the soul requires if it is to slip the tightly knotted bands of self-serving and move into the heroic self-spending company of the servants of God.'[45]

Spirituality has the primacy in all von Hügel writes, and it is well to approach his frequent technical digressions, understanding them for what they are: a probing, with whatever success, towards man's richer, more abundant life. The large resources of von Hügel's mind and learning are wholly at the service of his spirit and the spirits of his fellow-men. His writings are, in the deepest sense, apostolic and missionary. Blunt evidence of this primacy of spirituality and of the role of learning as servant of life and adoration is given by von Hügel himself in one of his last essays, 'The Facts and Doctrines Concerning God Which Are of Especial Importance in the Life of Prayer'. We shall therefore partially enumerate its contents at the end of this chapter.[46]

Friedrich von Hügel seeks a metaphysic of *life*, and not of the schools.[47]

> We religious men will have to develop, *as part of our religion*, the ceaseless sense of its requiring the *nidus*, materials, stimulant, discipline, of the other God-given, non-religious activities, duties, ideals of man, from his physical and psychical necessities up to his aesthetic, political and philosophical aspirations. The autonomy, competition, and criticism of the other centres of life will have thus to become welcome to religion for the sake of religion itself.[48]

But once *within* the circle of religious experience itself, man's spiritual life is seen to be,

> in proportion to the depth and delicacy of its spirituality, always simultaneously conscious of two closely interconnected things: *the more than human reality of the Object of its experience*, which Object indeed itself reveals itself in, and makes real, this experience, AND *the abiding difference between even this its present experience and the great reality thus experienced and revealed.*[49]

The testimony of such religious experience demands as its presupposition and vehicle a critical realism, where the mind reaches the trans-subjective thing-in-itself and where the trans-subjective is not limited to the empirical.

This realism is characterized by givenness as the first fact about *every* level of experience, 'from the givenness of the pebble and the star . . . on to the immensely greater givenness of the human spirit, and the primary, absolute givenness and reality of God'.[50] Religious experience, like all others, then, is '*une affirmation ontologique*'.[51] This God-experience, at least initially – and to a great extent, always – is dim, but its potential as vivid is limitless. As human, it is reasonable, but as experience, it is also compound of feeling and of willing. It is an intuition, then, which in the spiritually alert man increasingly apprehends a God who yet remains incomprehensible.

And this apprehension or intuition – this experience of God – occurs only on the occasion of and in contrast to man's experience of finite reality. *But the experience of God is direct.*[52] The unconditional is immediately given; it is neither deduced nor inferred. But it is given in and with the definite and contingent alone, lighting up the finite and contingent, and *contrasting* itself to this contingent even as it thus reveals itself with it. Finally, what is really already said – but what is crucial for von Hügel's description of religious experience as direct, as intuitive: *both* terms of this stated contrast fall within consciousness.[53]

We have here, surely, a description of religious experience as a closely woven, organic complex – which is not unexpected, given the systematic character of von Hügel's incarnationalism. And we have, by way of corollary, the explicit repudiation of any distinct faculty of mystical apprehension. Charges of ontologism, atomism and pure or exclusive mysticism are rejected too. Von Hügel maintains that religious experience is not ontologist because it does not 'deduce our other ideas from the idea of God', nor does it argue from Cartesian 'ideas and their clarity, but from living forces and their operativeness'. It is a metaphysic of life. It is not an atomism because the direct experience proclaimed is specifically rejected as an intellectualism and demands, on the contrary, the employment of *all* man's powers and experience, and it demands this precisely of man *in a society* 'affecting him from the rich past and the poignant present'. Finally, it is not pure or exclusive mysticism, 'for only in the shock' of finite mind on finite thing 'does the latent fire, the affinity to the Infinite of all true life, spring forth . . . ' And here too religious experience is insisted upon as social. For God is present to man primarily 'as the divine link between all moments and all souls, and as the centre of the Kingdom of God'. Men are intended surely to become unique personalities. But they do so 'only as necessary constituents and docile parts of the large whole, as members, through a visible organization of the invisible Church. Thus the test as to the reality of the divine contact will become ever less restricted . . . to the individual life, as the soul, dying to all solipsism, grows in true spirituality.'[54]

The foregoing statement of what von Hügel intends by religious experience may serve as general orientation. But if it has been dense and compressed and excessively technical, it is nevertheless also incomplete. We shall seek now to clarify and supplement it, and within a development that is von Hügel's own, by extensively reproducing one of his formulations of the problem, together with a commentary based on other texts. The central text to be given, a letter of 11 December 1918, to Gwendolen Greene,[55] has two advantages: it is synthetic in character, and – most importantly for this study – it was written by von Hügel specifically in the way of spiritual direction. If nothing else, we are afforded a bravura, but not atypical, display of the ambitious, freewheeling and demanding quality of that spiritual direction. For purposes of clarity, we shall, while commenting on it, set this letter, and only this letter, off from the main body of the text.

The question is put to von Hügel: 'What is the precise meaning of Thekla's[56] insistence upon religion as primarily an is-ness, not an ought-ness?'

A good question. Well, you see, Niece, when the Renaissance

> and the Protestant Reformation, and later the French Revolution came, they, in part, only articulated, but also they, in part, each differently, yet all greatly, fed and excited a reaction which had permeated the educated average man of Western Europe ever since, say, A.D. 1300. It was a reaction away from the (by then too exclusive) occupation with the object – with *things*, taken as though apprehended by us without our minds, and especially with *supernatural things*, taken as so different in kind from our natural endowments, as to require a sheer imposing from without . . . These doctrines, against which there came the reaction, are *not* the doctrines really held by the Middle Ages at their best – say, from A.D. 1100 to A.D. 1300, but they were the doctrines of the later, moribund Middle Ages, and they were doctrines by which those Renaissance, Reformation and Revolution doctrinaires were really profoundly infected – as is always the case with men who do not patiently study the past (also the more recent past) and who, instead of discriminating, condemn what is before them *as it stands* – who do not untie knots, but who cut them. Again, Dear, do you note? Life taken cheaply – 'cheaply,' I mean, because practised and sought outside of, and not within, and by working through, its entanglements!

Von Hügel elsewhere refers to this 'objectivism' as '*naif* realism . . . , so little conscious . . . of the always present, and often large, contribution furnished by the apprehending subject to this subject's apprehension of the object'.[57] The reaction he mentions, and which he now goes on to consider, strikes close to what von Hügel came to mean by 'modernism'. And he finds this 'immanentism' or 'subjectivism' common precisely among 'ex-clerics' trained in an excessive 'objectivisme'.[58]

> Well, now, these three (and other) specifically 'modern' movements have been very largely dominated by a most ruinous, excessive, or even exclusive insistence upon the

> *subject* – your own (or at least humanity's) apprehending powers, feelings, etc. *These subjective* powers get, here, more or less taken as alone certain, as always the first facts in the order of our life and consciousness. Thus a baby will be taken first to feel, know himself – or rather, his own feeling and knowing, and then gradually to discover an outside world – his mother's breast . . . , etc. – all this being really less certain (in itself, or at least for his mind) than is his thus feeling, knowing himself. You entirely follow?[59]

This passage echoes von Hügel's lengthy treatments of Feuerbach, where the latter is said to *assume* man knows only his own mind, with the inevitable result that man's undisputed *consciousness* of God as Other can actually only *be* man's own *self*-consciousness. He doubtless also has in mind Descartes's initial 'exclusion . . . of one entire third of every living experience'.[60] Von Hügel, nonetheless, is well aware of auto-suggestion. And he will brook no contempt for psychology. But he is clear that the psychological involves necessities and determinisms which are preliminary and instrumental to man's deeper *self*-determinations precisely as human, free-willing spiritual personality.[61]

> Well, then, even more as to God – the supersensible, the Infinite – he is pushed still farther back amongst the late-acquired, the more or less doubtful 'ideas,' 'notions,' 'perhapses.' – The regulative notions for our conduct, the useful, more or less, working answer to our real difficulties amongst our real facts.

Here von Hügel describes the God of the gaps. And for him, better no God at all, than such a manipulated and postulated, constantly altering and shrinking anodyne. Von Hügel's God is prior to any problem and to every answer. He is in the centre of life from the beginning – as suffering in Christ, and in himself, as joy.

> [God is, in this subjectivist view,] an hypothesis, 'it is useful

> to live *as though* there were a God', Kant's celebrated '*als ob*'? Conduct here alone is quite certain; but then, too, conduct alone entirely matters. Religion is here always directly dependent upon, it is but the (really derivative, though seemingly superior) sanction of morality.[62] How different is real life, and the spontaneous attitude of all unsophisticated religion! In real life (all good psychologists and all careful theorists of knowledge are coming to see it) there is from *the first* direct contact with, direct knowledge of realities other than ourselves. Light and air, plants, animals, fellow-humans, the mother, the nurse: these are known together with ourselves – we never know ourselves except with and through those realities, and with and through our knowledge of them. Indeed, it is them we know best first; we know ourselves, at all adequately, only last of all. This knowledge of other realities less than human or simply human is never a knowledge through and through – it never simply equals the reality known. But it is a real knowledge of these realities, as far as it goes; realities which reveal their natures in their various self-manifestations. I know Puck[63] as truly as Puck knows me; my knowledge of him does not merely extend to appearances of him – appearances hiding, and probably travestying, his mysterious, simply unknowable essence.

Reality, then, and here specifically on the human and less-than-human level, is *given*, revelatory. Subject and object interact.[64] This level, taken together with God, provides that two-step approach to the real which is the basis for von Hügel's doctrine of the natural and the supernatural.[65]

Von Hügel's use of the word knowledge in this passage is undifferentiated. Basically he means by it experience or intuition, which includes reason but is not confined to it (as we saw previously and which we shall soon see again). The remark about 'appearances . . . travestying . . . unknowable essence' is a clear reference to Kant, whom von Hügel, on very numerous occasions, accuses of agnosticism with respect to the nature of the real, with the single ruinous exception that the real is somehow known to be almost certainly heterogeneous to our impression of it.[66] For von Hügel, such a position 'tears up the elementary experience and affirmation of religion by the roots'.[67] In a largely admiring survey of Troeltsch, he contends that precisely this 'Kantian idealism' in one strand of Troeltsch's thought risks surrendering essential and 'critically established happenings' to the 'windy subjectivities' that are Troeltsch's Christian 'legend' and 'myth'. Mysticism is thus rendered rootless, since extra-mental reality is not a given, but is, at the very most here, an inference, with the further result that 'the need of sense-stimulation [hence, sacraments] for the awakening of the mind and of the soul, is, in religion, sheer "magic-mongering"; and the sense of the Contrasting Other comes late and upon reflection'.[68] Von Hügel's incarnationalism is radically challenged in such a view, and he knows it.[69]

> We thus certainly know other realities besides our human reality (whether individual or even collective). And mark you, if this very real knowledge of realities not ourselves, always lags behind those realities as they are in themselves: *this knowledge, nevertheless, is (or can be) fuller than any complete and clear analysis of it can ever be.* Thus reality comes first; then knowledge of it; then science of this knowledge.

As early as 1906 von Hügel writes: 'Man's spirit has ever lived in the first instance by experience and conscience, and only secondarily by knowledge and science.'[70] Inference is knowledge. But reality is immediately given, not inferred. Experience, therefore, is wider than knowing.[71] Man, neither now nor in his destiny, is merely intellectualist. He will always be multiple. The religious sense is both reason and feeling and, as such, is not to be identified with philosophy, which latter may indeed not have anything to do with spirituality.[72]

This passage under consideration also contains the nucleus of von Hügel's broad programme for a dynamic, even evolutionary view of religion itself and of that growth of the individual as a person which is the main preoccupation of his spirituality. The individual's, and society's, increasing *apprehension* of the real, always distinct from that real (be it God, or other finite realities), and always less than it, and man's increasing *comprehension* of those apprehensions – is an ongoing, inexhaustible adventure whose history is the history of each man and of the race. Here too we may locate von Hügel's thought on the development of dogma. But in each instance of this real progress, the 'persistent self-identity of the source', the self-revealing God, is to be insisted on.[73]

> What about God? Well, we must first of all become clear to ourselves that, *as with every degree and kind of reality*, we always apprehend him only in, and with, and on occasion of, yet also in contrast to, other realities.

Von Hügel affirms the necessity of finite and sensible reality for the encounter of man with God. *God, man, and the world* are the requirements for God's indeed direct meeting with man.[74] The otherness of God, immediately present to man, may be increasingly vivid, but the apprehension nevertheless remains 'dim' in the Cartesian sense. Whatever clearness it has is maintained only in the company of and in contrast with other realities. If one keeps this otherness of God apart for long or gets deductive or 'clear and distinct' about it, 'it will rapidly lose its life'.[75] Here lies the importance for religion itself of all the other, non-religious, elements ingredient to von Hügel's spirituality. And once again we see ruled out any doctrine of a separate mystical faculty – a conception violently at odds with incarnationalism and the whole press of Christ as God-with-us in and through the history of human becoming. Thus too, and importantly: 'God himself is apprehended *only if* there be action of our own.'[76] He is *given*, but only as offered to our freedom. Yet this affirmation does not displace the 'anterior and more centrally religious truth': God is 'simply given, not sought and found'. [77] This last is the truth in Jansenism.[78]

The word *contrast* in this same dense passage of the letter to Gwendolen Greene suggests a major theme in von Hügel's analysis of religious experience: the painful experience of *contrasting* contingency and the implications of the fact, not that man is anthropomorphic when he speaks of God, but the fact that he *knows* he is. It is God who '*awakens* and slakes our thirst'.[79] 'The great mystical saints and writers . . . have, in the very forefront of their consciousness and assumptions, not a simply moral and aspirational, but an ontological and *pre-established* relation between the soul and God; and not a simply discursive apprehension, but a direct though dim experience of the infinite and of God.' *An affirmation underlies all negative theology*, all conscious anthropomorphism, all awareness of contingency and the grief of limits. 'The growing experience . . . of the apparent inescapableness and yet pain of man's mere anthropomorphisms . . . makes the persistence of his search for, and sense of' God 'and the keenness of his suffering when he appears to himself as imprisoned in mere subjectivity,[80] deeply impressive. For the more man feels, and suffers from feeling himself purely subjective, the more is it clear that he is not merely subjective: he could never be conscious of the fact, if he were. . . . Only a certain profound apprehension of abiding reality, the infinite, adequately explains the keen, operative sense of contrast and disappointment.'

He cites Troeltsch: 'Are not our religious requirements, requirements of Something that one must have somehow first experienced in order to require it . . . , which, in the conflict with selfishness, sensuality and self-will, draws the nobler part of the human will, with ever new force, to itself? . . . All deep and energetic religion is in a certain state of tension towards Culture, for the simple reason that it is seeking something else and something higher.' A central point of our entire study emerges here, for the task will be to *encounter* this tension *incarnationally*, and not to refuse it in Neoplatonic flight.

Von Hügel then goes on to cite Tiele: '"Religion," says Feuerbach, "proceeds from man's wishes" . . . ; according to others, it is the outcome of man's dissatisfaction with the external world. . . . But why should man torment himself with wishes . . . which the rationalistic philosopher declares to be illusions? Why? surely because he cannot help it. . . . The Infinite, very Being as opposed to continual becoming and perishing, . . . *that* is the principle which gives him constant unrest, because it dwells within him. . . . The origin of religion consists', not in a 'perception of the Infinite', but 'in the fact that man *has* the infinite within him'. And Tiele concludes: 'It is the specifically human element in man.' Von Hügel agrees, and draws the consequence: 'The mystics are amongst the great benefactors of our race.'[81]

> Again, . . . this apprehension and sense of God is (where not worked up and developed by the great historical, institutional religions) very vague and general, if taken as something statable in theoretical terms. (Here again, then, is the difference between knowledge and science!) Nevertheless, thus defined, the religious sense exercises a *prodigious* influence. It is the religious sense, even at this stage, where it seems no more (on strict analysis) than a deep, delicate, obstinate sense of otherness, of eternity, of prevenience, of more than merely human beauty, truth, and goodness, which really keeps our poor little human world a-going.[82]
>
> . . . . We have to be truthful, conscientious: why? Because these are the dispositions for putting us into fuller touch with realities of all sorts, especially with the reality of God. Dispositions are the means to acquiring reality – towards knowing, loving, willing realities greater than ourselves – in which energizings we grow in our own smaller reality.

Here we see the role of the moral will and the importance of that responsibility for belief already touched on previously in this chapter.[83] Von Hügel faces up to asceticism too and believes that a generally severe form of it 'is ever connected with at least some one phase . . . of every genuine mystic's history'.[84] Reality, God, are *there*. But emotional and volitional activity, active receptivity, are required, for 'God is apprehended only if there be action of our own'.[85] And again, humility. We must care. 'Caring is the greatest thing. Caring matters most.'[86] Von Hügel writes of himself to Kemp Smith: 'Oh how humble, how unworldly, how unself-occupied, how pure of heart – pure, not only from all sensuality but from all hate, all jealousy, all rationalist forcing one's poor thinking machine, how passive (in the right sense) one has, I have, to be, to gain any steady, useful light in these deepest facts and burrowings. That is one, perhaps the chief, encouragement to such toil: it makes one better, smaller, in one's own poor eyes.'[87]

> When, then, Thekla says 'religion has primarily to do with is-ness, not with ought-ness,' she means that religion is essentially evidential; that it intimates, first of all, that a superhuman world, a superhuman reality *is*, exists. The first and central act of religion is *adoration*, sense of God. His otherness though nearness, his distinctness from all finite beings, though not separateness – aloofness – from them.[88] If I cannot completely know even a daisy, still less can I ever completely know God. One of the councils of the Church launched the anathema against all who should declare that God is comprehensible. Yet God too, God in some real sense especially, we can most really know, since as does even the rose, how much more . . . [does] he deign to reveal himself to us.

We are here at 'the religious truth of truths – God's own initiation of, God's own presence within, all knowledge and service of himself'.[89] Von Hügel is reminded of Augustine: 'Thou wast within me and I was without, seeking thee outside me. Thou wast with me, but I was not with thee.'[90] God's prevenient self-revelation condemns all attempts to construct him *a priori*. And here von Hügel remembers St Bernard: 'Do you wake? . . . Well, he too is awake. If you arise in the night time, if you anticipate to your utmost your earliest awaking, you will already find him waking . . . In such an intercourse you will always be rash if you attribute any priority, any predominant share to yourself; for he loves both more than you love, and before you love at all.'[91]

A further point here is God's incomprehensibility. We never completely know reflexively, nor even adequately apprehend intuitively, God's inexhaustible richness. Man's advance into the utterly eternal God who is present to man and within him, or better, his invasion *by* God, is for man a durational event and achievement that will never lack novelty. 'We are like sponges trying to mop up the ocean.'[92] The incomprehensibility of God also suggests to von Hügel the problem of God's absence, of desolation, 'the stress of dryness and darkness, and what to do then. . . . What is a religion worth which costs you nothing? What is a sense of God worth which would be at your disposal, capable of being comfortably elicited when and where you please? It is far, far more God who must hold us, than we who must hold him.' We get trained by 'these darknesses' and 'dirty weather', and 'many such sandstorms'.[93]

> He does so [reveal himself] in a twofold manner – vaguely, but most powerfully – in the various laws and exigencies of life, and of our knowledge of it; and clearly, concretely, in and by the historic manifestations in and through the great geniuses and revealers of religion – the prophets, and especially Jesus Christ.[94] These latter manifestations get thoroughly learnt only in and through the various historical religious bodies.[95]

God, then, is the God of *all* history. He is present, therefore, mercifully and usefully, if less adequately, in religions and

Churches other than von Hügel's own. God prepares, he surrounds and assists, he is prevenient and present to 'his own fully incarnate coming' in Christ.[96] And von Hügel is clear that 'no amount of simply exterior attestation or appeal, of whatever kind or degree, could occasion within our minds any answering perception . . . unless we already possessed . . . a sense and apprehension which could answer to those attestations and appeals . . .'[97] But this is only to formulate that 'truth of truths' about man: Man cannot search out and desire God (including God in Christ), unless God has already found man out and loved him first. That God actually *does* precisely this is for von Hügel the deepest *constituent* of man as man. And it becomes thereby the *requirement* of man's very humanity, a requirement of which he indeed becomes aware only by a free and active receptivity, which is yet also gift.

However, if this bold description of the fundamentally human is to hold, then von Hügel's distinction of subject and object, while primary, must be located within a prior unity of reality in which the distinction takes place. And this is the case. Man is *organic*, 'not only to the world of organisms, but also, with them all, to the inorganic world' (which last is 'the truth lurking in materialism'). And further, *both* man and his world, as the expressed mind of God, are thus organic to a pre-existing harmony and teleology *of all reality*: man's spirit – in and through and on the occasion of the human and the less-than-human real – met by Spirit.[98]

This organic condition of man among men, and of all men with God, as ontological and pre-established in the Spirit, leads von Hügel to a powerful faith in prayer and socially redemptive suffering: 'I wonder whether you realise a deep, great, fact? That souls – all human souls – are deeply interconnected? That, I mean, we can not only pray for each other, but *suffer* for each other? . . . Nothing is more real than this interconnection – this gracious power put by God himself into the very heart of our infirmities.'[99]

And then this letter of spiritual direction concludes:

> There is not a line of all the above which has not to be learnt in careful detail, in lowly practice, in humble daily fight with self – in docility and docility on and on. We will gradually, ruminatingly, get the whole unrolled before us. . . .
>
> Gradually I shall give you more directly religious books to ponder; yet, to the end, these should be made to penetrate and purify a whole mass of not directly religious material and life. God is the God of nature as of grace,[100] he provides the meal and the yeast. Let us act in accordance with this, his own action.
>
> Affec. Uncle,
> F.v.H.

Throughout this letter to Gwendolen Greene, and in all von Hügel's writings, this God who directly penetrates man's spirit is a personal God, and he reveals himself as personal in immediate religious experience, or will do so, upon the deepening of that experience. For von Hügel, God is concrete and immensely rich. He is not a generality, or an abstract Plotinian One beyond multiplicity.[101] And if he is certainly not just one subject or object alongside others,[102] yet he 'is the supremely concrete, supremely individual and particular'.[103] Von Hügel lives with this paradox. Here above all, the vivid and the dense must prevail over the clear and distinct: 'God is a stupendously rich reality.'[104]

> As to the personal God, it has now become a prevalent fashion angrily to proclaim, or complacently to assume, the utter absurdity of anything personal about the Infinite; since personality . . . is a gross anthropomorphism the moment we apply it to anything but man himself. Yet it is interesting to note the readiness with which these same thinkers will hypostatize parts, or special functions, of our human personality . . . Thus thought or love or law, or even substance

> nothing of all this is, for such thinkers, anthropomorphic or sub-human; but anything personal is rank anthropomorphism. Yet it is only self-conscious spirit that we know well, since it alone do we know from within. Self-conscious spirit is immensely rich in content; and self-conscious spirit is by far the widest and yet deepest reality known to us at all.[105]

The point here for spirituality is that God is *at least* personal. Von Hügel goes so far on this point as to characterize Christianity as the 'revelation, through the person and example of its founder, of the altogether unsuspected depth and inexhaustibleness of human personality, and of this personality's source and analogue in God, of the simplicity and yet difficult and neverendingness of the access of man to God, and of the ever-preceding condescension of God to man. . . . Christianity is thus throughout the revelation of personality.'[106]

As so often, on fundamental issues, von Hügel grounds this aspect of his spiritual doctrine in religious experience. We get a powerful example of this characteristic approach in a blunt response to Fichte's remark that religion's personal God depends on 'ingenious pleadings':

> The now immensely abundant testimony of religion lies before us as a warning that Fichte here confounded philosophical thinking and the general idea of religiousness with the specifically religious experiences themselves. Theological deductions and speculations have indeed at times articulated or analysed, in 'ingenious' ways, the deepest and most delicate experiences of living religion. Yet these experiences themselves always present their object as overflowingly existent; and, in proportion as spirituality becomes more conscious of its own requirements and more sensitively discriminating, the object is apprehended as perfect self-conscious Spirit, as very source of all existence and reality. We can indeed argue against religion, as mistaken in so

> doing; but that religion actually does so, and this, not in the form of deductive reasoning, but in that of intuitive experience, cannot seriously be denied.[107]

Elsewhere von Hügel notices that to hold 'even as the barest possibility' that God might not be conscious is 'to put a lump of ice at the very heart of religion, and to let death attack its very vitals'.[108] But to do this is to attack man himself, for religion 'is the specifically human element in man'. Man is made for adoration.

Von Hügel's spiritual doctrine is one man's lifetime effort to unpack the single dense experience of incarnation, which is at once that self-gift of God which is also summons, even as it is man's own task of response: an individual called by God through the now Christologically located determinisms of matter and science on to the free self-determinations of socially constituted spiritual personality. Von Hügel's treatment of God's self-disclosure begins and ends with the experience of that self-disclosure. The reflections of a lifetime, however technical, however tentative and in need of correction, derive from this experience and exist only to validate, purify and deepen it. As a living experience, it must necessarily be dense; hopefully it will also be vivid. The technical effort is to make 'discriminations' which yet leave the experience alive in all its mystery. And the effort must also be to avoid those abstract *separations* of the complex datum from itself, separations which, in return for their clarity and distinctness, risk the mystery's life. For then, what ought to have been prayerful reflection becomes an autopsy. But this last, where it appears to occur, would be an illusion too. For it would not mean that either God or spiritual life are dead. Rather, they would have eluded one particular thinker, or theology, or culture.

The previous part of this chapter has studied von Hügel's writings on the adoration of God as man's fundamental experience. Here, the aim will be simply to deepen and explicate further the content and conditions of this experience. Von Hügel enunciates our subject for us: 'God's otherness and difference, and his nearness. You *must* get that.'[109] The theme is explored first as agnosticism and pantheism, then in the resolution of immanence and transcendence as panentheism, and finally, in the Godness of God, his joy.

There is a legitimate agnosticism. And it grows large in direct proportion to God's gift of himself to man. This agnosticism has its own magnificence, for it is the condition of that splendid *trust* which marks all human love and which even more does and will always mark man's love of God. The more man loves, whether his fellow-man or God, the more mysterious the beloved will be seen to be. Von Hügel cites John of the Cross: 'One of the greatest favours of God, bestowed transiently upon the soul in this life, is its ability to see so distinctly, and to feel so profoundly, that . . . it cannot comprehend him at all.'[110]

But there is another agnosticism which, together with pantheism, threatens the undoubted quality of man's experience as religious, i.e. as yielding the *givenness* of God.[111] Paradoxically, it is often profoundly *religious*, anti-pantheistic man who finds his joy in so exalting God as to cut away the ground of the religious experience itself. Von Hügel profoundly admires Kierkegaard. He finds him, 'otherwise a modern among the moderns . . . , as massively ontological as any ancient'. But Kierkegaard's description of religion and of God as conflicting with man's essential nature is 'tragic', 'non-mystical', 'ultra-ascetical'.[112] Kierkegaard had written: 'What the conception of God . . . is to effect in man is that he shall remodel his entire existence according to it; but by this remodelling man dies to his entire immediacy. As the fish lies out of its element when left upon the sand, so is the religious man caught in his absolute conception of God; for such absoluteness is not directly the element of a finite being. No wonder, then, if, for the Jew, to see God meant death; and if, for the Heathen, to stand in relation to God portended madness.'[113]

Von Hügel comments:

> Here once more we see . . . the all-importance for religion of ontology and difference, yet also of likeness. Thus it is Kierkegaard's profound apprehension of the ontology and difference which renders him religiously deep and powerful, beyond all the subjectivists and identity-thinkers put together; and it is his lack of insight as to the likeness which leaves his life strained to the verge of insanity. . . . Christ's self-renunciation is here, but not his expansive tenderness.[114]

He agrees with Kierkegaard's commentator, Höffding, that 'qualitative or absolute difference abolishes all possibility of any positive relation. If religious zeal, in its eagerness to push the object of religion to the highest height, establishes a yawning abyss between this object and the life whose ideal it is still to remain, – such zeal contradicts itself. For a God who is not ideal and exemplar, is no God.'[115] Von Hügel sees the history of sanctity as quite other: 'In the case of the saints . . ., as the . . . body is more and more transformed by grace and devotedness into an instrument and expression of the human spirit, this spirit is, in its turn, found to be more and more penetrable by, and not all unlike, the Spirit of God himself.'[116]

Von Hügel attempts to strike the balance in 1907: 'What I cannot abide is any view that would make man contain God, instead of God contain man.'

> We shall ever have to look *up to* God, to apprehend, *not comprehend* him; and our reason will never become *the reason*. Yet our reason even here is exceeded only by a higher reason, – a reason indefinitely nobler and greater, but not simply contradictory of our own. We are not, and never will be, *God*; but already here we can be, and at our best we are, God-*like*. I hope that you will think that this will do.[117]

Fifteen years later he presses Maude Petre somewhat closely on the agnostic results of excessively historicizing and relativizing human knowledge. He is puzzled at finding her 'so transparently confident of uttering simply undeniable truths', all of which indicate to von Hügel 'an insufficient trust in the carrying power of human reason at its best – in human reason which is, after all, the gift of God'.

To Miss Petre's suggestions that scholarly criticism's massive accomplishments have rendered useless the believer's attempting to establish a satisfactory refuge from what criticism may further do, von Hügel replies: 'Well, I do not think this is anything like as true as it is plausible.' The history of geology *and* of biblical criticism, while definitely a history of increasingly and continually corrected facts, is also a history of *facts*, facts which remain, become permanent (because true), and which get extended – but which do not get simply changed or subverted. Further:

> You say that 'there is no religious conception which has not a human taint; we make God even in the act of worshipping him'; and you add that the Christ of the critic who remains a Christian worshipper – the Christ eternal, the mystical Christ – 'is an idol in so far as the conception is a creation of the critic's mind'.... Now it is, of course, true that in so far as these ... are *purely*, are *merely*, the creation of a critic's mind, they are idols, i.e. they are not what the realities aimed at are simply in themselves. But this, if a truth, is surely a truism; it is indeed a tautology. It does not follow, surely, that a conception which is the discovery, the creation (if you like to call it so) of the critic's mind, is *necessarily* utterly different from the reality aimed at.[118]

And this agnosticism takes a heavy toll in spirituality. For it leads – most sensibly – to a hedged commitment:

> You say that 'so long as we find and feel the highest teaching of spiritual reality in the Church we accept her doctrine, her

> discipline, *her objects of worship*, but we accept nothing with the absolutism of finality, because we know that it is only given us to see through a glass darkly'. . . . Now here I wonder whether such abstention from a quite final self-commitment could and ought ever to be accepted by the Church.

At the end, von Hügel praises her declaration that 'doctrinal development cannot be carried out in obedience to history and science alone; it must respond to religious needs also'. The conclusion to his comments is cool: 'Thank you then, once more, for all you have suggested to me and taught me.'[119]

The opposite extreme to this agnostic, 'dualistic excess' of overly, if not wholly, separating man from God in being and in knowing, is 'the counter extreme: the ultra-unitive or pantheistic. Here the better self simply *is* God.'[120] Von Hügel takes his clearest definition of what he means here from Edward Caird's description of Spinoza: 'God . . . is conceived as the immanent principle of the universe, or perhaps rather the universe is conceived as immanent in God. . . . If for him the world is nothing apart from God, God is nothing apart from his realization in the world.'[121]

Von Hügel fears pantheism as a dangerous error possessing a powerful and noble truth. He writes to Gwendolen Greene of the danger:

> What you say about prayer, Sweet, is all very true, very solid. I know well what you mean. But though we will most rightly shrink from saying that this or that in it is God: yet it is God, his reality, his distinctness from yet great closeness to us, it is this grand over-againstness which through, and in, and on occasion of what you describe we experience in our little degree. . . . I am utterly sure that this is the direct antidote to the all but universal pantheism of our times. Before people worry about the Church or even about Christ, they must be helped to get God . . . sound and strong.[122]

Elsewhere he puts the question to himself: 'But what is the harm, religiously, in such an identification of God and man?' If it is only man's '*depths* which are God', is 'not the difference . . . one simply of words? I think not. For such a view, if it were fully to determine the imagination, reason, emotion and will, would make adoration – the very centre of the religious life – impossible. . . . I cannot, in all sober, consistent conviction, adore myself; indeed in my *deepest* moments I shall be *most* removed from all such fantastic feelings.'[123] Further, the refusal or inability 'to conceive close spiritual experience otherwise than as based upon the ontological identity of the experiencing and the experienced spirit' ends by contradicting and destroying the religious experience from which this error arises. It 'would . . . bring the spiritual life to a standstill . . . '[124]

Religious experience yields a central paradox:

> That God loves man, and is man's friend and *socius*; that God begs man: 'My son, give me thy heart'; that God, very variously but continuously and most truly, reveals his real nature in the world and to man – a revelation at its fullest and purest in the life, teaching, character, death and living presence and power of Jesus Christ. But this same paradox simultaneously teaches that this love of God for man, that this self-revelation of God in nature and in history, is so great and so wondrous precisely also because there is no parity of nature or of need, no absolute correlation between God [and man]. . . . We miss the delicate tension of the deepest religious experiences, if we *will* thus force an 'absolute correlation.'[125]

As we have seen, von Hügel regarded the doctrine of the proximate Second Coming of Christ, this 'sudden illapse from without', as a massive affront to any such view. 'A great foot, a pierced foot, prevents that door closing there.'[126]

Yet pantheism approximates some powerful and noble truths. Von Hügel speaks of three great services rendered by the pantheistic *tendency*. First, this tendency allows, but refuses to restrict God to a deistic separation, whereby we infer him through nature and his restraint upon our consciences; it insists also upon our finding God within man and man in God.[127] Secondly, this tendency asserts the primacy of religious experience, of interiority, even for the development of historical Christianity in its full depth and truth.[128] And finally,

> pantheistic-seeming mysticism, – though always only so long as it remains not the only or last word of religion, . . . alone discovers the truly spiritual function and fruitfulness of deterministic science. For only if man deeply requires a profound de-subjectivizing, a great shifting of the centre of his interest, away from the petty, claimful, animal self, with its 'I against all the world,'[129] to a great kingdom of souls, in which man gains his larger, spiritual, unique personality, with its 'I as part of, and for all the world' . . . ; and only if mathematico-physical science is specially fitted to provide such a bath, and hence is so taken, with all its apparently ruinous determinism and seeming godlessness: is such science really safe from apologetic emasculation; or from running, a mere unrelated dilettantism, alongside of the deepest interests of the soul; or from, in its turn, crushing or at least hampering the deepest, the spiritual life of man. Hence all the greater . . . mystics have got a something about them which indicates that they have indeed passed through fire and water, that their poor selfishness has been purified in a bath of painfully-bracing spiritual air and light, through which they have emerged into a larger, fuller life.
>
> . . . There . . . can be such purification only for those who realize and practise religion as sufficiently ultimate and wide and deep to englobe, (as one of religion's necessary stimulants), an unweakened, utterly alien-seeming determinism in the middle regions of the soul's experience and outlook. Such an englobement can most justly be declared Chris-

tianity fully driven home. For thus is man purified and saved, – if he already possesses the dominant religious motive and conviction, – by a close contact with matter;[130] and the Cross is plunged into the very centre of the soul's life, operating there a sure division between the perishing animal individual and the abiding spiritual personality: the deathless incarnational and redemptive religion becomes thus truly operative there.[131]

But pantheism cannot be final if man's life is an answer to Christianity's revelation and experience at once of *unity*, of *self-surrender* and of *action*. For the unity experienced by the saints, and presaged in the Trinity, is not an empty oneness, but a harmony of selves. And the self-surrender asked and given is not a dissolution of personality, but the passage from a 'self-entrenchment' to the brotherly 'devotedness' of the Kingdom of the living God. And the action of the primal Lover on each man and all mankind is not a determinism or an emanation, but a libertarian and literally ecstatic gift, i.e. creative of truly free and really other – selves. God gives himself to man only 'as he gives a self to them'. And the infinity of this personal love does not argue against the independence of the beloved, against the independence of mankind. Rather, God creates the independence, creates the freedom, and the love as well, whereby each man and mankind may love Almighty God.[132]

Von Hügel's strictures on pantheism in no wise disallow an enthusiastic doctrine of the immanence of God. His basic source here is St Paul.[133] And he frequently cites Teresa of Avila's statement of this, the culminating experience: that man 'holds God himself as distinct from his graces':

In the beginning I did not know that God is present in all things. . . . Unlearned men used to tell me he was present only by his grace. I could not believe that . . . A most learned Dominican told me he was present himself . . . this was a

> great comfort to me. . . . The living God was in my soul. . . . My life . . . is the life which God lived in me.[134]

Von Hügel calls this indwelling of God in man *panentheism*. And he considers man's 'ineradicable capacity, need and desire' for this indwelling to be 'the intrinsic characteristic of human nature'.[135] In 1900 he tells Wilfrid Ward that man's response to 'the immanence of the divine in the human' constitutes 'the very soul of the modern spirit at its best'.[136] And he writes to Blondel of a God who raises man to himself 'by way of a going forth from himself and a permanent entering into us, by an eternal immanence in the depths of humanity . . . , a very delicate point, but one of fundamental importance'.[137]

But von Hügel is adamant that a candid reading of the history of religious experience yields an immanence precisely of a God who is *transcendent*.[138] His opposition to immanentism is early and constant, and the rejection becomes an anxiety as the years pass. In 1903 he gives Tyrrell his conviction 'of the large, spacious, range of our . . . capacities, and of the necessity and value of an ideal and indefinite exercise for them; *and* of all this not being God, not one bit, not one bit. . . . God is emphatically *not* simply our highest selves.'[139] A letter of 1907 to the same correspondent becomes urgent:

> I feel strongly, somehow, that your treatment of the old transcendent conception of God as requiring to be reformulated, *en toutes pièces*, by an immanental one, is . . . impoverishing. . . . If one were to take your clear-cut immanentism as final and complete, that noblest half of the religious experience of tip-toe expectation, of unfulfilled aspiration, of sense of a divine life, of which our own but touches the outskirts, would have no place.[140]

Von Hügel's God is immanent *and* transcendent: 'The joy of religion resides, surely, in the knowledge, the love, the adoration of One truly distinct from, whilst immensely penetrative of, ourselves.'[141] And von Hügel is insistent that *experience itself* delivers this datum of transcendence: it falls 'well within, the living, operative experience of all deepest religion'.[142] To dismiss this presence of God as the transcendent Other, or to deny its roots in experience, or – perhaps worst of all – to conceive it as a 'dry conclusion of common-sense, a sort of ultimate affirmation of the higher mathematics, which fantastic or fanatical theologians *will* try and force into the living energizings of man's life, is to attempt the blinding of one of the two eyes of religion'.[143]

Von Hügel is well aware of the commonly offered substitutes for this God-centred spirituality: 'social amelioration and a combatively sublunar sturdiness'. He calls them 'a dreary Gospel, . . . a negation of all that is deepest in the heart and soul of man, the God-touched and the God-hungry, so little and so great'.[144]

But von Hügel knows too that man's social situation is *also* 'God-touched' and certainly 'God-hungry', and that 'social amelioration' and the building of the material world are profoundly Christian opportunities and tasks. We conclude this section of the chapter, then, with von Hügel's understanding of social, worldly action *within* a God-centred spirituality. Our subject, then, is Christian humanism as holiness, i.e. the life of God in the city of man.

Von Hügel defines secularism, loosely but very sufficiently for his purposes, as an insistent and even angry *this*-world attitude.[145] Within his frame of discourse, such a view is, certainly, the inverse and the death of significant spirituality. Von Hügel suggests that such secularism has its partial cause in man's limited capacity of attention and interest. Wherever men, for whatever reasons, are without the basic commodities of decent physical and cultural existence, or where men must be unduly preoccupied with securing these basic commodities, only a moral miracle will allow such men spiritual experience, or even the awareness that a truly *human* condition requires it.

Coupled with this compelled 'absorption in the clear surface and away from the dimmer depths of life', secularism finds a second foothold in man's revulsion against religion's historical and contemporary role and reputation as 'ally of the castle'.

But the fundamental cause of the death of the religious sense, while occasioned and nourished by these other two factors, lies deeper down than either. And this cause is ignorance, ignorance of what religion is, and of what man is. Years and generations of excited absorption 'in the physical requirements and in the social-economical basis of our earthly existence', whether the absorption be caused now by necessity, habit, or sin, disposes a man to naturalism and silences his deepest demands.

There are deliberate architects of this mentality, and they project a millennium of universal peace, contentment, and absolute equality by means of social revolution within and through 'our simply human powers and earthly lives'. The faith demanded for such an enterprise is more exacting than the faith of any of the great religions. And since 'happiness is here to arise from the perfection of exclusively earthly conditions achieved by exclusively earthly means' – a surely difficult faith, not to say difficult result to come by – all more- and other-than-this-world responses are most sensibly suppressed. 'No distractions, no waste of energy, are permissible here. Man, even in his holiday dreamings, is no more to be an amphibious creature, longing somehow for the boundless ocean.' He is 'a land-animal, a creature of earth alone'.[146]

Von Hügel, of course, will have none of this. He believes, nevertheless, that Christianity has profound cause to be grateful for, and a deep need to learn from, the large amount of unselfishness and the deep awareness of the extent and magnitude of our social problems which such secularism gives witness to. Von Hügel seeks also to learn from it, to be reminded by it, 'how large is the dependence of the growth and power of . . . religious experiences and requirements, amongst average human beings, upon a certain security and stability in the means and circumstances of physical existence, and especially upon some family life and leisure'. The case 'of the Galilean poor . . . whom Our Lord declared to be blessed' is here 'nowise in point. The problem is not simply intensified for us; it is radically changed.'

Decency, then, and leisure are utterly necessary preliminaries to, as well as materials for, the very occurrence and the growth of significant spirituality. Von Hügel suggests that we see in this 'an admirable further revelation . . . of the costly twofold source of Christianity's perennial youth and renovative power':

> For Christianity is thus obliged to be, more than ever, busy with the temporal and the spatial, the physical and psychical . . . ; more than ever, any exclusive other-worldliness, all quietistic suffering and listless waiting, would be treason against both man and God. Thus less than ever is the . . . incarnational doctrine of Christianity an empty theory; indeed, its insistence that spirit shall penetrate and transform matter, *and shall thus awaken and develop its own self*, has never in the history of the world had so gigantic a field, and such immense difficulties, in which to show and develop its power, as it possesses now.[147]

But a God-centred spirituality is alone fully equal to the total claim that this social situation makes upon man's heart:

> Only a vivid faith in the utterly real and perfect God, only the experience and love of eternal life, are able, in the long run, to supply a sufficiently deep, steady, and tender love and service of our fellow-creatures, precisely where, in their actual condition, they most require, because they least deserve, such selfless devotion.

Von Hügel does not mince words here. It is an assessment of the cost of fidelity in human love. He is clear that the love required for effective social action cannot, 'in the long run', be sentimental, but often *must* be agapeistic, certainly if it is to endure, and perhaps even if it is to exist at all. That is, it must be *creative* of its object, creative of the very lovableness of the fellow-man to be loved. We have here an ardent, stern, and superbly realistic doctrine of supernatural charity. Not man alone, but only man alive with *God's* fidelity can love man in all his need, and to the end:

> This heroic love will thus be gained *for* men, but not simply *from* men; it will be acquired in close union with God.[148]

And asceticism, 'in its noblest and widest sense and forms, will thus again operate as the great instrument of love; and will ever purify and replenish that expansive outgoing to creatures and intimacy with them'. For the Incarnation is also compounded of and must also be maintained by that 'other-world movement' which is the element of 'transcendence in Our Lord's life and teaching . . . Only the two movements together, the transcendence in the immanence, and the eternal in the temporal – only this tension and duality in harmony and union . . . constitute the Christian spirit's flower and strength.[149] And surely never was there a finer field for the heroically joyous practice of these two movements together . . . than lies before us now.'[150]

In the consideration of the joy of God, of God as joy, von Hügel literally heads for home: 'The final note of religion is joy.'[151] Man is made for joy, because joy is what God *is*. Joy is spirituality's name for all man seeks to gain and be, because it is the name for all that has been given to man in the religious experience of God as *fully constituted* Being and as *personal* Reality. Joy is love, fully, inexhaustibly given and fully, unconditionally received: the mutual love of Father and of Son eternally, dynamically at that flood which is the Holy Spirit. Joy, then, is not something static, something over and done with, completed – but God ever superbly new, wholly and purely in act.[152] There is no becoming in God: no movement toward love which men call desire; and no grief for love gone, or still on the way. God *is* triune self-surrender, given, received, and shared. He *is* this, he is joy. And man's joy is to adore and delight in, and take hope that his own destiny is, this very Godness of God, his Joy.

In one of his last and major essays, von Hügel carefully considers the problem of suffering in God.[153] He enumerates and assesses at great length both the biblical evidence and the long history of philosophical argument: Yahweh's jealousy, the Suffering Servant, patripassianism.[154] But in a comment on Harnack he makes clear what is fundamental to his spirituality in this question, and therefore what is central to our study of it here.

> Harnack's very interesting discussion of the rights and wrongs of 'patripassianism' . . . curiously overlooks the point which this address especially attempts to establish; for he nowhere apprehends that, though this outlook was doubtless the expression of an intense, naïve, and massive faith in God, in Christ as God, and in the immense worth of sanctified suffering, it really omits, indeed traverses, a profoundly important *religious* element – the joy, the pure joy, of God. Harnack writes as though the whole *religious* worth were on the side of 'patripassianism', and as though only philosophical and other, not directly religious, needs had decided its defeat. I am convinced, on the contrary, that only a non-'patripassian' view could defend and transmit *the very deepest note of the religious consciousness.*[155]

Von Hügel insists that if this religious consciousness is to strike this its deepest note, it 'will not, must not, be restricted to the self-limited creative God, or (worse still) to the persuasion that . . . God in and for himself has been and is absorbed in God as Creator. The religious sense, on the contrary, must be allowed to press on to, to be moved and fully satisfied only by the Ultimate.' God's self-gift in creation (including God's humanity in Christ), *and* God wholly uncreated and in himself: von Hügel's spirituality formally requires that man 'essentially be busy with both'.[156]

Only in humility and creatureliness, only in alert and active receptivity, does man meet God, the 'Contrasting Other' who is 'perfect love, unmixed joy, entire delectation. He is all this, not as a bundle of separate qualities, however consummate each quality may be, but as a living, spiritual, personalist reality, who himself is all this overflowingly. I believe this to be a true account of the fundamental religious experience and apprehension.'[157] Once again, at the last, von Hügel gives us no 'proof'. The datum is *given* to the responsibly and humbly alert man *in his very humanity*. Von Hügel spends a lifetime trying to help us to see that this is so. But he does not prove it. Finally, we either see it, in and through free and graced experience, or we do not.

If we do see it,

> we will not admit the presence of any evil, be it sin or even only sorrow . . . in him who thus dwarfs for us all our little human goodness and earthly joy by his utter sanctity and sheer beatitude. And all this goodness and joy God does not become, does not acquire: He simply *is* it. [And we will *want* to guard] . . . his otherness . . . as essential a part of the facts and of the power of religion as his likeness can ever be. True, God is full of loving care for us, his creatures; he knows us each and singly in all our particularity, and can and does help us to become more like unto himself. But this sympathy is not suffering; and, again, we never will, indeed never can, become really identical with him. He has allowed real, direct suffering to come as close to him, in the humanity of Christ, as, in the nature of things,[158] suffering could come. Let us be wise and sober, and rest satisfied with that deep

> sympathy in God and this deep suffering in Christ. . . . We will admit indeed great tracts of dreariness, suffering, sin, in our human lives . . . ; but all the more will we treasure the pure and distinct, the personalist and abounding holiness, joy and delectation of God.[159]

Von Hügel draws a striking pastoral conclusion from this experience man has of God as already possessing 'immeasurably more than all he helps us to become – he who, even now already, is our peace in action, and *even in the Cross is our abiding joy*'.[160] He suggests to Gwendolen Greene the practice of '*at once* meeting suffering with joy. God alone can help us succeed in this; but what, Child, is Christianity, if it be not something like that?'[161] These texts lead to von Hügel's underlying point: that human life, even with its suffering, if lived in God's joy, increasingly leads to that transformation of duty and obligation in which human joy emerges as the rush of arduous moral becoming towards that durational but utterly dynamic still point of total self-surrender in spontaneous and perfect freedom. It is the disappearance of external law through that law's own perfect, and perfectly willed, *interiorization as love*. Man never achieves this fully, but the tendency of joy is to abolish responsibility: 'As well insist to Kepler on his duty carefully to consider the stars . . . , or to Monica on her guilt if she does not love Augustine, as to preach responsibility . . . to a soul full of the love and of the joy of God.'[162]

But the goal is joy, not pleasure.[163] 'No conception of religion as . . . an abstract law or a joyless duty can abidingly prevail. Man is made for overflowing joy, though not for shallow pleasure; and man's thirst for God, as man's sole full delight, must somehow be combined with a deep detachment and purity of love. Christian asceticism, its grand range from virile tone and tension to delicate tenderness and expansive happiness . . . here mediates a supreme acquisition: . . . spiritual joy.'[164] God, then, is man's joy, and it is this joy which is the measure of all negativities that may be required to mediate him to each man, and among us all.[165]

Von Hügel shares with us one particularly intense experience of joy, an experience of his own. We give the text here at some length, since it reveals von Hügel at his most personal and gives existential expression to much of the more technical content of this chapter.

'It was on a Good Friday forenoon in Rome, I think in 1899.' He had risen very late by mistake, rushed out to find church after church closed and locked, their services complete. He then finds himself, a half-hour later, under a scorching, uncomfortable sun, alone. 'Many green lizards were soon frisking close around me – otherwise nothing living was to be seen or heard':

> I sat there thus . . . , conscious of nothing but myself . . . ; of that mass of failures, disappointments, pettinesses, with a dim background, though, of men at large hardly more inviting or inspiring than myself. . . . Churchmen and agnostics, Jews and Protestants, also such souls amongst them all as were dear to me at other times – all seemed empty, irritating, oppressive. And then – I know of no transition or connection – then – well, suddenly, ah . . . another outlook. . . . I felt – I seemed to see – now without any straining, without apparently any action of my own – one great tender goodness and heroism pass before me after the other – the souls which in this 'eternal' Rome, had meekly suffered and had manfully agonised for God; also thinkers, and men of action, seekers after God. There were Peter and Paul, Caecilia and Agnes . . . , Rabbi Akiba . . . , Marcus Aurelius . . . , Plotinus . . . , Augustine now growing utterly weary and restless under his sins . . . And all of them were marked by suffering – and more or less marred by sin. But then, behind and above all these, appeared the Master of Masters, Suffering Love gently, pathetically triumphant – Jesus Christ, Our Lord, on

this the day of his utter Passion. And yet . . . , this utter woe, this day of that woe, they seem best expressed just simply as Good – as 'Good' Friday . . . For was it not *good*, supremely *good* for us? . . . The suffering, even here, was certainly an evil, but then its utilization, how good that was! And besides, here, no sin! Somehow here the intense suffering led on to joy – to the infinite good that had sprung from this infinite sorrow. And, then, came the final state of soul and outlook: God, God in himself. And here, in contrast with the first outlook, where fellow-creatures had appeared so largely suffering and so truly sinful, and even in contrast with the second outlook, where Jesus Christ had appeared, sinless indeed and joy-bringing, yet also bowed down with suffering, appeared joy, pure joy, an ocean of it, unplumbed, unplumbable, with not one drop of evil within it – not one drop of sin or suffering or of the possibility of either. *And I did not want it otherwise – far, far from it*! God was too much our friend, for us not to rejoice that he does not suffer; and this joy of God is too much our sustenance, it too much shows us, contrastingly, our indigence, a sight of ourselves which constitutes our specific dignity, for me, for any of those great lovers of his, to wish his joy mixed or limited or conditional. And yet this pure joy was utterly compassionate, utterly sympathetic; it bent down to, it entered into, the hearts of those great little ones; it was, indeed, at work all around me at that moment. What else, in the last resort, made those dear little emerald lizards so happy there, close to my feet? And then all ended with my receiving a happy impression that all the dreariness, which had preceded all this happiness, that that too, that it, especially for me just then, had already been an effect of that contrasting joy of God, or rather of my very dim but real apprehension of that joy.

For indeed dreary and petty, oppressive and imprisoning, is our poor little life, on its surface and apart from God and

> from his merciful condescensions towards us. But we would not know our misery, we would not feel it as such, were there not saints and heroes around us, and Christ our Lord above us, and, encompassing all and penetrating all, God – not a Sufferer, but indeed the Sympathizer, God Joy, the Ocean of Joy, our home.[166]

Our conclusion shall be to list, almost without comment, Friedrich von Hügel's seven 'facts and doctrines concerning God which are of especial importance in the life of prayer'.[167] This will enable the reader to have within a short space von Hügel's own witness to the relationship between prayer and his speculative-practical thought about God. The importance of this testimony is clear, for in any view of von Hügel, prayer, as stance and as act, is the fundamental human situation, and therefore of first concern to spirituality.

1. '*God is a stupendously rich reality*', richly bestowed in creation and incarnation, but superbly God quite apart from this preoccupation with us. We are emphatically taught this in the revelation of the Trinity, and it is the great truth of negative theology.

2. '*God is the author of, and God is variously reflected in, all nature as well as in all supernature.*' There is thus a tension, a polarity in man's life, and his prayer should witness to this: 'a tension, to the verge of strain; and a *détente*, to the verge of relaxation.'

3. '*God alone is fully free.*'

4. '*God is the supreme good.*' Religion, as distinct from ethics, goes straight to God as Joy and thus increasingly reaches beyond duty and obligation. 'The rivalry between God and creatures for the possession of our hearts will become less and less a struggle between a mysterious obligation and a clear fascination, and more and more a competition between an . . . all-penetrating joy . . . and feverish pleasures.' The competition, then, is not between flight and involvement, this world and

the next, or between God and creatures, but between joy and pleasure.

5. God, 'not all unlike man', is yet '*other than man*'. We must neither diminish God, nor dehumanize Jesus. Therefore we will hold within our single experience the pure joy of God and the sinless, deep suffering of Jesus. These are the imperishable truths secured for prayer by Chalcedon.

6. Man needs God utterly, and the converse is not so, however much and greatly God delights in the children of men. Man's most fundamental duty and honour is not petition, nor contrition, nor thanksgiving, but adoration. Augustine is a great witness: tenderly anthropomorphic, but profoundly aware of the non-equality of God and man. Modern man's prayer is exposed to 'subtle testing' by 'the sentimental anthropocentrisms which fill the air'.

7. '*The prevenience of God*' is 'the root-fact and the root-truth' of the six previous positions: He loved us first.

For Friedrich von Hügel, the heart of the matter for man is God – as it was for Christ: 'Did he not come to show us the Father?'[168] 'The most fundamental need, duty, honour and happiness of man is . . . adoration.'[169] It is the spirituality of the *Gloria*: 'We praise you . . . , we adore you . . . , we give you thanks for your great glory . . . '

CHAPTER FOUR

THE PRODUCTION OF PERSONALITY: INTRODUCTION

THE larger prerequisites, presuppositions and effects for Christian spirituality of Friedrich von Hügel's Christology and doctrine of God are already in view. Human existence is incarnational, conditioned by God and the world. Incarnation itself is the initial and the final dualism: finite and infinite, historical and eternal – perfectly integrated in Christ. Man is spirit in a body, embodied spirit in the world, summoned by Spirit, by God, in and through time, and during time too, to eternal life. But incarnation is not an abstract principle, nor even, as it might have been, only the real and truly effective, but non-personal presence of God in history. In Christ, incarnation becomes a concrete, historical event that is personal, who is God in history – and yet who is man too, himself sent and summoned by Spirit.

Human existence as Christian, then, and its theoretico-practical description, Christian spirituality, becomes the following of Christ, the study and appropriation of his mind and heart. It is then what it always was, even in the Old Testament, an incarnational theocentrism, but now and henceforth concretized by Christology, by the person and history of Jesus, and therefore by sin and the Cross, by the redemption and triumph of Christ, and by God's own joy, whose permanent mediator for man is the suffering, death and resurrection of Christ. All this is in function of love, which is personal. Love, which is the source, the goal, and primary means, the defining characteristic of personality. It is this question of human personality which will concern us in this chapter and the next. Personality, and the means to its production.[1]

Von Hügel's spirituality asks the question: What is involved for all of us and for our world – for all redeemed creation as the larger history of Christ – as we move in the Spirit, even now, and more fully after death, to God our home? This and the succeeding chapter, as a general answer to this question, move only to explicate and to draw the further consequences of what we have already seen. But it is a vast proposal, nonetheless, and if what follows is not to seem a veritable cookbook of disparate topics or recipes, it will be of central importance for the reader to see and to recall our many subjects in function of their relation to personality and the means to its production. The reader will need von Hügel's patience with the multiple and the gradual, his love of slow and costly, *incarnational* harmony, and of the durational, many-sided spirit which is man. For in von Hügel's spirituality, as Nédoncelle suggests, 'the development of personality is the final goal of the world, for which even the heavens wait'.[2] There shall be no conflict between this statement and the central burden of our previous chapter, which was the adoration of God and of our joy in God as man's defining characteristic. For as we shall continue to see, love, and Pure Love too, always incarnationally appropriated, is the deepest requirement and constituent of the fully developed human person.

The famous first two chapters of *The Mystical Element of Religion*[3] articulate the structure of von Hügel's problem and the general outlines of his solution. They concern both the *three forces* which history shows to be dominant in Western man and Western civilization; and the *three elements* of religion. It may be hazarded that von Hügel has written nothing which cannot be subsumed under, or at least related to, these two structures, if they are taken in the general and nuanced way that he presents them. We shall outline those structures now in the skeletal form that space allows. This will afford, and in the

way most characteristic of vo
entire thought. It may also ser
which to locate that thought
guarded against here would be
and not as a conclusion of ten
working inductively on the d
wide learning.

Von Hügel begins with 'an enig
we want a strong and interior, a
union between our own *successiv*
what is *abiding* in ourselves and w
fellow-men.'[5] It is reason and abstraction which deliver the general and the abiding, and in communicable form. But they do not seem to move or win the will, our own or others'. It is intuition and the concrete, it is feeling which moves and convicts us to action. But this seems individual and evanescent. Reason unifies, explains – perhaps explains away – experience, but it is the element that may be transferred to others, and to our future selves. Feeling, the moving power of experience, appears not to be transmissible. The deepest in man, what moves and convinces – and this in direct proportion to its importance and spiritual depth – appears without permanence or future, condemned to isolation, until it is stripped of that particularity which constituted its original appeal and persuasive power. The deepest in man and in cultures seems Heraclitean flux.

And is not this feeling, this emotion, whether it benumbs life as in the past of whole Eastern races ('in the midst of a world crying aloud for help and re-fashioning'[6]), or whether it maddens, as in Anabaptist excess – is not this emotion precisely what civilization, as we intend it, marshals and overcomes, reducing all experience – with but transitional outbreaks of the virulence – to the clarity of a knowledge which may be theorized and tested and made communicable through general statement and application, through law? Western polity, culture and religion, and the religious orders too, have shown neither long nor broad hospitality to the experimental-emotional in general, and especially not to the mystical. Within the history of religion, three major strains or elements appear: the historical (or institutional), the rational (or intellectual, philosophical), and the experimental (or mystical). And the last appears in that history as weakest for good, and with the strongest penchant for evil. But all this is preliminary and deceptive, and must yield to a larger view.[7]

Von Hügel concludes this analysis by returning to the original, apparent antinomy: it is the 'particular, concrete experience' which alone moves and determines the will, but which seems 'untransferable, indeed unrepeatable'; it is the 'general, abstract reasoning which *is* repeatable . . . , but which does not move us'.[8] Then he begins again, with a description of the three forces of Western civilization.

The first of the three forces is Hellenism, which von Hügel calls 'the thirst for richness and harmony'. Harmony is the goal, but *clarity* is the passion; and richness, multiplicity, will be substantively sacrificed, especially at the first in Parmenides and at the last in Plotinus and Proclus, for a harmony destructive of variety and difference, a harmony that dissolves union into unity, into empty oneness. Here generality and abstraction – and thus the impersonal – are the absolute, the perfect. And only mind is finally real: man's true self is reason. Variety and change, and persistent difference, especially in the spiritual order, do not, or only fitfully, survive. Yet von Hügel sees and loves the high philosophy and ethic born here: in the mutual identification of transcendent reality and absolute truth; in the Platonic themes of participation and conversion; and in the Aristotelian convictions that the absolute is dynamic act, that change is real, and (this only partially grasped) that virtue does not adequately consist in knowledge: a clear mind does not necessarily mean a clean heart. But von Hügel also watches

Greek philosophy end in the splendid and excessive mysticism of Plotinus, where man moves towards a One that is finally neither love nor will nor consciousness, but an anti-incarnational, empty transcendence. Thus philosophy's first problem, that of the one and the many, is brought to a solution vibrant with noble and deathless truths, but yet a solution which ends 'in an all-devouring abstraction, in an intense realism destructive step by step, of precisely all that concrete, individual, personal beauty, truth, and goodness, of all the spiritual, hence organic, interior, self-conscious reality, which had given occasion to this system'.[9]

The second force of Western civilization, as von Hügel reads its cultural and religious history, is Christianity, taken as 'the revelation of personality and depth'.[10] We may be brief here, since we have touched upon personality constantly thus far, and its fuller description awaits us further on in this chapter. Where Greek method 'identified abstractions with realities, and names with things, and reasoning with doing, suffering and experience; and sought for unity outside of multiplicity, for rest outside of energizing, for the Highest outside of personality and character',[11] where, in short, Greek method saw reality as a problem to be clarified and solved, Christianity is movement into mystery; it is a meeting of persons, and the penetration, by concrete, eternal Spirit, of concrete and particular, of historically developing spirit – and this pre-eminently in Christ. Simplicity here is organic and live, theoretically and practically bent on the ceaselessly tentative structuring of a mystery ceaselessly probed. The aim here is unity, or better, is harmony of *life*. And life for von Hügel, and therefore its unity (even for the inner life of God), is the *organization*, not the solution, of the *permanently* rich and deep and various. And the life to be organized is un-Greek indeed. It is the life of God active in the world, personally incarnate and historically embodied in the Christ whose flesh – and in him ours too – is become instrument and sacrament of Spirit.

The clarities of reason, and of negative asceticism too – we saw and shall see – have their noble and wholly ineluctable roles: but only as part and as *means*, in this organism of persons whose individual and communal harmony and growth – whose individual and corporate personalities have their source and materials in the breathtaking expanse of all that is human, *dinglich* and *secular* and, at those personalities' depths and as defining source and goal, in man's *religious* passion and capability for God's own distinct and prior joy, mediated, for sin's sake, by suffering and death, for personality's resurrection to God in Christ. Human personality is incarnation, both Christ's and our own. And again: as penetration of spirit by Spirit, full personality is eternal salvation, our own and the world's.[12]

Von Hügel finds in the Petrine, Pauline and Johannine literature of the New Testament three portraits of this 'rich unity of life' which is Christ. Despite the markedly different emphases and degrees of concern, he discovers at once historical (or institutional), and reasoning, and mystical affinities in all three biblical theologies. He finds it especially easy to observe in all three 'the two chief among the three modalities of all advanced religion: the careful reverence for the external facts of nature (so far as these are known), and for social religious tradition and institutions; and the vivid consciousness of the necessity and reality of internal experience and actuation, as the single spirit's search, response, and assimilation of the former.'[13] It must suffice our interest in von Hügel's detailed analysis of the New Testament writings to notice two things here. First, he finds that all of what we shall shortly describe as the three elements of religion are well within the second of the three forces of Western civilization: Christianity as revelation of personality and depth. Second, each of these elements, including the sensible-institutional, is explicitly affirmed to be ingredient to all three of the major New Testament sources, the earliest (the Petrine or Marcan) not excepted.

The third force of Western civilization is science and its

method, seen by von Hügel (and loved too) as the 'apprehension and conception of brute fact and iron law'.[14] And a first glance here, and even a second, suggest that metaphysics and religion (Greece and Christianity) 'evidently cannot ignore *it*; *it* apparently can ignore *them*'.[15] Science's three main characteristics are: a passion for clearness, expressed in mathematics and the quantitative view; 'the great concept of law . . . , one great determinism, before which all emotion and volition, all concepts of spontaneity and liberty, of personality and spirit, either human or divine, melt away . . . ';[16] and a vigorous monism, both as to means and to end. Our sources are one: 'the reasoning, reckoning intellect, backed up by readily repeatable, directly verifiable experiment.'[17] And the result is one: a strict unbroken mechanism. Von Hügel is not criticizing here. He is describing what he believes to be the case. He loves science and its utter secularity. It presents a great problem, but a great opportunity as well. As we shall see further on, he locates this science at the core of his spiritual doctrine.

In the light of the above inquiry, von Hügel sees man's task to lie, not in the subversion of any one or two of these forces, but in the harmonious interaction of the three. To summarize:

> There is the ancient, Greek contribution, chiefly intellectual and aesthetic, mostly cold and clear, quick and conclusive, with, upon the whole, but a slight apprehension of personality and freedom, of conscience and of sin, and little or no sense of the difference and antagonism between these realities and simply mathematical, mechanical laws and concepts. It is a view profoundly abstract, and, at bottom, determinist: the will follows the intellect necessarily, in exact proportion to the clearness of information of the former.[18]

The strength of this view lies in its 'freshness, completeness, and unity'.[19] And man must never lose this ideal of ultimate harmony, however much more difficult subsequent human knowledge and experience, and our sense of the developmental and especially of history, have shown the task to be.

> There is next the middle, Christian contribution, directly moral and religious, deep and dim and tender, slow and far-reaching, immensely costly, infinitely strong; with its discovery and exemplification of the mysterious depth and range and complexity of human personality and freedom, of conscience and of sin; a view profoundly concrete and at bottom libertarian. The goodwill here first precedes, and then outstrips, and determines the information supplied by the intellect: 'Blessed are the clean of heart, for they shall see God.'[20]

Von Hügel finds the strength here to lie in Christianity's 'being primarily not a view, but a life'.[21]

> There is finally the modern, scientific contribution, intensely impersonal and determinist, directly neither metaphysical nor religious, but more abstract even than the Greek view, in the mathematical constituent of its method, and more concrete in a sense than Christianity itself, in the other, the sensible-experiment constituent of its method. The most undeniable of abstractions, those of mathematics, (undeniable just because of their enunciation of nothing but certain simplest relations between objects, supposing those objects to exist,) are here applied to the most undeniable of concretions, the direct experiences of the senses. And this mysterious union which, on the surface, is so utterly heterogeneous, is itself at all explicable only on mental, metaphysical assumptions and on the admission of the reality and priority of mind. It is a union that has turned out as unassailable in its own province, as it is incapable of suppressing or replacing the wider and deeper truths and lives discovered for us respectively by Hellenism and Christianity.[22]

Von Hügel's spiritual doctrine will not admit deadlock in

theory, nor allow suppression in practice. Christian man must embrace the *entire* triad of his heritage, these three large facts of his own corporate experience. The goal is expansion, growth and harmony. The way will be suffering, friction, 'costly' joy.

Within the complex of Western civilizational forces, Christianity exists, we have seen, as the gift of, and summons to, deepened personal existence. And the profoundest impulse and need of human personality, among its other resources and achievements, is the specifically *religious* passion and capability under grace. But the term religion here, unlike its usage in the previous chapter, is wider than its own, mystical heart (the simple fact of God, and man's response to that fact and person). Here religion, as answering and expressing *man's* incarnational constitution as embodied spirit in the world, is a further complex of its own, another variety-in-unity and multiplicity-to-be-harmonized. The multiplicity also springs from *God's* revelational presence and action in history, a systematic and graded incarnationalism which achieves its fullest actuation within the created order in the personal presence and action of Christ, of the Eucharist, and of the mystery of his Spirit as community or Church.

Religion, then, is and must be complex because God gives himself to man and summons man to himself according to the total, the incarnational pattern of the real. Von Hügel, analysing this complex in the light of history and his own personal experience, suggests three elements of religion, understanding religion now from the human point of view.

Among the generality and, to a degree, for each man, religious life shows three modalities. The child's approach to religion depends on sense and imagination, and then on memory. The child is told or shown some religious fact or symbol. He accepts and trusts. It is the principle of authority and obedience in its simplest form. Error, even as a possibility, is not yet in sight. 'And at this stage, the external, authoritative, historical, traditional, institutional side and function of religion are everywhere evident. . . . Religion is here, above all, a fact and a thing.'[23]

But the growing youth begins to question, out of awe and wonder, and curiosity too. Hostile facts appear, and 'affirmation is beginning to be consciously exclusive of its contrary'.[24] The need for abstract reason, argument, and system, comes into play. And religion answers the need with its intellectual element. Religion here has become thought, theology.

The mature man, however, lives largely by 'intuition, feeling, and volitional requirements and evidences',[25] by the needs and exercise of suffering, effort and growth.

> For man is necessarily a creature of action, even more than of sensation and of reflection; and in this action of part of himself against other parts, of himself with or against other men, with or against this or that external fact or condition, he grows and gradually comes to his real self, and gains certain experiences as to the existence and nature and growth of this his own deeper personality.
>
> Man's emotional and volitional, his ethical and spiritual powers, are now in ever fuller motion, and they are met and fed by the third side of religion, the experimental and mystical. Here religion is rather felt than seen or reasoned about, is loved and lived rather than analyzed, is action and power, rather than either external fact or intellectual verification.[26]

Now this successive description must be modified, for all the elements are present to each stage, and especially to the mature religious life. 'Religion is at all times more or less both traditional and individual; both external and internal; both institutional, rational, and volitional.'[27] And here we repeat one of von Hügel's best formulations of the matter: 'I believe because I am told, because it is true, because it answers to my deepest interior experiences and needs.'[28] The richest spirituality will find all three motives richly operative. Yet man's movement into himself, his world and his God, involves transitions that are necessary and perilous, as the emphases widen and deepen. If he clings exclusively to institutional, external practice, his religion will contract and shrivel, and 'become a something simply alongside of other things in his life'.[29] But if he totally supplants this with the 'individually intellectual', a man's religion 'will grow hard and shallow, and will tend to disappear altogether'.[30] In the first case, superstition, in the second, rationalism and indifference, are in view. But to these two elements, singly and even more in their combination, the third element of religion, its experimental and emotional force and power, will easily appear as revolution, subjectivism and 'sentimentality ever verging on delusion'.[31] And where this latter force triumphs over the institutional seen as oppression and over the intellectual seen as rationalism, a subjectivist 'tyranny of mood and fancy will result'. And then 'fanaticism is in full sight'.[32]

Von Hügel finds parallels for his analysis of the three elements of religion in the processes of human knowledge and the stages of reflex action. And there too, the movement and interaction itself both

> *culminates* in a modification of the personality and . . . *prepares* this personality for the next round of sense-perception, intellectual abstraction, ethical affirmation and volitional self-determination, – acts in which light and love, fixed and free, hard and cold and warm, are so mysteriously, so universally, and yet so variously linked.[33]

The three elements of religion, further, are found distributed among man's various ages, sexes, professions, and races. Their varying history, moments of harmonious interaction, and the excesses of their mutual isolation, are the history of the great religions. Within Christianity, they tell the tale of the various

Churches and sects and, within Roman Catholicism, the story of the religious orders too.[34]

Von Hügel comes towards his conclusion with a description of the causes for the harassment of one element of religion by the others. The religious temper legitimately aspires towards simplicity, for God *is* the one thing necessary. But to speak this truth is not to solve, but rather to pose the problem. The task will be, as we have seen,[35] to assess and appropriate the rich, various, *harmonized* simplicity of the 'naked Jesus'. Von Hügel finds that even the most astringent, abstractive and absolutizing of the fully Christian mystical theorists, John of the Cross, in his actual practice *organizes* a *variety* of incarnational truths, and that the mysticism of Teresa of Jesus did not lose, but gained through her concern for the many-sided Church and its authority, and through her contemplation of God *through* the humanity of Christ. Yet von Hügel readily admits that the history of religion, and of Christianity too, teaches modern man that 'the elements of multiplicity and friction and of unity and harmonization, absolutely essential to all life, everywhere and always cost us much to keep and gain'.[36]

Von Hügel maintains that all higher religion is called into existence by a contingent historical event which rightly makes an absolute claim. But this claim will tend to impose itself as a '*spatial*, a *simultaneous* exclusiveness', and the traditional and institutional element of religion then starves or shuts out all else, including science and politics. Religion reigns in a desert. And there may be the further danger of an imposed '*temporal*, *successive* exclusiveness'. Here, historical event as contingent absolute is seen as fixed, utterly once and for all, unchanging, materially identical with itself. And thus religion becomes not a life but a stone, 'even though a stone fallen from heaven . . . And the two exclusivenesses, joined together, would give us a religion reduced to such a stone worshipped in a desert.'[37]

What this abuse forgets is that religion is 'the manifestation of an infinite Personality, responded and assented to by a personality, finite indeed but capable of indefinite growth'. The fixity, therefore, the identity of revelation with itself, must be vital, 'like the gradual leavening of bread'. And man's summons to surrender must be, finally, 'not towards some thing, but towards Some One, whose right, indeed whose very power to claim me, consists precisely in that he is himself, absolutely, infinitely and actually, what I am but derivatively, finitely and potentially'.[38]

On the other hand, however, this latter sense of the 'freshness and interiority' of God's and man's own action can imperil the external and institutional altogether. Maturity can seem to mean moving on and away from the definite and the repeated. Vocal prayer, for example, may be dropped. The 'indeterminate consciousness of Christ's spirit' may seem wider and larger than the 'apparent contraction of mind and heart' involved in contemplation of the Gospel scenes and in the precise localization involved in devotion to the Eucharist; a general regret for sinful dispositions may appear nobler than the 'apparent materiality and peddling casuistry . . . of fixing for oneself the kind and degree of one's actual sins, and of determining upon definite, detailed reforms'. For von Hügel, this full pendulum swing and reaction against the former abuse avoids the specific thrust of Christianity's central, incarnational temper, which 'nobly bends under the yoke and cramps itself within the narrow limits of the life-giving concrete act'. For von Hügel, it is a false escape, and a great betrayal of the incarnational *facts* and laws of human existence. Indeed he sees Christian life and history as 'a living commentary upon the difficulty and importance' of this truth.[39]

Finally, the institutional and mystical elements, singly or together, have manifold motives for hostility towards the intellectual element. The latter's historical criticism and philosophical analyses seem to threaten the institution, while man's emotional power and love seem undermined by the intellect's congenital impersonalism, which tends to represent all reality 'as something static, not dynamic, as a thing, not as a person or Spirit'.[40] Von Hügel asks for a solution here in a fuller conception of personality, where 'the human person begins more as a possibility than a reality'. And the production of personality thus understood, the actuation of its possibility, will take place, under grace, only through purification: the death of the *selfish* self in and through the growth of free-willing spirit. Human spirit ever requires three things: 'rest, expression, and purification'. And the intellect can contribute to each of these needs. Its abstractive processes *rest* the moral-spiritual activities. Its statements *express* the achievements of spirit, spiritual facts that require constant restatement for the successive ages and cultures of the world. And the intellect *purifies*, by placing 'a zone of abstraction, . . . of apparently ultimate, though really only phenomenal determinism, between the direct informations of the senses, to which the *individual* clings, and the inspirations of the moral and spiritual nature, which constitute the *person*'.[41]

Von Hügel denies that this conception of religion is excessively intellectual. The intellectual, determinist element he calls for is, in essence, simply the reverent 'attention to *things* and their mechanism, their necessary laws and requirements', which is present even in the 'rules of good washing and of darning of clothes'.[42] He denies the conception is Pelagian or naturalistic – that it represents a failure to present religious life as 'simply the gift of God, capable of being received, but not produced by us'. No. Grace and freedom rise and fall together. Our self-expression is 'a thing received as well as given, and that we have it to give, and that we can and do give it, is itself a pure gift of God'.[43]

Finally, von Hügel rejects the charge of Epicureanism. 'Where is the cross and self-renunciation' in this world-embracing scheme he gives us? Is not the doctrine of 'friction' a euphemistic, un-Christlike covert for gaining the whole world at any cost and for bidding a man to love his father and mother even if it introduces a conflict into his affections? Not, von Hügel replies, if the historical-institutional and the mystical elements are held in close concert with the intellectual. Personality is neither born from the intellect, nor crowned by it either. For life is finally not a problem for the mind to solve, but a mystery calling forth the whole man's love and self-surrender. Indeed, the intellect may do good service as 'the very measure of the soul's own limitations, and of the exceeding greatness of its love and of its Lover . . . ' The intellect, in fact, perhaps has its, otherwise necessary, but *particular* value just here 'for the planting fully and finally, in the very depths of the personality, the Cross, the sole means to the soul's true incoronation'.[44]

Von Hügel's three elements of religion, as sketched against his background of major cultural or civilizational forces, are a consideration of religion 'on its human side'.[45] They effectively amount to a description of man *as religious*. Now in our previous chapter on *God*, the heart of religion was the mystical, was just the fact of God in himself as self-conscious, self-communicating, free-willing Spirit. And here once again, in von Hügel's description of *man as personality*, the heart of religion, its dangerous, splendid heart, is the mystical: man as experimental, volitional spirit. For religion, besides being traditional and old, is that *novel* adventure which is *my* appropriation of its institutionally mediated truth. And before and besides and beyond being a matter of things and doctrines, religion is a person whom I encounter and love.[46] For von Hügel, all personality, and its fullest expression as sanctity, has its first source and final goal (from the human point of view) in man's power to love, his will.[47] The religious, then, and the personal, and the holy too, all have their centre in the mystical understood as free-willing spirit and what spirit was born for: love. Much else is required besides. But all else is means to the end. Love is personality in act and coming to being. Heroic love, sanctity, is personality arrived in triumph upon itself.[48]

In 1900 von Hügel presents for Maude Petre an extremely careful articulation of his fundamental thought on personality. That thought does not intend to contradict basic Greek metaphysic. It does intend to correct and radically to existentialize it as a spirituality. Von Hügel argues for a deeply true sense in which man is not born with character and personality but only 'with certain aptitudes within him, and certain mysterious helps within him and above him, of slowly, laboriously, painfully, obscurely *making for himself* a character and personality'.[49] The *ex nihilo nihil fit* objection to this cannot be allowed:

> We cannot imagine how a mere individual can become a person; a mere unit, a moral centre and force; an animal, a character. And yet it is clear, I think that . . . , mysterious though it be, so it is: that with God as supreme and absolute reality, the moral Person in the world, we have been created and are helped by him, in such conditions and according to such laws, as are conducive to our making ourselves into moral agents of a particular (our) kind and degree; and that he, being there to help us, he intends to help us only to make our own selves, and gives us to begin with our materials but not the results, and *never, at any time, in the materials practically the results already*.[50]

Indeed von Hügel goes so far here as to allow that, even as regards man's experience of God himself: '*He made us in order that in a sense we might make him.*' For von Hügel believes that the personality of God, even though it

> decides *in fact* even our first instant of existence, . . . [yet] *as a conception of our own* (if it is to become and remain at all not an idol or a caricature, but is to be as true and helpful as possible) must, it too, be conquered and again reformed and reconquered by us, with and through the conquest of our own personality.[51]

Such a view sees man's spirit not only and not primarily as a static, fixed quantity, but as a dynamic quality actualizing its own possibility. Man's spirit 'is not only an energizing substance: *it puts in substance* by right energizing, and only by this means'.[52] From the point of view of existence, the Greek mind puts essence 'at the beginning', while von Hügel, just here, asks for substance 'at the end':

> the former [Greek essence] is previous to and independent of action, the latter [existentialist essence] is posterior to it and its fruit; the former is fixed and stable, the latter is ever growing and shrinking; the former is adequately cognizable in its true concept, the latter is but partially apprehensible, from an analysis of the results of the experience of the reality itself, gained in and through action; the former can be as fully known by the bad as by the good, even though it be but the latter who utilize and build upon such knowledge, the latter can be really known only in and through moral devotedness, since it is the latter that alone supplies adequate material and sufficient earnestness, and the humility and livingness which will ever begin again and again the happy, enriching round of action and analysis, love and light.[53]

The Greek conception contains a powerful but largely abstract truth. It speaks of Christian personality in its moment as sheer and totally *unappropriated* gift, where it is project, proposal, and objective offer alone, and not subjectivity and achievement as well. The Greek stress here – and fully endorsed by von Hügel within its limits – is on man as an *invitation* to life. The emphasis in the complementary, existential conception, on the other hand, is on life as *met and engaged*, as an historical and rich variety-in-unity. It is this latter – concrete human personality as process – which is the subject of incarnational experience and, therefore, the primary object and concern of Christian spirituality.

Von Hügel structures and gives further content and direction to his view of personality and its production in a discussion of the three stages of the spiritual life. He is not referring here to the classical and at least theoretically progressive divisions known as the purgative, illuminative and unitive ways. Rather he treats of individualism, law, and personality. In this view, the first ought to yield to the second, but the second remains, in this life, as the perennial and honoured means to the third. There are, in the first place, men 'characterized, even to the end of their earthly lives, by that, more or less complete, naturalistic individualism, with which we all in various degrees begin'. Such are

> unmoral or even anti-moral men, who, however gifted and cultivated as artists, scholars, philosophers, and statesmen, must yet be counted as essentially childish and as clever animals rather than as spiritual men.[54]

Life here is shrivelled and disparate. Variety and breadth have not sought their unity and depth. Pleasure has been substituted for struggle leading to joy. Severe want and privation too, and the obsessive guarding against them, can arrest men at this stage.[55] Existence here, at any rate, is thin and distracted and – as categorized by time – discrete, unorganized succession. This is von Hügel's superficial man.

Men 'that have recognized and have accepted duty and obligation, that are now striving to serve God as God' belong to the second stage. Such men

> of necessity tend to suspect, or even to suppress and sacrifice, whatever appears to be peculiar to themselves, as so much individualistic subjectivity and insidious high treason to the objective law of him who made their souls, and who now bids them save those souls at any cost. The large majority of the souls . . . striving to serve God . . . belong . . . to this second, universalistic, uniformative type and class.[56]

The noble themes of conversion, austerity and sacrifice appear here, but their intended aftermath and final purposes remain, for this life, largely thwarted. The theme of purification as positive, as growth and love, is not, or is only fitfully appropriated. Successiveness is severe, ardent, and deepened. But it does not, for experience at least, blossom into duration, much less bask in the simultaneity of God as joyous presence. Law has not yet revealed itself as Lover, or as the *interiorized* rhythm of free hearts.

> The third and final stage occurs when and where that universality, obligation, uniformity, and objectivity, of the second stage and class, take the form of a spiritual individuality, liberty, variety, and subjectivity: personality in the fullest sense of the term has now appeared. And this fullest spiritual personality is the profoundest opposite and foe of its naturalistic counterfeit, of those spontaneous animal liberalisms which reigned, all but unrecognized as such because all but uncontrasted by the true ideal and test of life, prior to that prostration before absolute obligation, that poignant sense of weakness and impurity, and that gain of strength and purity from beyond its furthest reaches, experienced by the soul at its conversion.
>
> Yet that merely subjective, liberalistic individualism of the first stage can only be kept out, even at the third stage, by retaining within the soul all the essential characteristics of the second stage, – by a continuous passing and re-passing under the Caudine Forks of the willed defeat of wayward, self-pleasing wilfulness, and of the deliberate acceptance of an objective system of ideas and experiences as interiorly binding upon the self. For if the second stage excludes the first, the third stage does not exclude the second. Yet now all this... leads up to and produces a living reality bafflingly simple in its paradoxical, mysterious richness. For now the universality, obligation, and objectivity of the law become and appear greater, not less, because incarnated in an eminently unique

and unreproduceable, in a fully personal form. And at this stage only do we find a full persuasiveness.[57]

We have in this description of the three stages of spiritual life a most useful presentation of the whole structure and intention of von Hügel's spirituality. The false, wilful self as individualism and subjectivism is clearly distinguished from true liberty as personality and subjectivity. And the permanent, perennial means of passage is the *object*, the objective, the real: whether natural or supernatural; whether God himself or his graces; whether other human persons or one's own body, mind and emotions; whether things as mental, abstract idea or in their sensible physicality. The production of personality involves *both* man's rhythmic, grace-aided *outgoing* towards objects at every level of the real, in a loving, docile, attentive, non-violating surrender to the laws of those objects in their own respected interiority and autonomy; *and* it involves man's recollective *withdrawal* and repose from those objects. Von Hügel's production of personality demands *both* movements as agents of growth and of purification, of cross and resurrection, of humility and joy, where the scattered self, the incipient person, despising cheap grace, continually, increasingly and *wilfully*, dies-and-rises under the ensuing *friction* to the rich and organic variety-in-unity which is personality: self-conscious, free-willing *durational* spirit, whose source and pattern and goal is the dynamic simultaneity and vigorous social joy of the triune God.

There is question here of both means and end. The end is personality. And the twofold asceticism of the means is stern. Man must give himself to the object according to the laws of *his* own worth, and not be absorbed by the object in some behaviourist or 'humanist' levelling down. He must not even, finally, be absorbed by God, in some false, self-contemptuous, anti-incarnational levelling up. That is the first asceticism. Secondly, man must give himself to the object according to the laws of *its* own worth, and not dominate or impose upon or destroy its truth by some 'religious' fear or arrogant neglect, or by crude anthropomorphism. Man must ardently face the factualness, the *there-ness* of God and the world and his fellows, humbly seeking the stripping away of his own false self through his active and creative involvement with *their* truth, and gratefully striving for his constitution and growth as a person through *them*. It is a matter of both death and life, in and through both that life and death which is Jesus as struggle and growth and tension, for that eternal life which is Christ as harmony and joy.

Our following chapter will detail some of the incarnational objects and experiences of fully developed Christian personality, objects and experiences which are also means to its production: sense and the social as Church (the institutional element of religion); asceticism and purification; and science (which includes the intellectual element of religion, but is markedly important for this study precisely in its non-religious, its secular affirmation and concern). But here we continue with the exposition of the basic notion and experience of personality. It ought to be clear by now that von Hügel's use of the word personality is not answerable to any technically exact psychological or philosophical theory or school. Rather he constructs its meaning eclectically – not by defining it *a priori*, but by designating it the synthetic term embodying all that man already is as gift, and all that he must do and be as freedom.

Von Hügel's decisive but sympathetic denial of the doctrine of conditional immortality reaffirms what we have just seen and further helps to locate the place and the acceptance which both Greek and existentialist essence or substance find in his spiritual doctrine. It also affords an important glance at his view of personality as source and fruit of goodness and love – of personality as holy – and of his insistence on the very real but really subordinate character of evil precisely as reality *vis-à-vis* the reality of love and goodness. His view of conditional immortality will also briefly review for us the relation of personality and time.

Conditional immortality is not taken here as the annihilation of impenitent grave sinners. Rather, it

> simply holds that human souls begin with the capacity of acquiring, with the help of God's Spirit, a spiritual personality, built up out of the mere possibilities and partial tendencies of their highly mixed natures, which, if left uncultivated and untranscended, become definitely fixed at the first, phenomenal, merely individual level, – so that spiritual personality alone deserves to live on, and does so, whilst this animal individuality does not deserve and does not do so. The soul is thus not simply born as, but can become more and more, that 'inner man' who alone persists, indeed who 'is renewed day by day, even though our outward man perish.'[58]

Von Hügel places the *ex nihilo nihil fit* charge against this view taken strictly. Man must already be *given* as, he must somehow be and have responsibility for, what he is to become: spirit. And this is the Greek truth. If personality is growth and movement outward and beyond the preoccupied self, it is also the actuation of what was there *at the beginning* as offered, as gift. But von Hügel's criticism is gentle. For the position, though false by its excess, emphasizes the existential and 'profoundly expensive, creative, positive process and nature of spiritual character'.[59] And it leads to another, acceptable position: the shrunken, scattered consciousness of impenitent sinners. For '*love alone is fully positive* and alone gives vital strength . . . ' Here we discover that the heart of personality, even in man, does not lie in freedom of choice, but in what that freedom chooses and becomes. For von Hügel, it is Manichaean to suggest 'any serious equating of the force and intensity of life and consciousness between the saved and the lost . . . ' Those who love are not only '*other*', they are '*more*: for God is Life supreme, and, where there is more affinity with God, there is more life, more consciousness'. In short, more personality. Hell is man as largely successiveness, as animal unit – perhaps, in God's mercy, man as almost unaware. Heaven is personality: rich, successively acquired, *durational* self-consciousness, participating in the *totum-simul* awareness of God.[60]

In analysing the life and achievement of Catherine of Genoa, von Hügel speaks of the materials, the problems and possibilities, the multiplicity and '*beggarly elements* which she found, and of the *spiritual organism*', the variety-in-unity, the persuasive personality, 'which she left'.[61] His subject, then, is determinism, effort and grace, and he is seeking to identify, to understand and respect, and then to move on from 'the psychophysical and temperamental peculiarities and *determinisms* of her case, up to the spiritual characteristics and ethical *self-determinations*' of her sanctity.[62] The will must utilize all that is to become personal. Both the free possibilities and the determinisms of environment, background, ability and of psychophysical structure are of no spiritual significance in themselves. They are morally neutral or irrelevant until 'sifted, taken up, organized and transformed in and into a large and deep spiritual experience and personality'.[63] And there is nothing automatic or necessary about this liberalizing and never-completed constitution and growth of the spiritual self. Personality and that sanctity which is its fullness are an heroic achievement.[64] Hagiography, then, and spiritual direction, and each man's common sense too, ought to fear the admiration and perhaps ruinous imitation of saints which does not know 'how to distinguish between the merely given materials and untransferable determinisms of each separate soul's psychical and temperamental native outfit, and the free, grace-inspired and grace-aided use made by each soul of these its, more or less unique, occasions and materials'.[65]

Psychology, then, looms large.[66] And its honoured place in von Hügel's spiritual doctrine furnishes a concrete instance of the initial and continuous importance of that second stage and means of spiritual life: alert attention and respectful surrender to the facts and laws of reality at every level, both in our theory and in our practice. Theoretical and clinical psychology, together with the other contextual materials of personality, must receive such undivided attention and careful study 'as though they were *not* secondary and but the material and occasion of the forces and self-determinations' which must utilize, build up, and be assisted by them. Those forces are freedom and grace.[67]

Von Hügel's spiritual doctrine, then, assigns a most important place to psychology within the wider range of spirituality. But it assigns psychology's limits too. Psychology and its ideal of mental-emotional health are a means. Indeed, some psychological stability and some physical stability, as necessary conditions of significant freedom and as dispositions for grace, are indispensable means. But they exist within and for an organism greater than themselves.[68] The act of a man may be, humanly speaking, irrelevant, that is, not a human event. Or it may be of human significance, in which case it will serve either to promote or to diminish spiritual personality. Psychology and the other human sciences ought increasingly to clarify these situations and to enlarge their human possibilities. But such science cannot decide 'of itself, anything whatsoever about, and still less against, the objective truth and spiritual value of the ultimate causes, dominant ideas, and final results of the process'.[69] Something more organic is required. And modern spirituality must avoid 'the Philistinism both of the rationalists and of the older supernaturalists, and will neither measure our assent to facts by our ability to explain them, nor postulate the immediate action of God wherever our powers of explanation fail us'.[70] The final criterion, answerable both to good psychological counselling and to sober spiritual direction, is that test of 'spiritual fruitfulness' central to the great Christian mystical tradition as founded on the Gospel of Christ: do the alleged facts and acts of our spiritual life make us 'more humble, true, and loving' towards God and our fellow-men?[71] All psychological and other materials and phenomena, whether ordinary or extraordinary, must face the judgment of this great personal principle and test and be thereby accounted: either irrelevant; or destructive; or the perhaps expensive but worthy price paid; or finally, truly productive causes and expressions of spiritual personality.[72]

We pass now to the question of effort or human freedom – and grace. For Friedrich von Hügel, the elemental evil and goodness in the world are human: self and spirit.[73] And in that deepest sense in which God honours human freedom, man is his own responsibility. Therefore, while condemning strain at every turn, von Hügel sings a constant and unabashed hymn to strenuous, both positive and negative, effort, and to personality both as self-constituting and as destructive of individualism. The individual is required and enabled by God – 'he constitutes himself and is constituted into a person' through the interaction of, 'and in friction with, *complexes*, – complexes, profitable in proportion to their variety in unity'.[74] The effort is *positive*, towards the growth of personality; yet it is also profoundly a movement *against*, against the self. And it remains, on both counts, a human and strenuous *effort*. Even a woman very young in years, Juliet Mansel, is invited to the 'building up of interior unity in the daily watch and ward against the false self'. Human souls

> do not even begin to attain to their true unity, indeed they are not really awake, until they are divided up – until the spirit within them begins to discriminate itself against the petty self.
>
> In the Scottish rivers the salmon will leap and leap, and only after much leaping will they succeed in jumping up

> and into the higher reaches. Jump, Child, jump: *I* jump with you, look, we both manage it!
>
> Loving old Fatherly one.[75]

Many years earlier, when she was a young girl, he had counselled her to a

> simple, humble determination, with God's grace, quietly and wisely, with much breadth and ever renewed patience, to constitute yourself, on and on, into a spiritual personality.

And he warns her against that 'mere drift and fever of the surface, faddy, selfish life – so near to the best of us, as long as we are here below'.[76] He remembers at the age of seventy, for another young girl, his own experience of being seventeen:

> I saw young fellows all around me fretting to be *free*, to be their own sole, full masters. They fretted against this and that thing; against this and that person. They thought if only they could get away from these, they would indeed be free. But I myself *could not feel that to be nearly enough*; I was too little happy in myself to fiddle-faddle at such little things! I wanted, *I had to*, get rid of – not those outside conditions, not those other people and their orders, etc.: but I had, somehow, to become free from *self*, from my poor, shabby, bad, all-spoiling *self*! *There* lay freedom, *there* lay happiness! And I see now at 70, more clearly again than at 17, that I was right there.... Our service of God ... [which] includes also our service of others ... really means for us the fighting of self.[77]

Death and life are indeed distinct, but they are not separated, or separable, in this spirituality. The paschal mystery is an organic whole. For the pilgrim Christian, joy occurs and comes to be, in and through the Cross.

This doctrine of strenuous human effort, of man's *self*-constitution as a person, raises, of course, the question of freedom and grace, and invites the charge of Pelagianism. Von Hügel counters that thrust easily, I think, and without effort or heat; indeed, without much interest. He certainly never makes the *de auxiliis* controversy his own. Grace is not an addition to the will, but a modification of its *quality*. Grace 'does not check or limit', rather it is constitutive of the will's autonomy and therefore of spiritual, independent human personality.[78] 'Passive' prayer is perhaps man's *freest* act,[79] for grace and freedom exist in direct proportion: they rise and fall together.[80] And the doctrine of merit has its largest goodness in the very nature of 'rewards'. Precisely in their 'owed' quality they are the 'self-donations' of God.[81] '... The very self-donation of the creature is the Creator's best gift ... And thus ethics are englobed by religion, having by doing, and doing by being.'[82]

In this whole matter von Hügel settles for and frequently repeats St Bernard's formulation of the mystery:

> That which was begun by grace, gets accomplished alike by both grace and free will, so that they operate mixedly not separately, simultaneously not successively, in each and all of their processes. The acts are not in part grace, in part free will; but the whole of each act is effected by both in an undivided operation.[83]

What is needed philosophically, as we have seen, is the rejection of any quantitative, materialist view of substance, and the assertion of the penetrability of personal spirit by distinct and prior personal Spirit. A now distant, once-upon-a-time, deist creator God will not do; but neither will there suffice man's identification with an absorbing, or absorbed, pantheistic God. *Panentheism* is von Hügel's answer: a Transcendent Immanence, an intimately present creat*ing* Father whose ecstatic love *is* the deed of that dependent independence, that significant and adult freedom-in-humility which is Christian childhood.[84]

We have from von Hügel, in this context of God as 'distant' and as 'present', as both grace and freedom (therefore as neither separate from man nor as identified with him), an important appreciation of the psychological needs and laws of incarnational piety and devotion as they do and must continue accurately to reflect the theological doctrines of grace and freedom: of God as not man, yet who becomes man and dwells in men; of God as gift, and as gift received and acted with and on. It is a perennial question and of more than speculative import, for it concerns and will affect how man shall pray and act and be. It concerns those gestures, words and silences of liturgy which express *and* structure the contours of the Christian heart. Man, as finite, embodied spirit, is, must be, anthropomorphic. He *must* imagine – which is to spatialize – whatever is to have a vital role or is to exert true motive power in his piety and life. The continuing effort and point will be *accurately* to imagine the central *facts* of faith, and accurately to interrelate and purify them for a particular culture and experience, without reductionism:

> *Spatial* concepts and imagery play two important roles in the full and normal consciousness of eternal life. For whether or no the spatial category abides with man in the beyond, in this earthly life at least he cannot persistently and vividly apprehend even the most spiritual realities, as distinct and different from each other, except by picturing them as disparate in space. Now a vivid consciousness of the deep distinction and difference (within all their real affinity and closeness of intercourse) between God and man, and the continuous, keen sense that all man has, does, and is of good is ever, in its very possibility, a free gift of God, constitutes the very core of religion. Hence the spatial imagery, which, by picturing God as *outside* the soul and heaven as *above* the earth, helps to enforce this fundamental truth, is highly valuable – as valuable, indeed, as the imagery (spatial still) which helps to enforce the complementary truth of God's likeness to the soul and his penetration of it, by picturing God as *within* the soul and heaven as *in* this room.[85]

We return now to conclude our discussion of the journey from self to person seen as both effort and gift, both freedom and grace. Von Hügel sums up his position with fine pastoral bluntness in his spiritual direction of Juliet Mansel, eighteen years old in 1911. The upshot is a socially oriented love:

> I feel as though you are now getting thoroughly awake, Child, as though you sincerely long to fight, to drop, to overcome self. Without that dividing up of the true self against the false, without a fear and dread of self that will drive you to God and Christ, without a taking in hand daily, and ever humbly beginning anew, but *not in your own strength, but in a despair of self*, which, if true, means *an utter trust in God and Christ*, so utterly near you night and day – religion is fine talk.
>
> . . . I could, of course, try to help you to find peace, just simply in your non-combatted self, in the exclusion of the deeper promptings of the religious sense. Yet *not what you give will make you suffer, in the long run, but what you keep back; not the fear and hatred of self, but all temporizing with it. Every self-conquest will mean peace. . . . These* would be the chief points, I think, for your examining of conscience, for turning over at spiritual reading, and for your little silent cries to God, in your recollection, during the day: dropping quietly all favourable comparison of self with others, indeed all unnecessary self-occupation, all self-sufficiency, all self-completedness; putting in place of all *that*, love, service, adaptableness, attention to, occupation with others, *ever so much, to the verge of weakness* . . . with love, you understand love, Child, *love*! Mind, now, no naturalism, no goodness in your own strength. Pretty rotten rubbish that would be.
>
> God bless you, Child mine. Pray for me.[86]

Von Hügel's affirmation of multiplicity everywhere – so familiar now to the reader – occurs in the function of incarnational personality as a repudiation of the personal and the holy as something thin and unitary and unworldly. It rather views God and man as rich and full and various realities, organized for self-surrender. We have already seen – and we shall see it again in von Hügel's discussion of the Church – that man's body and man's status as social are not merely accessory means to personality (they are that too), but that they are constitutive of man, interior to his being and to his goal as person.[87] We have also seen that the *objects* of man's concern and attention, objects which are source and fruit of his personality, are multiple. They include art and politics and economics, as well as God and the three elements of religion as humanly understood.[88] And the multiplicity to be organized is not only one of quantity, but one of quality too. It involves nature and supernature 'as a [qualitative, not temporal] succession of steps in the becoming of personality', where personality 'arises, out of man, to beyond man . . . as a merely natural product – a personality achieved through a union of his will and deepest being with God . . .'[89]

Now this complex of issues raises the famous and even notorious problem of Pure Love, a matter to which von Hügel gives extended attention.[90] And here too he seeks that 'incarnational and synthetic' stance 'which finds spiritual realities and forces working' the one inside and through the other.[91] Basically for von Hügel, love, and therefore 'pure love' perfectly, is action centred in the other, and not in the self or even in love's consequences.[92] The doctrine of Christ's Spirit dwelling in man is the major presupposition here. [93] For pure love is that *human* act which loves – *with God's own love* – anything and any *number* of things at all – whether God in himself, or one's fellow-men, or oneself, or the wide and various world.[94] *This* is the surrender called for: not to love God alone, exactly (a true, but incarnationally insufficient and misleading formulation), but to love only with God's love – to *become God's love of all he loves.* It is a gift, of course. It is also, always, a free human act.[95] Von Hügel knows it is difficult, for it is the splendid climax of that austerity-in-liberality which is the basic proposal of his spirituality: utter detachment *within* complete involvement.[96] But moments of that splendour are not unduly rare. Strict contemplation, which *is* rare, will not occur without pure love, but the converse is not so.[97] In any case, pure love is not odd, inhuman, Platonist, or anti-incarnational, but the summation of the Gospel.[98] It has nothing to do with loving God alone – and here von Hügel charges John of the Cross with living better than he sometimes wrote.[99] Rather, it is to love God and all he loves with *his* love, according to his mind and heart. And this is its triumph and its sanctity: by moving out of self to love *all* with God's love, pure love defeats the self by a positive putting on of Christ. And this is personality.[100] Furthermore, pure love does not speak of any attempt to seek, through some anti-incarnational 'maximum possible degree of abstraction, to apprehend the absolute character and being of God'. Teresa of Avila learned this lesson with much trouble, but she learned it – and never forgot it – from the humanity of Christ.[101] Finally, pure love is indeed to love God directly, but von Hügel is valuably emphatic that pure love is to love all else directly too. We are to love with God's love, *as* God loves. And the Father's loving concern for the sparrow is direct and most detailed.[102]

The same affirmation by von Hügel of multiplicity, of personality as expansion and fullness, also suggests, as we shall see again later, the character of holiness, *and of purification too*, as positive. The static, negative, Platonist theme of the Christian ascetical tradition, where purity and perfection are the removal and the absence of stain, is true and essential, but it is preliminary, and radically to be subordinated to a conception and practice of love and purification as *creative* variety and force. 'Specifically human purity' embraces and *affirms* the body and the world. Christian personality is 'flame rather than snow', 'dwelling upon what to do and give and be, rather than upon what to shun'. Von Hügel sees Catherine of Genoa here as overcoming her Platonist *theory* through an incarnational *life* where 'purity is found to be love, and this love is exercised, not only in the inward, home-coming, recollective movement, – in the purifying of the soul's dispositions, but also in the outgoing, world-visiting, dispersive movement – in action towards fellow-souls'.[103]

The negative, then, is indispensable as a means, is subordinate even as a means, and is no part of the goal. Christian man worships a God not of the dead, but of the living.[104] Noteworthy here is that even the fight against self, while thoroughly negative in intent, is usually (though not always) conceived by von Hügel in positive terms. Again and again he asks for a 'dropping' of 'self' that is to be achieved positively, by 'gently' turning to 'God and Christ and the Poor', and by moving 'away out into God's great world'.[105] Further, this movement towards the personal is positive in its *incarnational and historical* quality: only fidelity to the definite and the particular, to time and to place, leads to the *concrete* universal: the *durée* of spiritual personality. The great maxim here is 'one thing, and only one at a time'. It is a 'severe successiveness' that builds up a 'rich simultaneity'.[106]

We have, finally, in this chapter, briefly to consider a whole tissue of questions relevant to von Hügel's description of moral personality: questions about the relation of acts and states; the plurality of acts and their freedom (quietism); and the permanent quality of free-willing spirit's deliberate character. Conduct cannot turn aside these issues as precious. The refusal to reflect on them, for whatever published reasons, does not avoid very practical pastoral stances that relate to them.

Von Hügel sees the doctrine of the responsibility of the individual for his particular, individual acts, rooted in Ezechiel, as a great incarnational truth which secures the dignity of man, of this individual man, and the significance of just today and of all history as component of time, as real successiveness. What *this* man does, today and in this place, makes a difference. But this doctrine must be located within 'the Gospel depth of teaching, (with its union of the social body and of individual souls, and of the soul's single acts and of the general disposition produced by and reacting upon these acts) . . . ' The alternative to this, not collectivist but organic, view is a 'solipsistic individualism and an atomistic psychology' offensive to 'Christianity and science equally'. There is argued here, then, the *durational* character of moral personality – successively indeed acquired and expressed; and there is argued the 'profound reality of habits, general dispositions, tones of mind and feeling and will, as distinct from the single acts that gradually build them up and that, in return, are encircled and coloured by them all'. This view does not wish to deny

> the possibility for the soul to express its deliberate and full disposition and determination in a single act or combination of acts; nor that the other-world effects will follow according to such deep, deliberate orientations of the character: it will only deny that, at any and every moment, any and every act of the soul sufficiently expresses its deliberate disposition. Certainly it is comparatively rarely that the soul exerts its full liberty, in an act of true, spiritual self-realization.[107]

In short, succession most often proceeds with laborious successiveness. And whether in the individual or in the social body, any one moment or act is possibly but rarely, and only at man's greatest, to be found laden with the *full* reality, splendour, and awesome responsibility which is moral personality as *durée*. There is obvious cause for both gratitude and humility in this circumstance. For if the rare self-possession required for such a wholly decisive moral option poses a great risk of sin and of human pride, such self-possession is also a great gift for the whole community to give thanks for, when it occurs in the hidden adventure of the saints. Von Hügel records it of St Catherine: 'she was kneeling on . . . , throughout a deep, rich age of growth, during but some poor minutes of clock-time.'[108]

In his discussion of quietism, von Hügel leads us more deeply into his understanding of human personality as a free and operative, incarnational multiplicity.[109] He asks for a 'distinction between experiences', their 'expression' and their psychological and theological 'analysis'. The entire mystical tradition, including the Christian, rightly emphasizes man's *receptive* stance with regard to God and to grace. Gift is the fundamental truth. But one current of the tradition makes the point at the risk of imperilling what a second current affirms with equal rightness: the correlative truth that this very receptivity is inevitably, and in direct proportion to its being such, also a free human act. The terms 'passivity' and 'action' (as distinguished from 'activity') characterize these different views. The experience of the greatest mystics, it is true, gives an impression of utter passivity, but this 'is an appearance only'.[110] The impression of rest is actually the *presence* and the result of much actualized energy, of action, and the *disappearance* and absence of feverish, distracted and distracting, activity. The aesthetic experience provides a parallel, as indeed does any willed and creative absorption with the *given*. In man's noblest responses to God – and to a great degree, in his noblest responses to an art object, his work, his fellow-men, his whole world – *not* consciousness, but consciousness of *self* is lost (and here lies, I suppose, the essence of ecstasy as Trinitarian and as incarnational). The personality

> energizes and develops, in precise proportion as it is so absorbed in the contemplation of these various over-againstnesses, these 'countries' of the spirit, as to cease to notice its own overflowing action. It is only when the mind but partially attends that a part of it remains at leisure to note the attention of the other part

and of the will. And this analysis applies to all 'the deepest, most creative, moments of full external action', such as Nelson at Trafalgar or Ignatius of Antioch in the amphitheatre – or the mystics in their most intimate union with God. Man is most free, is most himself as person and as lover when he is lost to himself in the other: whether an event, a friend, or God.[111]

In everything, then, and especially in what is most important – prayer – von Hügel (supposing just here their necessary quality) will argue for a multiplicity of acts, and of sensible acts too,[112] and for a multiplicity of social and secular action – and for a minimum of activity. What he means by this last distinction may be further gathered in his remark that 'activity and action . . . stand to each other something like scruple stands to conscience'. God is action and never activity, and is always at rest.[113] Action and activity spell the difference between the ardent and the feverish, zest and excitement, and that organization of the multiple which is personality and depth accomplished at the expense of the superficial, busy and scattered self. Cleverness, and theological cleverness too, is a gift that faces its great challenge here. Von Hügel presses the point home in his position on suffering. Jesus on the Cross, and all our *devoted* suffering ('passion') is 'perhaps the only quite pure form of action' achieved by man on earth.[114] We have here an ardent, apostolic humanism, deeply affirmative of man and directly related by von Hügel to the incarnation of God in Jesus Christ. But the condemnation of activism is total and unqualified.

Our last consideration of von Hügel's general doctrine of personality concerns the *permanent* quality of free-willing spirit's deliberate character.[115] Von Hügel is adamant that a view of man as incarnational *durée* demands what he calls 'abiding consequences'. It is true, of course, that any uncreaturely (pantheistic) spirituality must deny this doctrine, at least where the 'consequence' is hell.[116] And von Hügel readily admits too that any view of man's historical, time-and-space adventure as trivial, as a *sheer* process or succession, or where man's costly, incarnational action simply has no final significance or meaning (whether because man is not personal immortal spirit, or is not responsibly free, or is not sinful) – such a view of man may comfortably avoid the possible disaster which is hell. But it does so at the cost of the possibility of the specifically human moral splendour of great *worldly* loves and achievements *that make a difference for ever*. For von Hügel, this is not humanist, but anti-humanist, and a grave indignity to that time-space journey into the real, man's life, which at its best is the history of human love.[117] He is aware too of his own fundamental, anti-naturalist presupposition in the matter:

> . . . As soon as we hold the difference between various kinds of human acts and dispositions to be always potentially, and often actually, of essential, of ultimate, of more than simply social, simply human importance, we are insisting upon values and realities that essentially transcend space and even time.[118]

Von Hügel takes over from Catherine of Genoa the two root facts which structure his doctrine of human personality as finally being *itself* either heaven or hell. First, God is, in himself, dynamic, unchanging and ceaseless, personal love – and nothing else. Second, reward and punishment, heaven and hell, are not added realities distinct from man. Rather, they *are* human personality in its climactic self-determined harmony or disharmony with, its own presence or absence in love to, the real: God, its fellows, and itself.

> . . . Dispositions of souls . . . vary within each soul and between soul and soul, and . . . determine the differences in their reception, and consequently in the effect upon them, of God's one universal love:[119] but the soul's reward and punishment are not something distinct from its state, they are but that very state prolonged and articulated . . . Heaven, purgatory, hell are thus not places as well as states, nor do they begin only in the beyond: they are states alone, and begin already here. And grace and love, and love and Christ, and Christ and Spirit, and hence grace and love and

> Christ and Spirit are, at bottom, one, and this one is God. *Hence God, loving himself in and through us, is alone our full true self.*[120]

Heaven and hell are the success or failure of that adventure and event.

This last text from von Hügel also furnishes us with perhaps his richest, even definitive, description of human personality: 'God, loving himself in and through us, is alone our full true self.' Here lies the source both of his massive ascetical attack on the false self and his burning 'looking out' and through and beyond both 'contemplation and action, towards that Infinite Country, that great Over-againstness, God', and towards everyone and everything that this creating and redeeming Lover loves.[121]

For von Hügel here, as for Catherine of Genoa, the two great realities are Spirit and spirit 'in various states of inter-relation'. Now such a truth is easy where the importance of the human body and the social, of the historical and the secular, is largely disregarded, or denied. The priority of man as spirit is a dangerous truth, for it risks a 'diminished apprehension of the essentially complex, concrete, synthetic character of man's nature, and of the necessity for our assuming that this characteristic will be somehow preserved in this nature's ultimate perfection'.[122] But the truth that God and man are spirit remains a conviction 'as rare as it is admirable'.[123] Full, incarnational Christianity loves spirit dearly. However, it will also love to say and do the fuller truth that all men – including God-become-man in Christ – *precisely as spirit* are spirit-in-a-body-in-the-world. Spiritual personality thus broadly based can take upon itself the full task and the 'great truths involved in the doctrines of the Resurrection of the Body and the Communion of Saints'[124] and thus essay the rich harmony-in-tension of the total real which is the total Christ. And *only* personality thus broadly based and thus incarnationally essayed can be 'the final goal of the world, for which even the heavens wait'.[125]

We turn now to the two large and primary means of personality's production: man's *religious* and incarnational encounter with that history of Spirit which is part of Christ's 'larger biography': the Church;[126] and man's equally incarnational, but distinctly non-religious, indeed *secular*, encounter with the world in itself, and especially as science.

CHAPTER FIVE

THE PRODUCTION OF PERSONALITY: THE CHURCH AS INCARNATION, AND SCIENCE AS SECULARITY

VON HÜGEL'S entire discussion of the Church as incarnation, in so far as it will concern us here, presumes and acts upon the faith-*fact* and the lived *experience* of God as personal, self-communicating Spirit with whom man is in contact. It therefore builds upon and seeks integration with a logically prior endorsement and broad understanding of the mystical as an 'insistence upon immediacy, interiority, presence of religious experience'.[1] For von Hügel, the unmystical man 'remains or becomes but half a man, uninteresting and vulgar . . . '[2] But the mystical *attrait* must balance itself against, or rather it must express itself within and through, the wide world of incarnation, where a real God, everywhere most variously and, in Christ, particularly and *absolutely*, affirms himself within both creation and history, and where man affirms both God and himself through his own real structure and enterprise as spirit-in-a-body-in-the-world.[3]

Inclusive, balanced mysticism, therefore, as fully human religion, demands and must account for: sense, time and space, society, authority – and sacrament.[4] The 'I' of rich personality is an 'independence . . . only possible in a world saturated with the results of dependence'.[5] Creatureliness, then, and the organic, relational quality of all reality assign the Church a primary role in von Hügel's fundamentally incarnational religion.[6] And if closely attended to, this ecclesial quality of his thought happily embodies with particular emphasis the tension-in-harmony and multiplicity-in-unity of his spirituality as ascending and descending Christology. For von Hügel sees personality occurring neither in the 'pure reception of the purely objective' *nor* in some Neoplatonist 'incapacity to find any descending movement of the divine into human life'.[7] He rejoices rather in the Christian paradox as that adventurous scandal of the real where the givenness, the there-ness and objectivity of the infinite God is absolutely affirmed and realized in the finite contingency which is Jesus and the Church.[8] Neither the Church nor Christ are simply God. Nor is the Church simply Christ (who *is* God). But neither is the institutional Church no part of Christ, or simply the effect of Christ. She is, despite her radical contingency and becoming, and despite her obvious sinfulness, the 'continuance of incarnation', God absolutely proferred as gift and as summons within time and space. Here and not there, now and not then – even this *thing* rather than that one, will make a difference.[9] But if von Hügel's humanism is insisting here that the vagaries of *successiveness* and the particularities of historical experience be taken with entire seriousness, yet both that humanism's humilities *and* its ambitions strike their deepest roots in the *durational* permanence of man's worldly achievement as proclaimed in the resurrection of the body, and still more in the precisely historical triumph of the precisely *non*-successive, the eternal God which is Christ and the Holy Eucharist.

Much will be tolerated, and much will be done, fought for, criticized and condemned, precisely because so much is received in the Church believed on and experienced in this way. The listing of the abuses and evils of institutional religion is a lengthy task which von Hügel frequently performs, and with a daunting frankness. Personality is indeed a costly task. But von Hügel's sanctity is realistic, and not afraid of scars. 'Not the maximum of harmlessness, but the maximum of fruitfulness, together with what may be its unavoidable dangers, this is what we want.'[10] He reads the history of religions as a long and often useful argument between prophets, priests and professors. They represent here roughly the mystical, institutional and intellectual elements of religion. Each has a history of excess and of crime, and each is indispensable. But for von Hügel, the polemic so usually reserved for the priest is often, more often, properly directed to the professor. For the priesthood, not in its abuses of politics, authoritarianism or greed, but just in its essence, is representative of the *cardinal* mission of the Church: to minister to and to mediate the *fact* and the *givenness* of God in the world. Jesus focused his attack, not on the Levite, but on the scribe and Pharisee.[11] We have a very non-modernist showing of the colours in von Hügel's austere reminder that the Church's 'primary end and function' must remain the primary criterion of all Church-directed criticism and reformation. That *primary* end and function is

> the awakening souls to, the preparing them for, the holding before them embodiments of, *the other life*, the life beyond the grave. Very certainly, the Church has also to help in the amelioration of *this life*; but, I submit, always after, and in subordination to, and penetrated by, that metaphysical, ontological, other-worldly sense and life which alone completes and satisfies fully awakened man. And only thus shall we be in a position to be fair to the Church's work in the past; for the first object and range of this her labours will, and ought to be, distinct from and beyond social improvements.[12]

In his general stance here on the Church and the priesthood of the ordained, von Hügel forcefully reaffirms that centrality of descending Christology so characteristic of his entire spiritual doctrine of human personality and of creaturely subjectivity seen as *gift*. The position achieves almost notorious clarity in the classical sacramental distinction of *opus operatum* and *opus operantis*. For von Hügel, this distinction enunciates the heart of all religion and especially of all incarnational religion. *Opus operatum* seizes on the quality of the personal God as fully constituted *prevenience*, as utterly present and *there*, as totally gift and given. And this gift is severally announced as *incarnational* fact: in Jesus himself as Incarnate Word; in his teaching on the Kingdom as 'illapse from without' and above; and in his, the divine, institution of the Church and the sacraments. It systematically *has* to follow from this that von Hügel will suggest that the adoration of the Eucharist is 'the very heart of the Catholic worship'.

Von Hügel easily admits that this objectivity is wide open to objectivism, to mechanical piety, to superstition and to magic. But he would also cheerfully allow that any religion not in real *danger* of such real abuses is certainly false. Personality is man's confrontation *by opus operatum*: by what *God* is doing, by *his* deed and gift of self brought to almost scandalous exactness in the thing-ness, the *dinglich* quality of sacramental action. *And* personality is man *as* that confrontation, as *opus operantis*: as graced and free, as truly creative and really novel response. Man, of course, may refuse the encounter, but God's deed remains done, with the gift and summons still extant. Or man may surrender, but *only* to God as law – as fact and obligation. Here the false self begins indeed to be filed away as it yields to the laws of the real. But full personality will occur only in the *active mastering* of the gift, in the interior and ardent transformation and *appropriation* of God's fact and law until they structure and become man's freedom. Then are the objects and Object revealed as the Subject of all subjects, man's personal and loving Father. Adoration of the Eucharist, *of what God has done and does* becomes also, at this point, *what I am, and what I am given to do*. It becomes also my gift to God for others, and a meal that brothers share.

For von Hügel, therefore, Christ and the Church and Catholic sacraments are not myths or symbols projected by the religious community as some sacred sociology entirely the product of the community's own experience. The historical and present deeds of God in Christ are rather data *for* experience: objective (in their essentials), factual data prior to man and offered to him as materials for that 'action which makes the Christianity of the individual soul continually to re-begin with an experiment and re-conclude by an experience'.[13] *Opus operatum* and *operantis* is the Church as refusal of both subjectivism and objectivism. Christian personality is neither. It is subjectivity. Thus does inclusive mysticism (and the prophetic and the charismatic too) have both its roots and its finality in God as sensibly present and active within the community (as including the institutional element of religion).

This view of the Church as the individual's and the community's appropriation of *God's* deed of community and of personality is well expressed in von Hügel's affirmation of infant baptism. The statement occurs in the context of a criticism of the idealist strand in the thought of Ernst Troeltsch.

> Infant baptism . . . stands for the all-important fact of our attainment to personality, in the very first instance all but entirely, and up to the end very largely, through our birth and incorporation into a world of realized values, a world already awake to and penetrated by that spiritual life which, as yet, only slumbers within ourselves. I greatly wish that the later over-absorption in the individual contribution (real though it certainly is in conviction of every kind) had not pushed so very much aside this great insight into these other more extensive and equally necessary means and conditions of all growth. To see in such traditional training and illumination nothing but oppression and Eleatic fixity is as little just as it would be to see nothing but revolt and Heracleitan evaporation in that element of individual spontaneity, appropriation, and risk by which Dr Troeltsch had become so greatly impressed. That pre-existing, already awake and awakening world of the Spirit, and this later awakening single spirit, belong together, and the steady aim of our

> inquiry must surely be to determine how they act and react, completing each other . . . [14]

In von Hügel's spirituality, the Church is a primary created, religious means towards the production of incarnational personality. It is the *religious* object by which the individual at once undergoes that death which is the purification of the self and that growth which is personality. We shall shortly consider von Hügel's broad understanding of science as the *non*-religious, the properly secular, object by which personality, as gift and task, occurs. Prior to that, however, we shall briefly suggest some further views of von Hügel on sense, history, and the social, and on prayer too, as these realities affect the ecclesial aspects of his spirituality. To a great extent, our intention will be to confirm and give nuance to what has been said.

Von Hügel's very frequent and lengthy considerations of sense, history and the social, and his driving insistence upon them precisely as a spiritual director, stem from his faith *experience*, an experience carefully tested, articulated and purified by the study of history and psychology, and by philosophical reflection. It is the experience or the now-familiar, single yet twofold fact: God declares himself to man *and* summons man to himself *directly*, yet only in and through things, history, and community. The mysticism of incarnational religion is rooted in community, and both are utterly dependent on historical facts, facts which in turn are given in, and mediated through, the historical community which is tradition – a community and a tradition responded to and appropriated by – even as they constitute and are constituted by – individual persons. And this paradox, difficult to verbalize and no easier to live and love, is not to be simplified. It is to be embraced with all its tensions, for the sake of that rich and concrete harmony: the full, dynamic, incarnational personality which is man's holiness. Von Hügel writes in the introduction to *The Reality of God*:

> The ceaseless contention and implication of this long book is . . . that it is in the contact, as close and penetrating as possible, with the concrete, with history, with institutions, with social groups, that men are most fully awakened to and steadied in the sense of the Unconditioned, the Abiding, the Prevenient, the Beginning and the End and Crown of life and light and love.[15]

This view predictably leads von Hügel to sing an ardent song to sense. The mystical tradition has understressed it, 'in contradiction . . . to the incarnational philosophy and practice of Christianity, and indeed of every complete and sound psychology'. And the mystics have undervalued history too, whose 'dynamic and libertarian character' is an indispensable condition 'for the acquiring of religious experience'.[16] It is a very non-Kantian world indeed that von Hügel finds and loves, grounded as it is on a personal God penetrating a world of various and graded realities; a world basically knowable to one of its real constituents, man; a world in and through which alone man responds. Descending and ascending Christology is in full view. For von Hügel, this means, and necessarily, cultic worship: sacred time, and sacred space, specific sacraments, and definite acts of devotion. The fact that God is Spirit and that man is spirit does not alter this. God may be Spirit, but it is man, not God, who worships. And man is irreducibly and by definition *incarnational* spirit. And therefore God has chosen, for our sakes, in various degrees everywhere and in Christ and the Church absolutely and permanently, to be himself incarnate Spirit. And if the degree and mode of God's presence to Christ and to the Church radically differ – as just the sinfulness of the latter puts beyond dispute – yet the Church, as continuing incidence of incarnation and as *his* holiness, does partake of God's absolute gift and offer of himself within history.[17]

Von Hügel sees three options. Man may absolutize the Johannine 'God is Spirit' and then seek to make a purely spiritual response. In Quaker George Fox, whom he deeply loves on other grounds, von Hügel finds this position classically expressed in the repudiation of institution, tradition and history, and the affirmation of direct (i.e. unmediated) inspiration alone. Here sense is vehicle neither for the *achievements* nor for the *expression of the achievements* of either finite or infinite spirit. 'It is childish ingratitude . . . only possible *because this real world has not always been, has at no time predominantly been, a Quaker world.*'[18] The second option, characteristically Lutheran, sees sense as a vehicle only for the *expression* of spirit. Von Hügel is relatively harsh towards this 'pure' spirituality and 'pure' prophetism,[19] and ominously finds its 'very easy and most natural' outcome in the 'cold secularism of Benjamin Franklin'.[20] Pride of spirit always frightens von Hügel in a way that materialism never does. He finds that the fear of superstition and of Roman Catholic vulgarity often masks 'fastidiousness', 'a superfine refinement', 'a sort of Paterism' and superiority, 'really a very hideous thing' which only a deeply, *costingly* realized Christianity 'gets beyond'.[21]

Von Hügel discovers the third option where he finds the central test and text that shall judge all three: in Jesus. He asks Friedrich Heiler, the German historian and philosopher-psychologist of prayer, about what

> seems to be fully historical . . . , 'My Father's House', the Temple. Thither, to something local, actually concrete, the Jesus Child is powerfully drawn. And, as the last action of the earth-life of Jesus, we find him purifying this same Temple in high indignation – he risks his life in so doing. Yet in both cases, not as accommodation to the lower, local, material standpoint of the masses, but, quite surely, as animated himself by this 'superstition', the Temple is to him something especially holy. What, again, of the long fast of Jesus – not unhistorical, is it? And yet, if historical, not something unconcrete (*undingliches*)? Then again, the baptism of Jesus? There

something material (*dinglich*) is present, and the contact with this concrete thing is not simply the expression of already present fulness of grace, but rather works with it *towards the production* of a growth of spiritual life. – What was the hem (or seam) (virtue) of the garment of Jesus? . . . But it is a Thing, is it not? Again, Jesus heals the blind man not simply through prayer. He takes clay and kneads it, and wets it with his spittle, and lays it on the eyes of the blind man – only after that come prayer and healing. I think, in face of all this – the facts are similar in the case of Paul – the religious life of the Greatest appears actually free from that subtlety and doctrinairism of Luther's, which indeed permits the purely spiritually awakened belief to express itself in sensual forms, but strictly forbids anything sensual or factual to be used as a means to stimulating the spiritual. But what a curious psychology, unassociated with God's world, if not absolutely turned away from it, *which allows me, for instance, to kiss my child because I love it, but strictly forbids me to kiss it in order to love it.* Why not this latter? Is, then, the sensual necessarily a blind alley? Does it then derive from the devil, or even from papistry? Is it not coming from God too, intended for the spiritual, and to be used as a bridge to the spiritual, as well as from the spiritual? Why should, how should, my senses, my body, remain outside, when I pray? I shall find later, I hope, that you do not mean actually this. It will rejoice me immensely to find that you introduce no such subtleties into what is most deeply and purely Christian.[22]

As to the question of history, von Hügel adopts two main positions which directly affect his spiritual doctrine. First, the 'historical happenedness' of Christ and the Church. Von Hügel's incarnational *faith* demands as 'absolutely essential' that Christianity be 'revelational, evidential, factual'. His entire spirituality suffers structural collapse without the brute fact of a 'happenedness' available to the empirical methods of scientific history and exegesis.[23] It is true that von Hügel's own exegesis requires a broad understanding of 'divine institution' when it is applied to the Church, the sacraments, orders, primacy, etc. – perhaps much broader than some would wish. But the point here is that von Hügel – and throughout his life – does assert the divine institution of the Church in her *essential* structure. And it is a *faith* assertion, in the first place, and not a conclusion of his sociology, psychology or epistemology. But this faith statement, as incarnational, does and must rest on 'historical happenedness', on facts. Von Hügel's incarnational *faith* says that Jesus and his deed of the Church are imperishable data of secular history,[24] data which faith alone, of course, may discern as divine deeds, as God in history, as *opus operatum*: 'the eternal shown forth in time. . . . and in a unique and clearly historical way – the incarnation of God in a determinate soul and body, in Jesus of Nazareth.'[25] And not only Jesus, but the Church too as historically given, is clearly asserted by von Hügel in terms of descending Christology: ' . . . the movement here is down from the one invisible God, through the one, visible, audible, tangible Jesus, on to the twelve, visible men, etc.'[26]

Von Hügel wishes to point out the implications of this for Christian life, for spirituality. It is *not* just a question here of whether one agrees that scientific history and exegesis can and do, *as a matter of fact*, defend the historical basis of scripture and creed, but whether a man's *religious experience perceives the religious necessity* for such an historical basis. Only the latter suffices for an incarnational, i.e. a specifically *Christian* sensibility. Von Hügel is aware of 'still active members of the Roman Catholic Church' who may actually hold very traditional or highly conservative, and even fundamentalist views 'as to the degree to which *as a matter of fact*' the essential historical happenings underlying creed and scriptures can be defended *as* fact in terms of critical history and exegesis.

> But what has here disappeared [i.e. even from many conservatives], what indeed is recognized as having gone from out of these minds, is any belief in the abiding *necessity*, the irreplaceable function of historical happenings within the spiritual life.[27]

For von Hügel, Christianity here is religion no longer, but a lofty ethic at most. It has ceased as an incarnational 'isness' and become only, and at best, a noble 'oughtness'. The historical facts of the creed are here become ethical 'ideals' in 'pictorial form'. Von Hügel calls it 'impossible and ruinous . . . of Christianity's deepest characteristics'.[28] It is the evacuation of incarnation.

Religion and incarnation, for von Hügel, are, in the first place, ontology. And while Rome's abhorrent tendency to reactionary obscurantism and her slow progress in the face of very real difficulties are here 'specially great, yet they are so, in large part, because Rome sees so firmly and so very far . . . Rome is splendidly aware of religion's absolute need of a real God, manifesting himself in real happenings and effects.'[29] As spiritual director, von Hügel warns Evelyn Underhill, who came to him largely an idealist and a Unitarian, of the importance for Christian spirituality of *experiencing* the necessity of historical happenings. 'Let us work gently but wholeheartedly, at getting this principle to become one of the chief beams of your spiritual edifice, *part of the rock*, known and willed at all times *of your faith*.'[30]

The second position taken by von Hügel on history which deeply affects his spiritual doctrine and markedly characterizes his spiritual direction, concerns the *location* of the deeds and facts of past and present sacred history – facts and deeds of God such as Jesus and the sacraments. The upshot here is a splendid, energetic ecumenism. Von Hügel is well aware that to affirm of a particular history (even the history of Jesus, not to speak of the history of the Roman Catholic Church, especially in her sacraments) – to claim that God has and does *absolutely* affirm himself in this particular history (and von Hügel emphatically wants to do this) poses the grave dangers, for those who so believe, of narrowness and intolerance. It has in fact led, and may seem necessarily to lead, to a tragic arrogance, hostility, and even persecution. He rejects, however, any alternative that would suggest a tolerance that masks or results in indifference and which, in effect, has to deny that God may or does so affirm himself absolutely in the contingent particularity which is Jesus and the Catholic Eucharist. One religion or denomination is not as good as another for von Hügel.

Von Hügel's basic and frequently expressed solution to the problem is to locate the history of Jesus and the Church within *all* history, and to welcome the divine deeds of our historical redemption *among* the deeds of the one redeeming Lord of creation. Here, both good history and good theology must reject *excessive* preoccupation with the historical Christ and Church. And exactly parallel to this rejection is the repudiation of any 'curialist' *identification* of the visible and invisible Church and of either with the Kingdom of God. What *is* affirmed, however, is a *real relationship* between all three.[31] For von Hügel, *all* creation is incarnation.[32] The Father affirms himself, both in nature and in history, in very various but very real degrees *everywhere*, especially in *all* spiritual life and in all, past and present, *institutional* spiritual life. And the point here is that this continues to be so. Christ in von Hügel's own Roman Catholicism continues to appeal to, and to be answered by, God in the other Christian Churches, in other religions, and in the world. Perhaps the most exciting stress for ecumenical spirituality here is von Hügel's insistence on the *institutional* character of this continuing truth. 'The synagogue here in Bayswater is *still now*, on December 11, 1918, a fragmentary but very real revelation of God and, however unconsciously, a very real pedagogue to Christ.' And so too of 'the little mosque at Woking'.[33]

Now such a view is death to pietism, to all 'churchiness' and narrowness. It asks for a vast intellectual labour and active sympathy, in order to discover, appropriate and love *all* that God has done and is doing as he leads man to the fullness of Christ. The position does not level everything down, because von Hügel sees not only truth, but doctrinal and pastoral *truths* as concrete and definite and as varying in value.[34] Truths are objective and 'are never interchangeable'. God's real and continued affirmation of himself everywhere does not preclude, but continuously leads to, his absolute affirmations of himself in Jesus and Catholic sacraments. But those unconsciously or in good conscience without Jesus or those sacraments are by no means thereby without a rich experience and presence of God. And Roman Catholicism may and ought continually to learn from this experience and presence of him. Any religious man might say what von Hügel is saying here. Catholicism is chosen as the paradigm only because it happens to be von Hügel's own, deeply loved, confession.

Von Hügel is now in possession of what he wants, both for himself and for those he directs: a panentheism which is not pantheism. God is in all things, but not equally so. And the differences are real and qualitative. But there is achieved this splendid ecumenical insight and practice: that between the false or invalid and God's fully incarnated, institutionalized and sacramentalized truth, there lies, not an abyss, but *a rich and precious continuum*. Von Hügel's own charity and kindness further applies this point to the always present polarities, imperfections and errors *within* Roman Catholicism. And it obviates, for him, the need for Catholics 'to keep on shying "chunks of old red sandstone" at Rome and all its works, and to prod up others not to go to sleep over this sacred occupation: . . . could we not turn to a preponderance of pure affirmation in our lives?'[35]

This surrender of system-making and of pigeon-holing, in favour of whatever is true in its degree of truth, happily opens up von Hügel's spiritual doctrine to the influence of very various and very welcome bedfellows: to Plotinus and Darwin; to George Fox as well as 'Ideal' Ward, the violently institutional ultramontanist. Von Hügel is thus left with neither bigotry nor indifference, but with a generous and universal sympathy which yet repudiates that naturalism whose contempt for incarnational 'detail' subverts the scandalous particularity which is the foundation of Christianity: Jesus of Nazareth as God-in-flesh. It is no surprise that von Hügel's spiritual direction of Gwendolen Greene and of Evelyn Underhill very much consists in leading them *into* their Anglicanism, urging and guiding them to the communion table of the Church of England, as well as out into the world of the poor and of secular knowledge. And this, without the slightest prejudice to his own, notably dogmatic, Roman Catholicism.[36]

For Friedrich von Hügel, man is a social being from first to last. Socialization is not only a means to the production, but is interior to the goal, of personality.

> The family, the nation, human society, the Church, – these are the chief of the larger organizations into which the inchoate, largely only potential, organism of the individual is at first simply passively born, yet which, if he would grow, (not in spite of them, a hopeless task, but by them), he will have deliberately to endorse and will, as though they were his own creations.[37]

Here as elsewhere, 'the individual gets before he gives'. Further, man is ordered neither to collectivism (as the subversion of individual personality) nor, conversely, to the group as a discrete, atomistic 'heap of sand'. Religious man rather acquires that permanent and unique organic interiority which is his own individual personality in and through that larger 'personalist organism' which is, first and as means, the Church, and which, finally and as end, is the eternal, social beatitude of the Kingdom. Again, man for von Hügel is social both vertically and horizontally. He insists on this. The Plotinian 'flight of the alone to the Alone', therefore, is not simply denied outright; rather it is corrected and replaced, it is re*organized* by and within the mystical body. Here,

> the individual thus personalized is solicited, sustained, completed and crowned by God, the great prevenient Spirit who works within and through this his kingdom of spirits, yet who is not (any more than the created spirits composing this kingdom) simply a part of, or even simply the totality of, this spirit-complex.[38]

The disappearance of individual personality, then, whether in religious pantheism or in secularism, is rejected. But the social as Pauline body and as personalist *organism* remains primary. Man's personality is

> constituted in and through the organism of the religious society, – the visible and invisible Church. This society is no mere congeries of severally self-sufficing units, each exclusively and directly dependent upon God alone; but as in St Paul's grand figure of the body, an organism, giving their place and dignity to each several organ, each different, each necessary, and each influencing and influenced by all the others. We have here, as it were, a great living Cloth of Gold, with, not only the woof going from God to man and from man to God, but also the warp going from man to man, – the greatest to the least, and the least back to the greatest. And thus here the primary and full Bride of Christ never is, nor can be, any individual soul, but only this complete organism of all faithful souls throughout time and space . . . [As to] the social constituent of the soul's life . . . hereafter: the Kingdom of Heaven, the soul of the Church, as truly constitutes the different personalities, their spirituality and their joy, as they constitute it, that great organism which, as such, is both first and last in the divine thought and love.[39]

Religion, then, and personality, are social realities. Sanctity is a companionship, while suffering and weakness are the Church as a great 'interdependence'. 'We are fragments of the Bride.' The Mass is a sacrifice, *and* a meal.[40] Yet the fragments of the bride, the members of the body, are really distinct, really different. Each man has his bent, his temperament, his grace. And emphases, individual *attraits*, ought to exist, among man and man, and group and group. Monasticism and marriage, the scientist and the priest, all must partake of the mystical, the intellectual and the institutional, but the amount and the stress will and ought to be different. But all must be done in the body, with a consciousness of the whole, with a welcome awareness of one's own contribution and of one's own weakness too, of one's need of the others – of the brother's grace and gift. Only humility toward realities one has not grown to can accomplish this humility and love.[41] It is a point that calls forth a rare burst of sarcasm from von Hügel:

> I found Mrs — quite sensible, indeed truly sympathetic, toward our modern, active, directly philanthropic [religious] orders. But... she continues dominated by the severe warning the Protestant reformers addressed to the Almighty (without that the Almighty paid much attention to them), that he may *not* call any souls to a directly contemplative and adoring life – that this would be necessarily idle, useless, displeasing to the modern world and hence (of course) to him![42]

On the contrary, Gwendolen Greene and Evelyn Underhill are to follow their *attrait*, they are to take 'only what helps', and are to 'leave out all that does not help you'. But they are urged towards a fine humility, tolerance – and growth, in what they see, and what they don't 'yet see'. Von Hügel wants nothing forced, but he twice proposes the cows,

> with their great tongues drawing in just only what they can assimilate; yes – but without stopping to snort defiantly

against what does not thus suit them. It is as though those creatures had the good sense to realize that those plants which do not suit them – that these will be gladly used up by sheep, goats or horses; indeed, that some of these plants may suit them – the cows – themselves later on.[43]

For von Hügel, the supernatural, the holy, is social. It is an historical torch-race: 'you must get a larger experience – you gain it by a study of history; the individualistic basis simply doesn't work.' 'Behind every saint stands another saint.' 'That is the great tradition – I never learnt anything myself by my own old nose.' Spiritual direction is the great apostolate. For the apostolate is personality, the persuasiveness of a man through what he *is*. But spiritual direction, in the main, is not an imposition from without. It is rather the discovery and the bringing to light of the *other's attrait*, the affirmation and encouragement of the *other's* own insight and gift. Furthermore, both the director and the directed need to live deeply within the *community* where members of the body actively share definite religious fact and practice, if they are to avert both the dangers of, as well as any widespread need for, excessive spiritual direction. Individualism is thus once again avoided. 'For myself, I must remain in the crowd, not only for the crowd's sake, but especially for my own.'[44] Finally on this point, great spiritual direction is a death, where the great and universal ideals and facts of Christianity *precisely as strikingly persuasive* (if and where now concretized in the personality of the director), must fall into the ground like the grain of wheat if they, if Christ is to occur anew, living, *re*organized, novel again, in this the unique, unprecedented personality of the *other*, the one directed. The social life of the saints is an amalgam of self-surrender and the heroic reticence of abnegation.[45]

The whole question of the Church as institution, but particularly the question of the Church as social and of personality as socially constituted, raises, of course, the fact and the problem of authority. Von Hügel wishes to stress obedience. He fairly harps on Teresa of Avila's teaching that the charismatic in general and even the most insistent and convincing mystical graces and visions have their validity primarily measured and tested in the obedience of their recipients to Christian doctrine, to Church law and to superiors.[46] But the onus on authority is clear. The Kingdom indeed and the social are interior to man's finality as person. *But the institutional Church is a means alone*, and not an end. And it is primarily a means of life and expansion, and not of death and confinement. For von Hügel, then,

> . . . it is clear that, if the *mere* individual, the raw human article, the spiritually untrained or unenlightened man, is, as such, ever under authority in general, and, normally, under some particular authority conceived by himself as more or less an end: yet the person, the spiritualized and purified man, who, as such, is part and organ and product of the invisible Church in which God's Spirit dwells, as in his very Bride, is bound to such external authority only as to an instrument, realized by himself as such, for his own further progress, and for his social-religious union with his fellow-men. And thus some degree and kind of official authority will be, in this double way, necessary for us all, and right up to the end of life, since we ourselves will never be quite completely 'personal persons', and since, even if we could be, we shall have to live with and to love, help and be helped by, a large majority who have hardly ceased to be mere individuals. And yet one of the tests of our advance will be the degree to which, in a very full and devoted life, we shall not actually require the pressure of that official authority, whilst nevertheless never ceasing to believe in, and on occasion practising, the necessity, for our own selves as for all men, of deferring to and executing its legitimate commands and counsels.

Von Hügel argues that the mediatorial and the ministerial

priesthood are related, but they are not identical. The latter is 'entirely subservient, as means to end'.[47] Further, the Church 'in none of its members is simply teaching, in none of its members is simply learning'.[48] And it must be remembered just here that von Hügel's whole spirituality insists that religion is not everything, though it is connected with everything. Freedom, therefore, and legitimate authority too, are as graded as the many realities they serve – and learn from. In any case, absolute authority tends 'to destroy authority's own *raison d'être*', paralysing instead of stimulating personality.[49]

Within its area of competence, official authority may not bind except to the extent and degree and finality with which it binds itself. Von Hügel sees here a basic dialectic: God and Christ give us the Church, which in turn, in giving us God and Christ, purifies and sobers our Church allegiance.[50] And the Church must recall that, as the 'extension of the Incarnation', of the precisely human and historical experience of God in Christ, she must not look for or pretend to find in herself a knowledge or certitude greater in extent or degree than the knowledge and certitude of her Lord: Jesus in his humanity, as the Synoptics depict it.

Institutional authority, then, *is* from God, as he expresses himself in the historical Jesus. Its single aim and truly authoritative role is to propose, and to assist in, the production of the *self*-determinations of free-willing personality. Church authority, in a word, is 'the consecrated, ceaseless servant'.[51]

Von Hügel is interested primarily in truth by truthfulness and conscience, rather than by orthodoxy. However, if his writings offer scant comfort to legalism or to some unreformist integralism, yet even the most casual reading of the man must prove ominous for anyone of antinomian preference. The Cross, suffering, mortification, asceticism, all loom large, simply everywhere. The birth and growth of personality through *self*-destruction is the goal. It is possible, but not easy, to read von Hügel selectively. The polar but inseparable themes of the double ethic, of life and death, and of freedom and obedience are, almost always, struck together.[52] During the 'modernist' period, von Hügel knows constant stress on this question of authority, and some storm too. Yet the far more conservative Wilfrid Ward kindly wrote of him not long after the crisis: 'He was a saint and a mystic as well as a scholar and a thinker. His general position was that, provided you have the spirit of the saints, intellectual freedom is as safe for a Christian as it is desirable. Sanctity and freedom of mind agree well together, he maintained.'[53]

In concluding these thoughts on personality as a community experience, as a socially and ecclesially constituted reality, we ought to return with von Hügel to God, the great fact of experience where he always begins and ends. Friedrich von Hügel loves to cheer on 'that man-seeking, world-seeking movement so necessary to the religion of the Incarnation', for he has a deep faith in man's ability and need to act and do. Man must

> throw himself out towards the painful making of history, the helping to put something where nothing is, the helping on that new creation, without which truth itself dies out amidst us, poor makers or marrers of our own spiritual destiny, entirely though this is, at the same time, in and through us, from God.[54]

But the warning remains: it is God, God in Christ, who creates personality and who creates community. Von Hügel knows well enough that, just as the healthy individual comes to himself in another by giving himself to that other, so too the Church, as personalist organism and as total community, has and must *consciously* have its roots and its primary delight, not in itself, but in the Other. The 'beloved community . . . as the great means of spiritual growth . . . remains vague and weak . . . without a distinct Christ and a distinct God'. Von Hügel sees widespread *malaise* with regard to this truth. But he is confident that it will pass. He looks for 'not merely good people, not merely lovers of their kind – but believers'. 'The Church will again be loved for other than itself, for Christ, love made visible, and for God, our home.'[55]

Predictably, and splendidly too, von Hügel's perhaps most profoundly social comment concerns joy – joy as a gift. Our final joy will not consist in what we have or do, 'but in what we get': what *God* gives and does. Yet this is not enough. For we find that 'we have soon reached the limits of what we ourselves can ever become'. Rather, it is in 'the joy for the others', it is in the joy for all God is and for all that our brothers shall be, that our hearts shall 'find their peace'.[56]

We come now to von Hügel's discussion of prayer, always seen incarnationally, and as radically a harmony-in-tension, i.e. as *mysticism in the Church*. Von Hügel's references to prayer are frequent enough, but it might be claimed, both of him and of this study of his writings, that the treatment of prayer is neither systematic nor central – an odd thing in a man and a study so ostensibly preoccupied with spirituality. But this, I submit, is a superficial view of the matter, and what immediately follows asks to be a formulation and not an interpretation of von Hügel's own thought.

We have seen that von Hügel's foundational requirement for human personality and his foundational description of human personality is man as free and conscious encounter with the reality and fact of God. And we have seen too that this is also and exactly von Hügel's description of prayer as adoration. Personality, then, as praise, and as petition too, *is* prayer.[57] For man, in his mystical centre as personal, *is* a 'let it happen'. Let it (the real, what is, and, in the first place, he who is), be, be so, let him and *all* that's real, occur. Let (as an *active*, creative, 'costly', free-willing and personal appropriation, an ardent letting be) – let the entire real, finally personal, initially and ultimately Personal, happen to me. Von Hügel's whole effort and argument begins and ends in his experience of man and his world as that deed of God who is destined also to be that reply to God: hallowed be thy name (let God be God). Once again, then, man as personality is prayer as adoration. And man as petitionary prayer is nothing, finally, but a request that man may become and be this adoration: Thy will be done (which is also Mary's reply to God as newly proposed *incarnate* fact: let it happen to me).

Prayer is *religion*, then: man before the *is-ness* of God.[58] Only after this and because of it does ethics occur as what the individual ought to do and become and be: that is, personality, in order that God may be what he is: God *for him*. Man as *individual* and as becoming is the *project*; as *personality*, he is the on-going, always increasing *achievement* of the conscious, subjective appropriation (Christologically, incarnationally, historically, socially – therefore ecclesially – and secularly achieved) of the fact of God, a fact and deed done and being done Christologically, incarnationally, historically, socially – therefore ecclesially – and secularly. To any accusation that he is climbing the heights of the mountain of God, von Hügel can only plead guilty. But the admission may come without apology or compunction, because the incarnational character of his doctrine is a standing counter to the charge that the climb is too steep or the air too rare and unworldly. Von Hügel's God comes all the way down to man in Christ.[59] Two points are made here, and both are stressed: God *comes*, and it is *God* who comes. And man is a reply that receives its structure from God's deed: he is a reply to God in *Christ*, and to *God* in Christ.

Von Hügel is well aware that prayer and religion as mysticism (broadly understood here, as usual) – as a response to *is-ness* –

> has not, for most of the more strenuous of our educated contemporaries, become, so far again, a living question at all. A morally good and pure, a socially useful and active life, –

> all this in the sense and with the range attributed to these terms by ordinary parlance: this and this alone is, for doubtless the predominant public present-day consciousness, the true object, end, and measure of all healthy religion; whatever is alongside of, or beyond, or other than, or anything but a direct and exclusive incentive to this, is so much superstition and fanaticism.[60]

We have seen von Hügel deal with this (for him), almost by definition, pre-prayer situation. When he treats explicitly of prayer, however, he is generally on other ground: he is presupposing a belief in, and a contact with, a real, personal God; he is presupposing too a real desire and a real effort to pray. Our brief further remarks, then, are some few of the implications he draws from doctrine already seen, doctrine already held and now brought to experience in love. The reader may recall that we have already touched on von Hügel's assessment of what are the 'facts and truths concerning God which are of most importance in the life of prayer'.[61] Here our concern is more with prayer from the human point of view. One way or another, incarnationalism as a Christologically structured theocentrism seems the point throughout.

1. Von Hügel's remarks on spiritual reading set the tone of Christian prayer as primarily a personal self-surrender of the whole man to God as given and received in the community.

> Of course, *such 'reading' is hardly reading in the ordinary sense of the word at all.* As well could you call the letting a very slowly dissolving lozenge melt imperceptibly in your mouth, 'eating'. Such reading is, of course, meant as directly as possible to feed the heart, to fortify the will, – to put these into contact with God – thus, by the book, to get away from the book, to the realities it suggests, – the longer the better. And, above all, perhaps it excludes, by its very object, all

> criticism, all going off on one's own thoughts as, in any way, antagonistic to the book's thoughts; and this, not by any unreal (and *most dangerous*) forcing of oneself to swallow, or to 'like', what does not attract one's simply humble self, but (on the contrary) by a gentle passing by, by an instinctive ignoring of what does not suit one's soul. This passing by *should be without a trace of would-be objective judging*; during such reading, we are out simply and solely to feed our own poor soul, such as it is *hic et nunc*. What repels or confuses us now, may be the very food of angels; it may even still become the light to our own poor souls in this world's dimness. We must exclude none of such possibilities, the 'infant crying for the light' has nothing to do with more than just humbly finding, and then using, the little light that *it* requires.[62]

Now only the family and the community of the Church make possible this childlike openness and trust. Therefore does this 'modernist reformer' and this scholar who spends long working days devouring Feuerbach and Hume declare

> that my own practice has always been, and (I doubt not) will continue to be to the end, only to read, in such purely receptive devotional moments, such books as are either formally approved by the Roman Church, or, at least, not formally condemned by her.[63]

And if prayer has its 'decisive preparation . . . not in the prayer, but in the life prior to the prayer', so too of spiritual reading. Von Hugel observes to the dying Wilfrid Ward: 'L — told me of the help you were finding in the Gospels and the *Imitation*. How almost purely literary their effect is upon us, when we are not suffering, or (at least) when we have not suffered – *and much*!'[64]

2. As to prayer itself, Huvelin had told von Hügel: 'For you, prayer should be more a state than a precise and deliberate

act.'[65] And von Hügel rejoices to find in others this grace of a more formless and simple prayer, which he often calls the prayer of quiet. He writes to his niece:

> I take it that God in his goodness has granted to you the simple prayer of quiet – or, at least, that you get given touches, short dawns, of it, now and then. . . . Such formless prayer, where genuine, is . . . a deep grace, a darling force and still joy for the soul.[66]

It is fed by silence, whose last and most important mercy and function is interior: 'Certain it is that at no time is overmuch talking compatible with spiritual growth; [but] to learn interior silence, the not talking to self – our little notions petted as our own, etc. – is fundamental in the attaining of the spiritual life.'[67]

Yet this strong, lifelong affirmation of this prayer of quiet, and of strict contemplation too, is always subject to the discernment of incarnational Spirit. What are the Christian criteria for such intensely personal prayer? 'What are the tests, the conditions of . . . genuineness? They are two. Such prayer may never become the soul's only form of prayer; formal, vocal or mental prayer – the reciting of e.g. the Our Father . . . must never completely cease.'[68] Von Hügel repeatedly demands of those he directs a prayer that is *also* vocal, sense-and-spirit, tangible, sacramentally oriented. And privileged importance accrues to such prayers of the whole community, 'the mind of the Church'. In the same vein, he also argues for liturgy, for public, corporate worship, rejecting as exaggeration here any 'either . . . or' instead of 'both . . . and' with regard to personal-individual and personal-corporate prayer. 'Public worship requires much care, much nurture: does it deserve all these pains? Why, of course, *yes*, and YES again.'[69] The intention is clear. It is through the sense-and-spirit humanity of Christ and through his body the Church that God declares and man replies to Presence. Spirituality must utilize 'the whole of man'.[70] Von Hügel deplores in an acquaintance that

> Greek (not Christian) contempt for the human herd, superiority to its needs. There, Catholicism – humbly received and faithfully practised – say even only a decade of the Rosary every day – would be the cure, the completion of the man. There is not enough in him of the Incarnation, as a fact, and a force especially.[71]

The second, and social, test of the genuineness of prayer is 'if, in coming away from it, you find yourself humbler, sweeter, more patient, more ready to suffer, more loving (in effect even more than in affection) towards God and man'.[72] Therefore, if prayer itself is directly a preoccupation with God and a dis-occupation with self, it is, in its intended result, not a dis-occupation with the world, but rather the 'loving of God, Christ, and others'.[73] Indeed, healthy prayer leads beyond itself, into the world of men and projects, to

> something more active for all, than standing by helpless at the side of the Cross and praying. I say this, knowing well that prayer is the greatest help – it and example . . . And yet, – is it not in part through such an ideal as the former that they have got so sleepy and stony in Catholic countries? I find for myself that, everywhere, if one will but care, and look about, there are men and women . . . who are, in the world of learning or of action, working and living for true bettering.

Von Hügel asks to 'join myself on to them, encourage and get encouragement, to find active work without presumption'.[74]

3. The prayer of intercession gets illuminated in a brief but beautiful exchange between von Hügel and Evelyn Underhill. Von Hügel's belief in all reality as organic, in all men as a great 'interconnection', and in 'the continuity and immediacy of the divine action involved in any adequate doctrine of creation' provides an ample background for the great adventure intercession is seen to be.[75] Underhill begins by confessing that her

prayer would have more intercession in it 'if I could feel it did real work. But it is so unreal to me that I forget all about it. Yet I know, when you pray for me, you do somehow bring a tremendous force to bear! And even in my tiny way I ought to be able to do something . . . ' Von Hügel knows she is worth more than this. He waits her out, commenting only that she is not yet fully awake 'to its [intercession's] reality and power. But pray do not strain after a comprehension of it. Be very faithful in your service of the poor, in your Holy Communion, and . . . it will come, and perhaps soon.' Underhill's magnificent reply to this shows her true mettle – her very fear indicating her grasp of the size – the cost and triumph – of the enterprise, of what Calvary is all about: 'As to intercession, if I ask myself whether I would face complete spiritual deprivation for the good of another . . . , I can't do that yet. So I have not got real Christian love: and the question is, can one intercede genuinely for anyone, unless ready to pay, if necessary, this price.' Von Hügel's conclusion to the exchange is gentle. He asks for the final humility which frees a man to trust. The generosity demanded for the task of intercession indeed requires courage. But *all* is a gift: the intercession and the courage too. Whatever God asks for, he will give. Underhill is to live only with the present, serving the *real*, as and when it occurs. She is to pray for others as and when God asks it, remembering that in his very asking it of her, *he will give her asking*, and its cost. ' . . . Possible demands of God . . . lack all the corresponding support which they bring with them the minute they become actual.'[76]

4. Finally, von Hügel speaks of deliberate prayer, which should be of a more or less definite amount, irrespective of consolation or desolation. The old social and apostolic criterion determines the kind and amount: 'whatever . . . most strengthens you to love, to work, to suffer'. On the other hand, the *spirit* of prayer 'should more and more penetrate all your

waking hours'.[77] Here von Hügel is asking, as an ideal, for 'a sense that all you are doing is, in its perfection, always beyond you [and therefore always being given for man's appropriation and effort]. All that you are doing should always have a certain awe-inspiring over-againstness; something of the great *contrata*, the infinite country of God. You will find that this will not split up your attention, for it does not consist of any direct consciousness of God himself. I would only ask you, over and above this, for a little aspiration to God or Christ, at the breaks or the movings away from one occupation to another.'[78] The vast erudition and concentration required for his own books apparently does not preclude the living of his own advice. Of *Eternal Life*: 'I wrote the thing praying. Read it as written, Child!'[79] Or again, at the end of his life: 'Have, at last, plunged again into my big book composition [the unfinished *Reality of God*], which I find turns into a prayer and makes me very happy.'[80]

But von Hügel's emphasis here on the spirit of prayer, and his own penchant for prayer as a state, in no wise supports that *interpretation* of Ignatian 'contemplation in action' where the *tension* of work *and* prayer – and the time and the habits such definite, regular prayer requires – disappears from view. Von Hügel's man is never a one-ness, and he is an *accomplished* harmony only rarely, at his best, and at moments. Von Hügel's man is a durational multiplicity *aimed* at harmony; he is an on-going, unending rhythm and tension, always in *process* of overcoming and resolving itself in the dynamic, utter fullness, the perfect coming-to-self in the other which is personality as found in God alone. Only as perennial action *and* prayer does man move *towards* the goal of his becoming: his harmony as *fully* personal being, as prayer-in-action. ' . . . Without . . . contact with the material and the opposition of external action, recollection grows gradually empty; and without recollection, external action rapidly becomes soul-dispersive.'[81]

In Gwendolen Greene, his niece, von Hügel finds a mind

and heart of 'continuous openness to the impressions . . . brought you by all things beautiful and true and good'. It is 'one of the most precious of the gifts of God . . . a true prayer'. He asks her to *receive* this gift – to admire this world and to work in it – with a cry of adoration. And he hopes that she will 'gradually develop this into spontaneous habit'. *Spontaneous habit*: both terms should be stressed. Von Hügel is rejecting any mechanical, impersonalized, objectivist reaction. And he is rejecting any subjectivism too. He is asking for the *interiorization* of the *real*, both secular and sacred, in their objectivity, until the real God and the real Christ, and the real world as seen and directly loved in God, become the very structure of that true freedom which is selflessness, subjectivity, and fully human personality. Von Hügel then concludes, with a gift to his niece, a prayer given to him in the Church:

> For years I have loved and prayed this prayer, Dearie. If it makes sense to you, you too might begin your day with it. 'Receive, O Lord, my entire liberty – my understanding, my memory, my will. From thee I have received all things – to thee do I return all things. Give me but thy grace and thy love. I ask not anything else of thee.'
>
> Loving old Uncle,
> Freddy H.[82]

We are approaching the conclusion of our exposition of Friedrich von Hügel's spirituality as given in his writings. And here we come to an explicit consideration of perhaps the most original of his insights: the importance of the secular, the importance of science, for personality – first within religion itself, and more fundamentally still, within spirituality as a larger whole. However, we must first consider the question of purification, because von Hügel deals with science largely as a *positive* agent of purification and growth, as a means in the production of personality. But prior even to this occurs the question of purification in its *negative* moment, i.e. as asceticism.

Von Hügel is a man of affirmations. For him, personality and holiness are life: that gift which is both birth and costly growth of self-determining personal spirit. But for fallen, sinful man – as the rhythm of paschal existence declares (an existence *given*, for our lifelong *appropriation*, in baptism) – Christian personality and life are also and always a death: a death to self, a death actively to be brought about, a false life to be destroyed. Von Hügel, as pastoral theologian and as spiritual director, lays overwhelming emphasis on the indirect method here: die to self *by living* to God and others; kill the animal individual *through the achievement* of personal spirit. Nevertheless, he does affirm and, to a degree, require the directly negative, *both* as a frontal attack on the self *and* as the dramatization within history of the infinite reality of God as Other. In the latter case, we have in von Hügel the paradox of the classical mystical tradition: *affirmation* through negation, where *experienced* absence proclaims the presence, and silence peals the thunder, of eternal life within history. Von Hügel sees well enough that 'the deepest insight of all asceticism' is its affirmation that 'the beyond is, in very truth, the power of our here and now'.[83] From a considerable literature, then, we shall briefly see the measured place and stringent limits von Hügel assigns to the negative within incarnational spirituality.

Both Schopenhauer and William James confirm von Hügel's main contention. James had said:

> The metaphysical mystery, that he who feeds on death, that feeds on men, possesses life supereminently, and meets best the secret demands of the universe, is the truth of which asceticism has been the faithful champion. The folly of the cross, so inexplicable by the intellect, has, yet, its indestructible, vital meaning.... Naturalistic optimism is mere syllabub and sponge-cake in comparison.[84]

Von Hügel agrees. 'Ultimate optimism' is cheap grace without a corresponding and 'preliminary pessimism'.[85]

Now it is true that most men are rarely, if ever, called to striking choices of the directly negative. The generality of men are rather called to *accept* the negative (though spiritually significant acceptance is always also to choose) as occuring and imposed in the duties and obligations of normal life. And yet, 'the man who laughs at the plank bed and the discipline is a shallow fool'. In any event, not hate – never hate, even here – but only love, love of God and man and the world, decides.[86] The negative, even when *directly* chosen, is a means, not an end. Von Hügel repeats and repeats this. Detachment must occur within, and for the sake of, the larger whole which is attachment. The incarnational movement of Christ as grain of wheat is always for the sake of fuller involvement, of deeper, more abundant life.[87] The deeply ascetical, yet far more deeply human and joyful Huvelin had told him: 'I practise detachment only for the sake of attachment.'[88]

Coming now to the Church as total community, von Hügel asks for an awareness of, and a witness to, her entire patrimony and her total task as paschal and as creaturely. He conceives this, *as it concerns the negative*, both as a direct denial of the Church's communal false self *and* as the Church's first and final, always halting effort to banish every idol from sight as she affirms, by naked, wordless faith, the reality of God in her life. This is surely one of the most superb inner moments – and perhaps the most dangerous – in the *multiple* witness and truth that the Church must do and be. The *legitimate* Christian pursuit of the directly negative is, for von Hügel, then, a gigantic affirmation, as the joy of the mystics testifies.[89] And the importance of the Church as community looms especially large just here. For if all must directly choose death a little, some few must do so publicly, massively, if the Church as witness and sacrament, as embodied symbol of Christ's full mystery is to be maintained. And it is importantly not a question only of this life *and* the next, of the natural *and* the supernatural, but of the supernatural *within* the worldly, of eternal life *within* the here and now of history. The Parousia as eternal life is 'the deepest and most operative revelation concerning the *temporal* and the eternal ever vouchsafed to man'.[90]

For von Hügel, only marriage *and* the monk, the family and the desert, the homely and the heroic, tell the Church's whole *historical* truth about man: that he is made for God who is not man, yet for a God who has become man; that he is a sinner whose life must be destroyed, yet a redeemed man whose life is holy and to be aggrandized through a world that God has saved. Only a few are led far into the desert. But at the peril, both of those who go and of those who stay, the journey must occur *within* the communal body, within the community whose basic task remains incarnation: the ever deeper taking flesh of Spirit, the ever further conflict-and-tension-filled personalization of man in and through man and his world. Love, love alone, will decide.

It is in this context that von Hügel affirms repeatedly the *Christian* reality of celibacy. The witness of the Baptist, of Jesus and of Paul is part of the permanent truth, not to be historicized, relativized, about historical man and God. This leaves von Hügel quite free to inveigh against the abuses of tradition, as regards both celibacy and marriage, and to question the Roman Catholic discipline of celibacy as required condition of priesthood.[91]

Von Hügel also argues that the negative is simply required if the three elements of religion as means to personality are to flourish. *Incarnational* harmony means conflict and tension: the institutional, the intellectual and the mystical will each have to be denied and curbed, if religious man is to occur as the achievement of an integration, always in process, of the three.[92] And religion as well, we have seen and shall see further, must be subject to the continuous inner rhythm of a vigorous negation of itself, in order that a fully emancipated, autonomous and flourishing secularity (brute, sensible things; political and cultural relationships; scientific law as impersonal and necessary mental category, as abstract thing and fate) – in order that this secularity may play its own indispensable role in the constitution of the individual, and of the community too, as personalist organism. And the negation of secularity will be demanded in its turn. But the surprising, profound and marvellous thing here is to find the negative-creative demand von Hügel makes on religion in function of affirming the whole realm of the secular as *interior* to spirituality. Von Hügel couldn't be clearer:

> . . . Religion will have to come to see that it cannot attain to its own depth, it cannot become the *chief thing*, if it does not continually renounce to aspiring after being *everything*; for it cannot become its own fullest self without, not merely occasioning the love of the Cross in other departments, but also taking the Cross upon *itself*. And then *all things* will become food for such a faith, and it will become the base, and transfigurer of all things.[93]

Just a few words of summary conclusion. Von Hügel, we have seen, bases the negative, both as a moment in the practical spirituality of self-denial and as a moment in faith, on the affirmation of man as, in part, positively selfish, and on the affirmation of God as *Deus semper maior et alius*. And he sets the *limits* of the Christian negative with even greater force within what God has done and what man may do and be as declared in the Gospel of the Incarnation and the Resurrection of the Body.[94] Pastoral practice must find a conduct that expresses this death and life, this likeness and unlikeness, in the tension of their real distinction, and then bind them together in love.

Von Hügel sees two large ascetical trends in tradition, each with its history of glory and abuse. The first is wholly, directly negative; it abstracts and 'turns away'. It is valid, and required, as a part and means, and it is very dangerous.[95] The second trend is already purification as positive. It is incarnational asceticism, where unity is grappled within and through multiplicity;[96] where death to self is directly intended indeed, but is indirectly achieved as a function and blessing, a *by-product* of life; where the childish becomes childlike and the individual becomes personal *both* through that *love* which seizes and appropriates all the richness of the total real in all its harmony-in-painful-tension, *and* through that *humility* which knows and experiences that both the multiple real and man's free appropriation of it – are a gift. The Gospel of Jesus gives witness to both ascetical trends, for it tells us of sin and of death, as well as of life; it tells us that God is not man, and that he has become man. But von Hügel believes that it is the second trend, with all it holds for secularity as a goodness of God and a task for man, that especially for modern man, must dominate Christian spirituality as the achievement of personality.[97]

Purification as positive is multiplicity-in-unity, that reaching for an ever *richer* harmony through tension and conflict. It is the death of *self* achieved, not by direct negation, but through self-surrender to and appropriation of the objective and *other*, of the total, multiple real. It is actively and 'expensively' to allow this multiple real, this 'over-againstness', to invade and become, to constitute and aggrandize, spirit – so that self and selfishness perish in direct proportion as subjectivity occurs. Personality as *durée*, as self-conscious, free-willing spirit, is both agent and achievement of this process historically attained through close and severe successiveness. Within these Bergsonian categories of our second chapter, the ever wider seizure and acceptance of this multiple reality – and its organization for a unity that is vivid, complex and deep rather than clear, unitary and thin – aim at a personal and social expansion-and-cohesiveness, and at a contemplation-and-action which increasingly approximates the divine simultaneity: that eternal life which is partially within history even now and which will finally be the personalist Kingdom of God.

Personality as positive purification, therefore, is both creaturely humility and confident, energetic love. The multiplicity to be organized is simply the total real: God, God first and last and in himself; then the sacred realities which are Christ and his Church as they structure and summon man's incarnational, his embodied spirit; and finally the secular, given in all its variety and mystery, the pain and appeal of all its precisely *impersonal* things and facts and laws. For von Hügel, human spirit comes to itself, becomes personal, through this last encounter too. The more meal for the yeast, the more bread, the more life, the more personality, there will be. And man does not come to himself richly by a precocious escape into God. The encounter between God and man must be personal. And man becomes personal, and thus comes to God with much richer praise, by *doing* this world: not by tampering with it, but by letting the world be world, by actively allowing and assisting it as other, as itself, to happen to man. The structure is still Marian: let it happen to me.

Friedrich von Hügel writes at length on God in himself as purification and growth. We have touched on this.[98] He also treats the incarnational, the sense-and-social quality of the institutional Church in this light.[99] But since we have already treated God and the Church somewhat fully, we will now consider purification as growth only under the rubric of secularity, which von Hügel calls science.

Here once again, von Hügel *presupposes* for spirituality an ardent love of God as personally experienced, and a love of the Cross. But spirituality is a larger reality than religion. He is convinced that

> the Christian, indeed the man of any religion, who wishes to make and to keep his religion strong, will doubtless have to live it with all he is and has; but that Christians, and indeed religionists of any kind, cannot (all of them and in the long run) ignore the other activities of man's manifold life,

> nor simply sacrifice either their religion to these activities or these activities to their religion. Christianity in particular will be unable to do so, because gnosticism is not true to life. God is the God of the body as he is of the soul; of science as he is of faith; of criticism and theory as of fact and reality. And thus, in the long run and upon the whole, man will, even *qua* spirit, have to grow and to be through conflict and temptation, through darkness and humiliation, and through a triumph hardly won. . . . The official Church [despite ascetical and curialist abuses to the contrary] especially has, from very early times, persistently conceived and practised life, not pietistically, but in a Catholic, i.e. an all-inclusive manner.[100]

These 'other activities' are what von Hügel means by science. Clearly, the intellectual element of religion is largely involved. Here science has a task to perform *within* religion, as when the biblical exegete renders the givenness, the *opus operatum* of faith more exact and authentic, or when the philosophical theologian structures and formulates its unchanging truth anew for a particular and changing spiritual-cultural environment and experience. Science as intelligence, then, according to laws that are autonomous and *interior* to itself and to the object of its study (and not, therefore, imposed on the object from without, either by subjectivist mysticism or by institutional authoritarianism), is thus, and only thus, directly *purifying*, even as it serves the *growth* of, both legitimate mysticism and legitimate institutional authority. For, as in the example at hand, science's more exact discovery and more successful pastoral expression of the *opus operatum*, of the simply *given* of faith, ensures to mysticism the full reach of *its* proper, experimental, charismatic freedom, even as it concomitantly offers to authority the area, whether modest or ample, for its legitimate service of command. Science, then, with its increasing knowledge, assists both the mortification and the building up of the mystical and institutional elements of religion. Its permanent and evolutionary function of discovery and criticism puts freedom (the mystical) and authority (the institutional) at the ever greater service of the real.[101]

But this concerns intelligence alone, and indeed intelligence as *within*, as an element of, religion. Von Hügel's view is far broader: it seeks to harness the total secular for spirituality. Therefore, *within* the spiritual life, and precisely in view of its initiative and finality as libertarian, concrete and *personal*, von Hügel asks for a middle distance, an *intermediate* stage which involves and encourages: immanentism, and monism; phenomenalism (as a non-metaphysic); brute, mechanical law; a 'preliminary pantheism', and even atheism. The proposal, frequently repeated and developed, is clear as early as 1898:

> . . . if we look back, around us, and within, we shall find two great tendencies. There is that of seeking and finding personality in self and the absolute, so, with Christianity and such types as St Augustine in the past; with the Church and the Churches around; and with our religious and moral life within ourselves. And there is that of flying from and losing personality, both in self and in the absolute, so, with Buddhism, Neo-Platonism and Spinoza in the past; with the laboratories and factories around us; and with our scientific life within ourselves. The former has person joined to person, and love; the latter has thing lost in thing, and law. And neither seems capable of suppressing the other permanently. Now here . . . we have a means and an end, *but the end here . . . must not attempt to suppress the means, but should help to keep it vigorous and autonomous, even from the sole point of view of its uses as a means* [and herein lies the polemic against religiosity, pietism, 'churchiness', precisely as enemy of religion]. The pantheistic self-losing of a Spinoza has too persistent a hold upon noble minds not to contain an element of indispensable truth: apply it to man's way, more or less generally, and to all science in particular, and you have found its enriching truth

[thus far, with *brio*, and no farther, von Hügel's 'religionless' Christianity]; apply it to his end, and to metaphysics, ethics, and religion, and it has become mischievous error. Let us conceive of science as the observation and registration of all phenomena, and of these as determined; and of philosophy and religion as the discovery and revelation of metaphysical reality, and of this as reaching and requiring self-determining personality, as the highest within us and without; and of both as insuppressible and requiring each other *unmaimed*, and of man as requiring both if he would reach his true depth. In this manner we have found its appropriate, safe bed for that purifying depersonalization, that fatalism and relentless law, which for the Greeks stood fixed, an iron firmament, above the gods, but which for us must flow, a fiery Lethe of tonic self-oblivion, between the clamorous, greedy individual self on this bank of it, and our true personality and God's on the other. . . .

And for the rich development and full purification of our own personality, and our consequent increasingly worthy conception of his [hence a real *and* continually-to-be-purified anthropomorphism], we shall want work and recollection, the visible and invisible, science and morals, nature and grace, a true self-dying and a true self-finding.[102]

Before proceeding to final implications, it may be well to remember or notice several points now. For one, von Hügel is not guilty of a snobbism here. He is not describing a spirituality that is intellectualist or élite. By science, he means the *serious* curiosity, discovery and observation of things and their activities, and the serious effort to understand and to act according to the laws (the 'science') of the objects in question. This broad understanding of science applies equally to geology and biblical exegesis; to art, politics and economics; to the beautifying of a public square, *and* to the sweeping of a house, to the laundry girl's application of 'the laws of successful washing', or to the rhythms of the human heart and family that are involved in being a devoted wife and mother. Only what is done without love, with supercilious contempt, or as mere hobby or in dilettante fashion, is declared outside this definition of science.[103] Man is to engage the world of things, be they sensible or mental (concepts), whether the data and law of physics or sociology. And he is not selfishly, egotistically to patronize and manipulate them. Von Hügel grows reverent – and he loves Darwin for his humility – before 'the individuality and interiority of all existences – all that *is* at all, has an inside to it'.[104] Man as steward and co-creator of the world of things and facts and ideas, is humbly to assist in order that things may become and fully be – *fully be themselves*, at whatever cost to man's self-centredness. He is to face, and fight through, the resulting multiplicity, enduring and growing through the friction that must come, and not imposing quick solutions that must suppress or distort the real; he must rather harmonize slowly and *successively*, by and for personality as *durée*, what faith knows already to exist as dynamic *simultaneity* in God.

There will often be temporary, even lengthy disarray. But both religion and science must speak their truth, however great the friction, however slow the harmony. Von Hügel believes that the early Church used the doctrine of a proximate Parousia to detach both the individual and the community from themselves and that for centuries afterwards the doctrine of original sin and its effects performed this function. He sees science, as he understands it here, as the purifying bath given by God to *modern* religious man (only as religious does he fully have the problem) for that separation from himself which is his constitution as a loving, outgoing person. Two things are therefore asked: an ardent curiosity for facts, together with a deep wish to experience the full dimensions of the real; and honesty, and independent responsibility, however painful and expensive, before whatever the facts and the experience declare themselves to be.[105]

But the fulfilment of these requirements, of course, will prosper man only on the presupposition and condition of his experienced dependence on and deeply exercised faith in a personal God. Once again, Huvelin had told von Hügel as much: 'There are no security rules in scholarly work. Prayer – to avoid obstinacy – is everything.'[106]

Von Hügel also asks that this attitude towards science and the secular be thought nothing extraordinary, but 'have *its normal necessary place in the very theory of spirituality*'.[107] Even *within* 'the directly religious life', he sees the Church's genius in the same steady incarnational emphasis on the *thing*. God in himself, and especially God in Christ, both as concrete, sensible thing (Eucharist) and as abstract, mental thing (whether as Word or in the doctrinal propositions of the creeds and Councils) offer the same incarnational challenge and summons which the secular does. They invite and compel man to die to himself in and through the Object as other, as over-against, as *there*. It is in and through this death and surrender that man comes both to God and to himself as alive and personal and free.[108] The whole conception of thing here is analogous and parallel to von Hügel's view of heaven, hell and purgatory as chosen *places* or determinisms which are then experienced and revealed as states of personal being: they speak of the presence or absence of a personal and loving God.[109]

A further comment is suggested here by the possible impression that von Hügel is not interested in the world, but only in man; that for him the world and all secular activity is nothing but a means in the production of personality. In a way, this impression is correct. But it may also misunderstand. Von Hügel's world *is* for man. But it is for his *love*. As object of that love, the world creates and develops its lover, and it survives in him even as it is created and developed by him. It is by a reverent, humble, joyous *building* of the world, it is through the discovery and the development of secular structures as well as of religious ones, that man comes to himself as personality. Just as God must invade man as a gift for man's appropriation, if man is to be fully man, so too must the world, and for the same reason. Human society becomes personal, becomes religious – becomes Church and begins to be Kingdom – in the world. For human personality, and the ecclesial community too, are *embodied* spirit, as von Hügel's insistence on the incarnation and the resurrection of the body makes clear.[110] And the world survives. The world of things, of science and of law, as personalized in man, survives: 'I have been realizing, with such happy vividness, that *nothing* in my past life, that was worth abiding, has gone, but that it is either still within me, or, what is better far, held and kept alive by God elsewhere.'[111]

Von Hügel is clear that to refuse either to relate or to differentiate religion and science must end either in a secularism which leaves personality truncated, or in a sacralism and religiosity that starves and sterilizes religion itself and leaves man's spirituality so thin and shallow that the journey from petty, self-occupied individualism to loving, expansive, other-directed personality is largely arrested and aborted.[112] Divided man *must* pass beneath the 'Caudine forks' of the impersonal, simply factual and real, he must *choose* this fire and bath of objectivity if he is to move from self to that self-surrender, from sheer distracted successiveness to that deep and rich *durée*, which is incarnational personal spirit.[113] Von Hügel draws the alternative for us clearly in the following passage. He describes first the man who seriously chooses only science, only the world and other men; and then he incisively observes the man who, *seeming* to choose *only* God and the personal, is found to have chosen them too quickly, too directly, too cheaply, and thus has risked not having seriously chosen and effectively accomplished, either the world *or* God:

> Once again: take the intermediate, the thing-level as final, and you yourself sink down more and more into a casual thing, a soulless law; materialism, or, at best, some kind of

> pantheism, must become your practice and your creed. – Take the anterior, the individual-level as final, and you will remain something all but stationary, and if not merely a thing yet not fully a person; and if brought face to face with many an agnostic or pantheist of the nobler sort, who is in process of purification from such childish self-centredness by means of the persistently frank and vivid apprehension of the mechanical, determinist, thing-and-fate level of experience and degree of truth, you will, even if you have acquired certain fragmentary convictions and practices of religion, appear strangely less, instead of more, than your adversary, to anyone capable of equitably comparing that agnostic and yourself – you who, if faith be right, ought surely to be not less but more of a personality than that non-believing soul.[114]

Now these convictions govern very much of von Hügel's advice to others. They are seen especially in the largely and consciously non-religious, yet overwhelmingly God-centred and specifically spiritual, direction and education of his niece, Mrs Gwendolen Plunket Greene, a fully matured woman at the time, with a son of her own at Oxford. God is indeed directly given and directly met within immediate experience. But not pietistically. He is to be found out in 'God's great world'.[115]

Yet it does remain true – and we have already quoted von Hügel in this – 'that God, the Spirit upholding our poor little spirits, is the true originator and the true end of the whole movement, in all it may have of spiritual beauty, truth, goodness and vitality . . . '[116] This, the first, the *religious* experience and conviction, must initiate, alternate with, and finalize all that von Hügel has just been saying, if the encounter with science and secularity is to be an *incarnational* moment integrated within a larger *incarnational* whole, and if the pantheistic or mechanistic and immanentist moment and 'way' is not to prove a secularistic cul-de-sac. And a second conviction, permeating and giving intelligibility and motive to all the conflict and tension and friction that this struggle for harmony and expansion and inclusiveness must cost, 'is the continuous sense of the ever necessary, ever fruitful, ever bliss-producing Cross of Christ'.[117] Von Hügel's spirituality as personality is paschal, a death-in-life, a 'painful-joyous expansion and growth'. God as joy in himself for man's adoration and love, and God in the suffering, perfectly human Christ as man's way to joyous life – these are 'the two eyes of religion and twin pulse-beats of its very heart', which must 'waken up and themselves be vivified by, *all the other activities and gifts of God which we have studied*'.[118]

At the beginning of *The Mystical Element of Religion*, and in our own previous chapter, von Hügel asks: what makes life genuine, authentic, *persuasive*. Only truth as concrete and vivid, as unique and emotional, only the subjective moves and convinces a man and his fellows. Yet it is the abstract and clear, the general and intellectual – it is the objective that is transferable from one moment to the next of a man's individual life, and from one man to his brothers. What is 'the secret of spiritual persuasiveness'?[119]

We have von Hügel's answer here at the end, in the dialectic of incarnational personality. Spiritual persuasiveness is personality as *concrete universal*: the unique, organic unity of loving self-determination *accepted as a gift and achieved as a task*, through and in the face of the multiplicity to be organized which is the total real: God in himself; God as incarnate in Christ, *religiously* mediated for man in the institutional, the intellectual and the mystical elements of religion, and *secularly* mediated in the autonomous but related world that science loves to know. Personality is the concrete universal, an effort always in process towards the personalization of being through its historical becoming. Its structure and example is Christ, the one perfectly personal, perfectly embodied human spirit, whose constitution and whose death and life are exemplary of the rhythm of man as individual successiveness moving ceaselessly towards and down into personality as *durée*: Christ as life and/in death, joy and/in suffering, contemplation and/in action, detachment and/in attachment, withdrawal and/in involvement, the other world and/in this world, eternal life and/in history. Only the whole Christ – in himself as principle and in the total history of the total community of his body[120] – only he *seizes* the total multiple real which ultimately is the Father as creating and redeeming. And only he perfectly *organizes* and personalizes this multiplicity into an organic unity and harmony, at the cost of his own struggle with tension and friction.[121] Each man else is ever on a journey towards a 'relative unification'. And hence the necessity of each man's incorporation within the community as that larger personalist organism which shall finally be, in Christ and for his Father, the social Kingdom of God. 'We make up and supplement each other. We give and others give to us.'[122] An incarnational theocentrism, where grace and glory are structured Christologically, binds the whole *theory* together, because of von Hügel's *experience* that the many-graded *reality* in question is thus bound.[123]

For von Hügel, the facts of the real are not so much complicated as they are complex and extensive and profound. And a man must decide how much of reality he is prepared to greet and love.[124] Von Hügel has to agree with the judgment that says his spirituality is very joyous – and very difficult. 'Christianity is a heroism.' Man, therefore, must go into training, 'grasp the nettle', and choose prayer and work that will 'brace' him.[125] But it is what man is born for. Full personality is sanctity. And 'to sanctify is the biggest thing out'.[126]

We have seen the whole rhythm of von Hügel's spirituality – the multiplicity-in-unity, the detachment in and for attachment and involvement[127] – we have seen this formulated as an ethic, and we repeat it here, where von Hügel, citing Troeltsch, asks for 'the deepening of the humane ends by Christian ethics, and the humanising of the Christian end – so that life, within the humane ends, may, simultaneously, be a service of God; and that the service of God may, simultaneously, transfigure the world'.[128] In 1918 Friedrich von Hügel joyfully throws his net still wider to embrace the entire world of his thought, experience and aspiration. He asks for nothing less than the 'Civilizing of Spirituality and . . . the Spiritualizing of Civilization'.[129]

CHAPTER SIX

CONCLUSION: THE CIVILIZING OF SPIRITUALITY AND THE SPIRITUALIZING OF CIVILIZATION

WE have come to the end of our study of Friedrich von Hügel's spiritual doctrine as found in his writings. That doctrine begins with experience, rests in its dense, rich ambiguity, delays upon it, and ends with it too. To that extent, von Hügel's spirituality is mystical, intuitive, emotional, sensuous.

But it is a criticized experience, an evaluated and tested experience that makes for spirituality as doctrine, and so von Hügel thinks, relates, distinguishes. The function of intelligence here, however, is not to solve mystery and life, much less to create them. The effort here is rather critically to report the data of experience – as much of it as possible – and critically to allow the distinct realities experienced to be what the experience says they are. And to this extent, von Hügel's spiritual doctrine, as an on-going attempt to probe and organize the *durational* experience of the historical and contemporary community within conceptions emotionally available to a given moment within *successive* cultural history – to this extent that doctrine, while ceaselessly empirical, is intellectual, rational, metaphysical.

However – to pause a moment – the validity of the experience itself cannot be finally judged by this reflexive enterprise of scientific intelligence. Intelligence indeed ought to deepen and purify the experience from which it gets its blood. But only the *experience itself* can ultimately judge the success of this. And the final discernment and validation of experience must lie in its *own* aftermath. For Christian spirituality, this will be the presence or absence of charity as the unconditional love and service of God, our fellow-men, and the world.

Further, von Hügel's doctrine, as a tested and formulated experience, wants to be product and expression of experience far broader than von Hügel's own – though the effort will always be to narrow this gap ('My faith is not enough – it comes and goes'[1]). And this will mean deliberately and docilely to structure and enrich the perhaps thin spontaneities of personal piety, thought and social concern within the broader experience of the contemporary community of both Church and world and within the experience of the historical community too, especially of the saints, across the centuries ('So we make up and supplement each other. We give and others give to us.' 'Behind every saint stands another saint'[2]). This will be, then, intransigently to fear the impoverishment arising from any arrogant absolutizing of a particular experience (whether one's own, or one's culture's, or some previous culture's). All the varieties of pietism and secularism bear witness to the truncation and distortion of man as fleshed spirit that result from any such foreclosure on the experienced real in its full and historically cumulative drama as God and world. To this extent, von Hügel's spiritual doctrine, as contemporaneously and historically social, is both institutional and traditional.

By way of summary, then, we have in Friedrich von Hügel's spirituality a vigorously criticized, historical, socially appropriated – mysticism.

Mysticism, for von Hügel, is human spirit's always incarnational, *immediate* experience. It is a conscious and free apprehension. It is an appropriation too, because man's actuation of the given *for himself* is a true making of what yet remains pure gift ('I am to incarnate, in my turn, the incarnate God'[3]). It is the appropriation of the total, complex, differentiated, organic real (though von Hügel, and this study, reserve the term mysticism to name the immediate experience of God alone).

Asceticism appears immediately here as the energetic, though largely indirect, attack on whatever (mostly selfishness) prevents this encounter with the real from occurring, either at all, or in the full drama of the multiple real's own otherness, interiority, actuality and promise. Here asceticism, as negation, is a condition of experience. And sufficient physical, economic and social well-being figure as positive conditions here too. Asceticism itself occurs again as positive, here as both principle and effect of that purification of self which results from positive, *loving* actuation of the real as delivered to experience. It takes a homely and a humble heroism to let the world be world (secularity) and to let God, and only God, be God (religion). And this self-surrender to the other and the Other, to world and God, *is* the self's aggrandizement as personality through its death as selfishness.[4]

Personality – man as both historical process and durational achievement – is the continuing and cumulative, dynamic victory of this historical interaction between graced freedom and the multiple reality offered to this creaturely freedom as both gift and task. As an always historical offer to always historical freedom, man's exploration into, and his invasion by, both world and God ineluctably says time and space and other men. Thus human personality, and its triumphant mode as sanctity, is durational fleshed spirit, a journey within community and in the world.

The incarnationalism of von Hügel's spirituality – as experience, as problem, and as achievement – is clearly deriving from the reality which this spirituality seeks to report and grapple with. The real in question, including the experiencing self as fleshed spirit in history, is a vast, complex, potential organism of mutually distinct, mutually inseparable, graded realities which for each man and every culture are initially in tension (and even in conflict) and which are destined for the simplicity, not of empty oneness, but of that living harmony, that multiplicity-in-unity which is presaged in Trinitarian life itself, but especially in the person and work, the death and resurrection of Christ. And the graded reality in question, including the self, is knowable to human spirit and available for its self-actuating love (indeed truly knowable only as loved). That complex, graded real comprises both finite and infinite Spirit; finite spirit and flesh; fleshed spirit in community and world; change and history and eternity (as succession, duration and simultaneity); things, their ideas and their science; determinism and the self-determinating love of conscious freedom as personality; and secularity and religion as personality's true making of both God and world a God and world *for man.*

This multiple, graded, always mysterious reality is indefinitely apprehensible (for experience), less so but really comprehensible (for knowledge and science), and in the case of God and the supernatural, modestly but truly analogical for reason. This makes von Hügel's spirituality – and on principle – a ceaseless task, an endless march into God and the world, an arduous effort to admit and speak the evidence, in order to live in terms of it and according to *its* highly differentiated structure, its formidable terror and inner hope. Experience itself, therefore, and hence its testing and formulation, ought to be coterminal with each man's and every culture's, and the race's, lifetime. Where this process, this contemplation, is blocked, concluded, or becomes selective (through laziness, selfishness or social injustice), ideology, fanaticism, idolatry, impoverishment are at hand. And the size and shape of both secular and religious *action* will alter constantly – towards enrichment or towards narrowness (however clever) – in direct proportion to the quality of each man and the community as *contemplative* of both God and world.

From this point of view – as a wish and effort to be an ever-deepening and broadening discernment of the real – von Hügel's spirituality, like every other inductive and existential enterprise into mystery, is incomplete. It remains as unfinished as man and the world are, and as unfinished as man's corporate becoming and being as an historical people in God. It is a cumulative, open-ended moment in the history of prayer and secularity as incarnational, worldly mysticism. As a record of life and love, it is a stage on the way, and as doctrine, it is work in progress.

Clearly, von Hügel wants reality to be his single subject. And this is perhaps the most impressive part of his achievement. He wants to *know* the evidence, all of it, and from whatever source (which therefore means, for example, *both* faith and empirical science, both dogma and biblical exegesis, both the theology and the psychology of mysticism). And he wants to *live* in terms of the evidence, all of it, at whatever cost to self (which is to choose, as well as to endure, the patience, and waiting, and darkness involved). Reality is what there is. It is a gift – which includes man himself, and his freedom. It is what and who man begins with – a 'given' and grace, an 'overagainst' and 'there'. But not in any objectivist sense. For man, *precisely as given*, is a coming-to-self as personality only through a true human making of God and the world.[5] Reality is there for man (indeed man is there for himself) only as subjectivity, only as relationship and incarnational love. God and world, therefore, come to be a God and world *for man* only as creatively loved.

Von Hügel understands this creative love by which fleshed spirit occurs as personality imperatively to involve a rhythm of detachment and involvement, of contraction and expansion. For man himself is multiple – he is spirit and flesh. And the reality creatively to be loved is multiple as well. Only by a descent into, and a movement through, thing and law, art and politics and science, will human spirit – and religion too – at once be purified of selfishness and *gather a flesh* for personality as a *human* praise of God. Yet conversely too: only as *spirit penetrated by Spirit*, only as *spiritualized* flesh, will man be a truly creative, an agapeistic love and service of his brother and his world. Now this is to say that only *religious* man, the man who prays, can fully manage the terrors and wholly accomplish the joys of his destiny as thorough secularity. But it nevertheless remains for this secular destiny to be accomplished, if man is to be man. A valid man and a robust world, and not their shadows or stunted distortions, are the truth. If only the real God, therefore, is to be adored, only a real man can adore him. And this imperatively suggests that only a man come to prayer with a deeply worldly heart is the full adoration of God.

It is the experience of reality as multiple which decides this repudiation by von Hügel of both pietism and secularism. Man must civilize his God and himself, and he must spiritualize himself and his world. He must be thoroughly secular, and deeply religious. And in this rhythmic movement out into the God and the world which are given to him and which invade him – in this conscious choice of the multiple real ('let it happen') – man *presses* (it is a journey) to be *contemplated action*: he presses to do and give what he is (which is gift) and to become what he does (which is given): *God's love of man and the world, and man's worldly adoration of God* (which means the structure of secular man in the Spirit as a descending and ascending Christology).

Now von Hügel's spirituality, in both these religious and secular dimensions, is the record of a *faith experience* of reality. There is no bracketing of existence here, or of faith either. And while the experience is vigorously purified, tested and formulated, it is never doubted. As a faith experience, this spirituality delivers the multiple realities we have been considering both as existentially distinct *and* as existentially inseparable. The relationality suggested here has three inner moments. For von Hügel's faith finds reality to be at once *organic* in God, *organized* in Christ, and, *to be organized* in the full reach of human history as personality. The realities thus organic, organized and to be organized are basically spirit and flesh, God and world, and man's own complex, flesh-and-spirit self. Von Hügel's spirituality, therefore, is a systematic incarnationalism *because* incarnationalism is the content and the structure of reality itself. We will look now at these three inner moments separately.

In the first place, religious experience as mysticism in the Church – as ecclesially appropriated faith – knows the multiplicity of finite reality to be *initially and ultimately organic in God*, and organic *with* him too. It is God's creative love which is the root and source of graded reality's being at all, and it remains the indispensable milieu of that reality's nevertheless fully autonomous becoming and of its final destiny and victory as unified in human personality as love. One of the main presuppositions and linchpins of von Hügel's whole spiritual doctrine is this faith in the classical Christian doctrine of creation, especially in its more dynamic formulation of God as eternal life present to and within history as simultaneous dynamic act – as *creans* rather than as *creator*, and of God's creative and redeeming love as a *self-limiting* putting-in-substance of both man and world as independent interiorities, as *projects* with developmental dynamisms of their own and, in the case of man, with the responsibility and destiny of making for himself a God and world.[6] This faith emancipates von Hügel's secular energies precisely as a *religious* man. He is thereby free enthusiastically to seek and patiently to endure (without scandal to either his faith or his humanism) the slow, costly, harmony-in-tension-and-through-history of incarnational existence. Concretely, he can allow both his secular and his religious experience their full head: patiently striving for, and humbly awaiting, the complex mystery's further emergence in both his prayer and his science, his asceticism and his sexuality, his faith and his biblical exegesis; effortfully organizing the disparate data, but taking no short-cuts; repudiating both the cheap grace of the God of the gaps and any lowering of man's wager through the quick solutions of those authoritarian legalisms, pietisms and secularisms which mangle reality; watching to be worthy and childlike before the evidence and light of the morrow; *trusting the one God* of his religion, his mind, and his world.

Secondly, this faith experience finds the multiple real to be *initially and ultimately organized for history* in the love of the God-man, Jesus Christ. That love permanently appears, for history, at once as suffering and *Cross* (for the defeat of *dis*order as sin and selfishness), as ardent striving and gentle *growth* (because the human is a durational journey), and as *Resurrection* (as declarative of the *present* significance of all flesh and world because of their destiny as total body of Christ in what was always social, but is now forever also, incarnational Trinitarian joy). Along with the doctrine of creation, this Gospel of the Resurrection of the Body lies at the very heart of von Hügel's experience and enterprise. It is outright notification to him of the full, *essential* dimensions of Christian personality as spirit-in-a-*body*-in-a-*world* – which dramatically liberates his doctrine from every ghetto of religiosity and grounds his secular concerns as profoundly *interior* to spirituality. And while the classical morality of intention continues to decide here the humanizing and sanctifying character of human spirit's entrance into friendship, sexuality, science, politics and art, the resurrection of the body decisively restructures and gives new direction to that intention as love. For it will not be a question now of using and encountering the finite (world, flesh, civilization) as *only* a means, as only an occasion of loving God *alone*. Nor will it be even a question of loving the world and the brother quite directly, but only for God's *sake*. Rather, it will mean to love the world and the brother *as God loves them* in that ceaseless resurrection act by which he makes all flesh and history Christ's: directly, ardently, in detail, in all their autonomous and to-be-developed otherness; as *in themselves* the place of personality's purification and aggrandizement as self-surrender, and as in themselves (where well done and loved *for* themselves) the eternal flesh (however to be transformed) of immortal personal spirit as the total Christ. It is the *religious* experience of the resurrected Christ which drives von Hügel into the world and which makes whoever loves the world and its materiality generously – men such as Darwin – von Hügel's blood-brothers. Of course, to love the world as God loves it is to love it *with his love* – in his world-affirming Spirit. The indispensable roots of full-bodied secularity, then, continue to be prayer.[7]

Finally, this multiple reality as flesh and spirit, as God and world, is experienced in faith as *to be organized* by each man in community and by every culture. Here we have both the faith experience and the convinced hope formulated as a proposal for loving action – for a larger putting on of the total Christ. As a task and journey done by sinful man in history, the proposal shows itself a stubborn multiplicity-for-unity, a slow and costly harmony-in-and-through-conflict-friction-and-tension. As an ongoing, mostly hidden achievement, the proposal is the harmony itself: personality as finite fleshed spirit's incarnational self-surrender of love to both God and the world in history. Where this is triumphantly given and done, it is personality as sanctity.

Now it should be noticed that this multiple reality, however mysterious and unfinished for man's experience, has real definition. The polarities of von Hügel's spirituality are hard-edged, however dense and developmental, and they have detail. And it is important that the largely thematic approach of this present chapter should not obscure this circumstance, so crucial for the incarnational, *dinglich* quality of von Hügel's doctrine as the civilizing of spirituality and the spiritualizing of civilization. It is through the definite and the particular and the ever deeper taking flesh of Spirit that the concrete universal of *persuasive* personality occurs. Further, the religious mysticism in which both von Hügel's religion *and* his secularity are rooted always has its occasion and its validation in both nature and history, and its advance is always in the direction of the increasingly concrete. For the God who is revealed and greeted is the very definite Creator of the particular world, the particular history, the particular rocks and human society von Hügel knows. And where his faith experience presses on to its own full incarnation as a *mysticism in the Church*, then the God who is met, while remaining (indeed increasing) in his apophatic and hidden otherness, also becomes the almost scandalously precise God of Abraham, Isaac and Jacob, and the Father of Jesus Christ. And if it is true (and it is for von Hügel) that this God beckons man directly to himself – even in history – and that he even – and in history – beckons man beyond himself as Creator and Redeemer to his innermost reality as sheer Trinitarian joy, yet he does so only *in* history, in community, and in the world. And the *validation* of the encounter, however superb and dark its crucifying splendours, remains the encounter's own aftermath as *Jesus*, the lover of sparrows, and the lowly servant of his fellow-men.

Friedrich von Hügel's spiritual doctrine, as a Christologically structured theocentrism, as the production of personality, as the civilizing of spirituality and the spiritualizing of civilization, has both its *problem* and its *achievement* in terms of this incarnationalism. For the insistence on *reality* as both complex and one, as flesh and spirit – as Christic – accounts for the dense, highly differentiated quality of von Hügel's *experience*. It indicates too the general shape of the central *problem* to which this experience gives rise. It is primarily a problem of dynamic *ordo* – of organization and harmony, of *more abundant life*.[8] The problem is *also* – really, with intrinsic necessity (for sin's sake) but secondarily and as an inner moment of *ordo* – a problem of *conversion*, of sin and redemption, of *death and life*. And these two polarities must be grappled in a still richer organization (through the rhythmic paradox of detachment-in-involvement, of ascetical mysticism, of supernatural worldliness) for that *life in and through death* which is personality as *paschal* self-surrender. For the pattern is the historical and eternal reality of Our Lord, where suffering and Cross and gentle growth as Jesus mediate Christ and God as harmony and joy.

Finally, the intended *achievement* is adumbrated for us in this *ordo* as a refusal at once of simplism and reductionism, and of all absolute dialectic and relativism too. The achievement also appears in the insistence on reality as interrelational (both in itself, i.e. ontologically, *and* as historically experienced) and as analogical for reason. Now this is a systematic repudiation of all radical discontinuity. Only in the case of sin is the theme of conversion warranted (as the deliberate contradiction and destruction of the lying self). Here alone von Hügel asks for something *else*. In every other situation, personality and sanctity lie in the *magis*: the choice of something *more* – more reality, more Christ, more God, more world. Once again, and finally, we may repeat here von Hügel's profoundly characteristic riposte: 'Indeed the Professor loves the *aut-aut*; whilst I believe real life mostly demands the *et-et*.'[9]

Because of this passionate desire for the *more*, von Hügel's prophetism (as spirit of protest) remains an always lively principle of purification, creation and reformation. But it is conservative too, by current standards, in that it will rarely recommend or condone revolution. For it sees both reality *and* its human actuation (as the history of culture and religion) to be developmental and durational, and not an absolute process wherein successive absolutes are dialectically overcome. The effort here to relate, to enrich and to organize, is then seen to be what it is: the refusal to relativize. Von Hügel takes no pleasure in the strict opposing of one culture to another, nor does he enjoy any *excessive* periodizing of Christian faith as Augustinian, Thomist, etc. (except in service of a subsequent, richer synthesis).[10] For him, this is what both the 'scholastic' and the 'modernist' do, the one by an extrinsicism which absolutizes one moment, the other by an historicism that relativizes all moments, of a history which he, von Hügel, rather experiences – and which his spirituality records – as the surely ever-to-be-purified-and-enriched, but nevertheless *cumulative* and *durational* human love of a reality which is organic in itself *and* in its history as loved and thought and said. Human personality and its holiness, as a gift of the real in history, once again emerges as an individual and corporate dynamic *wholeness*, a developmental *harmony-in-tension*.

Now this element of complexity at the level of *experience* fairly substantively determines – and from the outset – the conditions under which we can hope to find von Hügel's spirituality both as problem and as achievement, a matter – not for agreement, necessarily – but just of serious interest. The central issue of secularity and religion makes this clear. Friedrich von Hügel locates with some clarity the place of the secular within spirituality, where the latter is seen as a total purview of human existence. He speaks with force and even passion of secularity's beauty and truth, its non-religious character and autonomy, and its role, precisely as non-religious, in specifically Christian, i.e. incarnational, sanctity. But von Hügel also speaks, and with equal conviction, of the Trinitarian structure of man's properly Christic engagement with reality. His spirituality has to conclude, therefore – and it certainly does – that where Christ and world are not seen and met within a Trinitarian reference, i.e. in terms of a direct relation to the *Father* in the Spirit through Christ (as an incarnational preoccupation with also *dis*carnate transcendence), then world, and men in community, and Christ too, may become idols. Indeed Christ here may become the last, most subtle (because so splendidly humanist) idol of all and the formal occasion and pretext for personality's escape from that *religious* experience wherein man centrally occurs as man: the direct, immediate love – in Christ and through the world – of *God* in Christ.

Now where these *two* central experiences, convictions and preoccupations (world and God as secularity and religion) are well recognized and understood by von Hügel's reader – where this complexity's status as datum and fact of *experience*, of life and of prayer (and not of some *aprioristic* philosophical, sociological or theological postulate of thought) – where this crucial circumstance is respected even if not agreed to, then von Hügel's spirituality as a problem of order and its achievement as an effort towards incarnational balance and harmony – whatever its success – can have a real excitement and importance, and a deeply suggestive value. On the other hand, where the central data of this spirituality (*both* God and world as the irreducible, immediately given of man's personal experience and of his historical becoming in community) – where these central data are not shared or are not allowed, at least provisionally, to be what von Hügel says they are, then the effort of his spirituality as a harmony-in-tension may well seem bland and boring, and his achievement – as the grappling with a non-problem – will of course seem trite. Von Hügel does not prove anything – nor does he intend to. It is a question of experience, tested and discerned.

The great strength of von Hügel's spirituality lies in its openness. And as the record of a ceaseless experience of a reality ceaselessly to be organized as love, it supplies its own principles of enrichment and reform. It actively invites the addition of a more intense and a broader experience of the real; it invites an always more accurate description of the reality experienced; and it invites a continually more adequate philosophical, psychological and theological formulation and organization of the data thus described. It is on principle, as we said earlier, a work in progress.

Another significant strength of von Hügel's spirituality – and where the substance is also the style – is its quality of *respect*. It may be that the word lacks resonance today, but von Hügel, I think, makes it amount to a very great deal. We catch the point in his request for a 'homely heroism' and in his description of Christianity as the 'bending down to the little in full confidence that it will turn out great'.[11] Von Hügel bends down. He looks hard at the facts. And he does not assume that this 'look' will be easy. It will take time, and patience, and humility. He asks to be worthy. He also wants the generosity and courage to respect what he manages to see, to admit 'certain great facts' and not 'tidy things up' – to deal with reality according to the evidence. And he prays for this too. He is aware of the respect for the other demanded if he is to see this other according to *its* existence and need, its tangled complexity and promise – whether this other be his daughter, some rock of his geological outings, the structure of a mystic's ecstasy, or the whole gamut of fleshed spirit's difficult, lovely advance. The alternative disrespect is 'life taken cheaply – "cheaply," I mean, because practised and sought outside of, and not within, and by working through, its entanglements'.[12]

The limitations in von Hügel's achievement, it seems to me, occur where we would expect, and where von Hügel would hope, to find them – in an insufficient experience. They are not systematic, therefore, in the sense of being defects which follow as a matter of course from the incarnational structure of von Hügel's thought. They seem due, as we said, rather to temperament and culture, to a narrowness of experience – his own and his community's. As such, they do not substantively affect the viability of his achievement, but rather suggest, and by way of example, every spirituality's need ceaselessly to broaden as well as deepen (rather more than to alter) its experiential basis. One of these defects is a certain distance in von Hügel's grasp on the importance of play. Now it is difficult to be a man, and the production of personality is therefore rightly treated by von Hügel as a most serious business. But keeping pace with von Hügel is heavy going all the same. There seems a lightness of step in the Gospels that we do not find here. It is true enough that von Hügel conventionally lists 'art' among the properly secular pursuits of man, and that he shows real interest in his niece's study of music and the violin.[13] But none of this amounts to that considered and lengthy appreciation of the purely aesthetic, the playful, and even the wasting of time which would significantly estimate the role of these activities in the humanization process and see them, not just as means whereby to recover from and prepare for the serious business of life, but also as ends in themselves which, when pursued *for* themselves, are values to become man by.

A far more serious limitation in this spirituality – and one needing far-reaching supplementation – concerns the narrowness of von Hügel's social and political consciousness. Here we have the experience, or lack of it, of a man little larger than his own time and personal situation. For in the face of social questions above all, von Hügel is a baron, a Victorian, and a victim of the isolation caused by his deafness. Now it ought to be clear from our study of his writings that von Hügel enjoys a strongly developed conviction at once about experience, about thought and about life – about all secularity and religion – as only *socially* appropriated gifts and achievements. Further, this conviction about man's essential sociality is not casual, but is central to von Hügel's incarnationalism and one of its greatest strengths. And our criticism here must not be allowed to slight that accomplishment. But if this powerful understanding of individual personality as *gift* as well as condition of community is noteworthy (and it is), and if the ecclesial, communitarian sources and goals of fully Christian personal piety are impressively clear (and they are), nevertheless the social and liturgical *expression* and *actuation* of that personality and piety find only brief and thin consideration in von Hügel's writings. Here above all, however, supplementation, 'more abundant life' – and not alternatives – is what von Hügel's spirituality calls for. For his doctrine of individual, socially actuated personality – of each man as uniquely loving and loved by God – remains both an indispensable condition for civil and ecclesial community as well as their great bulwark against their own dangerous false selves as collectivist self-idolatry. The tradition of devout humanism is mighty and alive in von Hügel, and if this tradition has very much to learn from, it has equally much to contribute to, our current liturgical reforms.[14]

A second social failure concerns the poverty of von Hügel's

political vision. It is a question that goes far beyond the limits of this study. But we can see here how the moderate quality of his prophetism can conventionalize the creative quality of his experience. Now von Hügel's concern for the individual poor, as expressed in his direction of Evelyn Underhill, is simply classical. And his reflections on the substantive justice of Marxist criticism of industrial society clearly indicate that he knows that this classical approach, while not thereby undermined, is not enough, and that something far more organized, massive and public is required. But he seems without suspicion that a truly political act, and that a new political reality, perhaps of actually revolutionary proportions, just *might* be, or even could be, indicated and demanded precisely in terms of his own, von Hügel's, understanding of man as autonomous secularity, with responsibility for building the world and himself in freedom. Briefly, in the realm of polity, von Hügel seems more adept as an ecclesiastical than as a secular Christian, being far more prone healthily to demythologize an authoritarian Church than imaginatively to reconsider, and from a spiritual perspective, the secular structures of social and political life.

Yet it remains Friedrich von Hügel's triumph and very original contribution to have seized upon a significant amount of modern experience, especially as controlled in the methods of scientific history, biblical exegesis, and of philosophy, and to have confronted his religious experience with his findings. In doing this, he places the individual Christian and the Christian community squarely in the world, where alone spirit finds flesh and where alone religion and prayer get all their blood and find their body. Other spiritualities have taken God and the next life with complete seriousness, and von Hügel continues this great tradition with undiminished vigour and, I think, real excitement. But that excitement and drama are particularly due to his heightening of the traditional wager by including within the formal thematic of spirituality man as also historical product of, by being also historical mission to, the world. I suggest that this is secularity in its proper role as an inner moment within the larger whole of civilized spiritual life. Man as the love of God alone and of other men for God's sake remains intact here. Yet the real enrichment and reorganization of the experience emerges in a significantly enlarged appeal for *man as the historical, autonomous love of all God loves: himself, a world, and a world of men.* Herein we have incarnational personality as the civilizing of spirituality and the spiritualizing of civilization.

To enlarge man's wager, of course, is also to increase his risk. And a spirituality of incarnational harmony-in-tension-and-conflict is not without its problems. The broader the experience, and the more multiple the evidence in terms of which one seeks to live and love, the more difficult personality – as the organizing action of love – will be. Without a rhythm of detachment, the friction could be unbearable, and chaos, not harmony, is a real possibility. Possible too is that failure of nerve, or that selfishness, which reduces the real and silences aspects of the mystery until it appears in those manageable proportions which man can dominate instead of serve. Von Hügel's spirituality of harmony-in-tension for more abundant life is emphatically an adult's adventure,[15] which yet only a child can accomplish. For the roots of its great ambition are creatureliness and humility. It does demand too both involvement and recollection, both prayer and action. For the whole basis of the risk is that mystical, *experience trust* which knows that the multiplicity to be organized is the gift of the one God of man's faith, reason and action, and that the harmony aimed at is already victorious and human, however hiddenly and inchoatively, in Jesus Christ.

Finally, on this question of risk: however energetically von Hügel seeks really and seriously to enrich and purify his religious experience through its ever deeper engagement with the world of men, of science and of history, that religious experience does remain primary. Von Hügel's spirituality, therefore, most certainly does not suggest living in terms of the most recent speculative thought – even one's own – or in terms of other men's opinions. For von Hügel, this, and not the converse, would be to live inauthentically, dishonestly, irrelevantly. So while remaining insatiably curious and very well versed in passing intellectual fashions and trends, he also wants deeply to be detached from mood theologies, including certain aspects of his own research and wonder. There is a difficult dialectic here. But the primary root and organizing principle of this spirituality is not thought, however assured, except that thought be fired in the joy of God and the Cross of Christ as delivered in religious experience. And as we have said so often, this experience is an *institutionally* mediated mysticism, an incarnational mysticism in the community of the credal Church.

The prize of more abundant life, of ever greater love and service, may well be thought worth the risk. At any rate, as a passionate openness of mind and heart to the distinct, organic realities of both God and world, and as the organization of this experience in a Christologically structured theocentrism wherein man as incarnational personality occurs, Friedrich von Hügel's spiritual doctrine – whatever the dated quality of some of its detail – remains a still significant reading of the Gospel, and a still valuable proposal for full and fully human, Christian existence.

We conclude our study now with the full text of what is perhaps von Hügel's finest letter of spiritual direction. It is a gift from an old friend to a young Anglican girl of seventeen, on the eve of her confirmation in the Church of England. Von Hügel *invites* her into the real – gently, almost shyly, but with a firmness and deep seriousness that measures the respect he has for her promise and for her freedom before his very real authority. That authority is markedly uncoercive. It is declarative – revelatory – of a real that is at once religious, social, and secular. Authority stands in fine relief here in its gracious role as servant: it seeks to assist this young girl to be herself, to be her own best self.

All the themes of our study appear here, and in their most attractive form, because stamped with the originality of the occasion – with von Hügel's particular care and love. In this letter we see proposed worldliness and deep piety, spontaneity and habit, transcendence and massive incarnationalism, immediate union with God and social involvement, sin and forgiveness, weakness and strength, and life as both effort and grace, as both achievement and gift. And we see that giving and receiving of self through God and the world and our fellowmen which is 'that complex, powerful, costing thing, the true, spiritual human personality'.[16]

It is valuable to part from von Hügel at this level of his rhetoric. For all his more technical writings – and hopefully our study of them too – are only a preparation for, and a commentary on, a letter such as this. The philosophy of religion, the psychological and exegetical indirections of this learned man are brought here to that crucial *inter-subjective* focus where von Hügel himself seeks the testing of their vigour and validity as existentially, spiritually, *persuasive*. I would suggest that in this letter we have such a convincing human act.

Civilization and spirituality are programmatic words, and we have seen the breadth and spaciousness, and the quality of existence von Hügel means by them. But they can have a pompous, abstract ring about them too. A letter such as the following has value from this point of view as well, for it shows these great themes seeking to find a flesh and a history in the homely particularities and simplicity of a young girl's life and love. And conversely, a careful listening to the words, the phrases, and to the letter as a whole, will easily identify the separate sounds, the fugues, and the full, ambitious, orchestrated harmony of Christ's Gospel as read in Friedrich von Hügel's spirituality. The letter is given here without alteration of any kind. We end our study with it in the hope that that study may be the letter's adequate exegesis and commentary – and in the hope too that the letter may in turn confirm the central statements of our study.[17]

Kensington, 11th March, 1910

My very dear child,

I am putting upon this paper for you, with much quiet reflection and prayer, those *four great religious principles and practices*, which we considered together, by word of mouth, a week ago. I shall here try to make them still clearer and more precisely applied to your own case and use. And I am sending you this letter in time for you to go through it all, in a leisurely and browsing fashion, so that it may help you to form your resolutions before and on Monday next, the 14th.

But before developing those four principles and practices, I want to bring home to your mind three prerequisites of their proper, fruitful use as clearly as I can.

I. 1. Religion is indeed authoritative, since *only if felt and accepted as not of our making but of God's giving is it religion at all*. And it is deeply social, since we shall never learn much about it, except souls more experienced than ourselves are touched by God to come and start us and help us on our way. Yet that authority is exercised and experienced in and through our human religious sense and conscience; and this social aid can (in proportion as we begin to attain the age and maturity of personal responsibility) act wholesomely *only in and through the unforced insight of our own, docilely inclined, minds and the free, loving self-dedication of our own wills*. Hence, Blessing, you will not *for one moment* strain, or torture yourself, to think or to do any one of the things here proposed to you. Only in the degree and manner in which, after thinking them well over, in a prayerful and open disposition, they really come home to your mind and really appeal to your own heart and conscience, will you quietly accept them and try and work them into your life. And after having thus helped to awaken your own mind and conscience to these great realities and practices, I can be of use to you in sustaining you to follow these lights, now your own, in times of darkness and of trouble. *These are the only two wholesome helps one soul can give another, as concerns such fundamentals.*

2. *The following four realities and practices combine with, condition, contrast with, and correct, each other*, if and when we try and live them, in endless manners and degrees; and for this reason also, they prevent the interior life from ever growing really stale or essentially monotonous. But, though my separate enumeration of them necessarily impoverishes them all, such enumeration will help you to understand the rich reality somewhat, against the time when such experience will have made you apprehend it all so much more truly, Blessing.

3. And, above all, even these four realities and principles taken together, indeed *the whole of the specifically religious world and life*, ever presuppose, if and when we poor humans use them wisely and well, *quite a number of other lives that we have to live*, each with its own specific laws, objects, organization and end. These lives, religious, moral, political, social, intellectual, aesthetic, physical, have each their immanental laws and range, yet each requires also all the others, and they all require to be wisely and courageously penetrated and purified, yet never really atrophied, by the higher and highest, and to be ever re-harmonized into an ever-growing and deepening whole, into that complex, powerful, costing thing, the true, spiritual human personality. Hence though I have described to you the most important among these many things, and point out to you those that should purify all the others; yet those others too are *strictly* necessary even for religion itself.[18] For without those other things religion would not have the fullness of the materials for it to penetrate,

nor the occasions of conflict, friction and of humiliatingly slow advance without which itself (that is our own hearts and wills when religious) would not be purified. For we are so small, and the work is so great, that not only must religion ever purify the rest of us, but the difficulties arising over this purification have to help us ever to purify our religion itself. You will then, Child, even for the sake of religion itself, ever eagerly love your games, your dancing, your hunting, and such other physical pleasures and activities as suit your health and social circumstances; you will enter delightedly into your music and poetry and other art; you will devote yourself to your studies of history or science; you will wholeheartedly care for, and help (in proportion to your special gifts and *attraits*) in – social, political, moral questions and necessities. And in each case, at each level, you will, in the first instance, simply try and discover and obey the laws immanent to that particular case and level. *The more varied and vigorous is your general, not directly religious life, the better for your religion, on condition always that you never do so much and so great a variety of things as to lose your power of recollection away from it all and your ability to harmonize it all with some difficulty and fairly well.* All real racket, all actual fever, all vehemence, strain and bitterness are weakening and sterilizing. Let us drop these, as soon as we see them, and get, as far as ever we can, physical, or mental, or spiritual rest and expansion.

II. 1. *The reality and practice of the presence of God.* I mean the sense, and the cultivation of the sense, of his omnipresence, of his *prevenience*, of all things, in their essence (which is beautiful, true and good) coming from him, and especially all our very capacity for, and slightest wish for, goodness and him. It is, at the same time, a sense of our pathetic limitations, as against the great background and presence of the infinite and abiding; of the utter unsatisfyingness of whatsoever is but scattered about space, or can or does pass away in sheer succession. And this *sense* it *is* which is *the centrally human sense*; without it we would be no more truly men. Yet this sense comes from the actual touch, the enveloping and penetrating presence, of the infinite Spirit, God upon, around and within our spirits which, finite though they be are sufficiently God-like to cause them to suffer under the keen sense of contrast of the two worlds which both touch them, and both of which they touch; the abiding, infinite, spiritual; and the fleeting, temporal, material.

You will, Blessing, gradually get your life saturated with this sense. The following texts express it grandly: Rom. xi, 33: 'O the depth of the riches of the wisdom and the knowledge of God! How unsearchable are his judgements and his ways past finding out.' I John iv, 8, 10: 'God is love. Herein is love, not that we loved God, but that he loved us.' Acts xvii, 27, 28: 'He is not far from each one of us, for in him we live and move and have our being.' II Cor. iii, 5: 'Our sufficiency is from God.'

It will be especially in your *daily quarter of an hour* of spiritual reading and direct recollection that you will be able to foster and feed this sense. But throughout the day (as you learn to take one thing at a time and ever to let drop all sheer bustle and fever) you will have many opportunities of, more indirectly, encouraging it, until, at last, it will become an ever, more or less perceived, background and support, a light and balm and refreshment to your life, Child.

And then, and then alone, will you have gained, with this sense of this presence of the infinite Lover and comprehender of your soul, a truly efficacious means against impatience, intolerance, injustice towards all and any of your fellow-mortals, and against the danger, that ever dogs the steps of all very sensitive souls, of becoming embittered, or gloomy, or broken, when in the course of life, keen disappointments or grave misunderstandings come to them. For, once you have learnt that the infinite Spirit alone can, but that he indeed does, completely, ceaselessly understand you, you can and will be sufficiently satisfied and moderated, gratefully to realize how much he and that fellow-mortal can and does understand you – most certainly at times, far better than you will ever understand yourself.

Besides, this sense, when strongly developed, will teach you more and more to live, not so much in order to get, as in order to give; not so much in order to be loved as in order to love; as Our Lord has said: 'It is more blessed to give than to receive' (Acts xx, 35). 'Nearer we hold of God who gives, than of his tribes that take.'

2. *The reality and practice of contingency, of creatureliness.* As a matter of fact, a wholesome, full sense of the infinite arises and is renewed, within us, not only by recollection but also by contact with the contingent, with matter, time and space. It is not only that we have a body and (partly physical) fellow-creatures, so that we have duties towards all these visible palpable things; but that *the sense of the infinite and of the finite spring up together and condition each other.* Hence we shall never attain a thoroughly wholesome, deeply spiritual religion, unless we take care to give it, and to keep for it, a body.

It is no doubt certain that at the time of such attention to particular, institutional acts – the kneeling for, and the recitation of, formal vocal prayers, the attending of church services, even the reception of Holy Communion – we often feel as though contracted, as though all these things were dry and petty; and as though God, Spirit and Infinite, must be right outside all such temptations and materialities.

Yet life shows us everywhere how necessary, for our fuller expansion and true deepening, are such seemingly narrowing, humblingly obscure contacts with the visible – such contractions of our attention and feeling to *things*, to matter, to the little Here and Now. The narrow mountain defile, 'the warm gates', *Thermopylae*, was the one entrance, from outside Greece to the broad plains of Thessaly and on to rich, free Hellas beyond. And so in human affection, however spiritual, some 'contraction' and contact, by sight, or handshake, or letter, is necessary for its fuller elicitation and maintenance. The pathetic narrowness of birth and babyhood precede, and are the necessary vehicles of, the larger and ever larger adolescent and adult life. And suffering (seemingly so opaque itself, and tending, if alone, to obscure and to contract the soul) in reality, if taken up by a will full of faith and love, enlightens and expands, in unique fashion and degree. So too *religion requires some apparently unnecessary, emotionally more or less irksome contractions and attentions to visible and audibly institutional and social acts and rites.* Without *some* such, we cannot fully capture and maintain a deep wholesome recollection and spirituality.

Christianity is specially great in that it does not ignore or neglect, but that it enters into and sanctifies, the body. For it consists, not simply in the great doctrine that 'God is a Spirit, and they that would serve him, must serve him in spirit and truth' (John iv, 24), but also in the doctrine that 'The Word was made Flesh' (John i, 14). It represents to us, not only Christ as saying to the Samaritan woman 'the hour cometh when neither in this mountain nor in Jerusalem shall ye worship the Father' (John iv, 21), but it also describes to us the sick woman cured by the touch of the hem of Christ's garment – the woman who said 'if I touch but his garment, I shall be whole' (Matt. ix, 20, 21).

These two things, together or in alteration, and not either of them alone constitute the very soul and force of christianity. And indeed, here as elsewhere, this its soul so reveals and meets the deepest, implied requirements of the human spirit, as touched by God, the infinite spirit in all lands and times, that there is no more certain way towards separating us from our fellow-men, and producing spiritual emptiness, restlessness and inflation, than contempt for, or absence of all reverence towards and practice of, the visible, audible, institutional idea of religion.

We have, then, simply to find out the amount and kind of such outgoings to the contacts and contingencies, and the amount and kind of such homecomings to the (thus awakened) sense of the infinite and to largely formless recollection in it, which our character, grace and present development may best grow by and require; and then faithfully and generously to practise this kind and degree of both, as thoroughly as we can. You will, in any case, practise your morning and night prayers, on your knees, for such outgoings; and attendance at church service, I should say once every Sunday and, I take it, on Christmas Day, Good Friday, and Ascension Day. And Holy Communion would, I suppose, be received once a month. I put the amounts here tentatively, since it is not *they*, but the presence and regularity of *some* such institutional acts which alone I can be sure of. And this *presence and regularity are indeed so essential, that, in the long run, you get two contradictory outlooks on to life according as they are present or absent*. You, Blessing, will, please God, ever re-decide for the deep, incarnational reality of all fully living life.

3. *The reality, and practice of the sense of, our human weakness, error, sin*. It is very certain that we can most easily endanger or ruin our religion and its helpfulness, by straining after too direct, or excessive, or continuous, a sense of sin, or by a too frequent and lengthy or too detailed a preoccupation with our own precise offences and evil tendencies. It is also certain that Calvin, indeed, in a lesser degree, also Luther and Pascal also, gravely exaggerated in this matter. Human nature is *not* essentially vitiated, and the whole of religion does *not* consist in a sense of sin and of our redemption by Our Lord from such sin. Even already St Paul concentrates himself with an intense exclusiveness, in most of his moods, upon our utter sinfulness, and, in the whole range of Our Lord's earthly life,

upon the Passion, as the ransom for these our sins, alone; whereas in the synoptic Gospels we get Our Lord's life and teaching as well as his Passion, and all these activities there constitute his great self-offering to God and his redemptive office and example towards ourselves, and we there find him insisting chiefly upon our blindness and weakness – thus with the cures of the blind men (Mark viii and x) and the great saying at Gethsemane, 'the spirit is indeed willing, but the flesh is weak' (Matt. xxvi, 41).

Yet it is also true, and especially for us nowadays, that we can easily grow morbidly fearful of morbidness, and can become unreal and dangerously silly in this matter. For, after all, we *are*, within limits, possessed of free will; we *are* responsible; we *do*, often, more or less continuously, not follow our better lights, our nobler promptings, the ways that we feel would teach us more of wholesomely costing truths about our duties and our faults; we *are*, often, more or less cowardly, indolent, double, severe or thoughtless towards others, meanly soft and touchy about ourselves; we *are* readily puffed up by insincere praise and dejected by deserved blame; we *are* ever very imperfect, we *are* insincere. Hence even in those excesses of one-sidedness there is a deep truth, apprehended by deep souls.

As to yourself, I should like you to *occupy yourself directly with your own particular faults and sins, only in two connections.* You would make a short and quiet examination of conscience, as to your doings of the day, every night at your night prayers; turning to God at the beginning and asking for light, and turning to him at the end and begging pardon and determining, with the help of his grace, not to commit whatever you may find pricks your conscience again. And, if and when you find yourself self-complacent, or markedly tempted to it, turn your mind (for a moment) to any act or fault of your past that you especially regret. But, outside of these two occasions (the one regularly recurrent, the other incidental, and both of them short and precisely limited) *live*, Child, *habitually occupied with God and his love and greatness, with your work and with all things as souls beautiful, true and good* – with all that God has given you to love. Joy, expansion, admiration, adoration, gratitude – much, very much occupation with others, with God in and through it all – let this, at other times, absorb you away from all direct occupation with yourself. To love dearly, to contemplate habitually the right things, to grow unconsciously like what you admire, what deserves admiration, with all you are to have: this should be the primary, prevalent preservation against, and purification from, your very real evil inclinations, faults and sins. And yet if others, even roughly or unjustly reprimand or criticize you, try hard, not only to be patient, but also gratefully to learn; and if you find this difficult or impossible, recognize that in *this* at least you are very faulty, and try to do better another time.[19]

4. *The reality, and the sense of the true function, of suffering.* Christianity is unique in the fulness, steadiness and fruitfulness of its doctrine and power as to this fundamental point. And here again we all of us have, nowadays especially, an immense, immediate, need of this insight and force.

Two extremes and errors, each showing the profound weakness and blindness of religiously unenlightened and unaided human nature have, outside of christianity and its devoted acceptance, ever prevailed, both produced from the same root, and each ever ending by calling forth the other. Either suffering, pain, death are taken, are attempted to be declared and made into, nothing, mere subjective creatures of our own minds, which these minds can and ought, consequently, to dissolve into the utter nothing from which they came (stoicism, etc.); or suffering, pain, death are taken to be all, or at least final, to be the reality, the end of all things (pessimism). The secret terror that the latter is the truth in the (most well-grounded) sense that man cannot (in the long run) stand such a doctrine, is doubtless the fundamental cause of the creation of the former, otherwise profoundly artificial and ever precarious system. And both are godless; indeed it is because they have no God, no experience of a real goodness and love which really triumph over evil, that they thus teach and reel from side to side. Christianity alone fully faces and exhaustively admits the mysterious depth and poignant reality of all the woe, the pain, the suffering, the loneliness, the misunderstandings, the war, the defeat, the death that permeate life around us and within us. And yet, not simply as a fine theory, or haughty doctrine, but *as a force and a fact, Christianity's ultimate note, the end of it all, is with the help of Christ's spirit, purification, acceptance, expansion, intimate union with God and man, spiritual power, joy overflowing*. And all this not because the evil itself becomes good, not because we judge it differently, but because, on occasion of the evil which, of itself, only darkens, weakens and stains the soul, God's, Christ's strength has come to, and has been accepted by, the soul. There is nothing so great in life, darling spiritual daughter, as this large, tender asceticism, nothing we all want more than this noble, utterly unmorbid, alone quite wholesome, virile understanding and willing of the great cross of Christ.

St Paul has it so gloriously: 'We preach Christ crucified, unto the Jews a stumbling block, and unto the Gentiles foolishness; but unto those that are called, Christ the power of God and the wisdom of God. Because the foolishness of God is wiser than men, and the weakness of God is stronger than men.'[20] 'Dirige me recto itinere in regnum tuum' we will pray with Thomas à Kempis, to Christ Our Lord. This *rectum iter* will not only lead to, but will largely consist of, much admiration, expansion, love and joy; but, inevitably, it will, not lead to, but will in considerable part be made up of, increasingly endorsed and willed suffering, also, Blessing.

For your practice here you will just simply, when suffering, physical or mental, comes, try promptly to accept it, and gently to utilize it towards loving God and man more fully and strongly than before – of course in and by prayer, by a soul's look to God. It would be well too if you had some external symbol or action to incarnate for you this great, glorious truth; a crucifix, or crucifix picture, however small; or a little sign of the cross, before and after meals; or sleeping with your arms crossed.

Largely formless recollection, a prayer of quiet and love; a small number of carefully selected and persistently repeated institutional acts; a short, but recurrent and direct, occupation with your definite faults and sins; and a learning to accept and utilize all such suffering as God may send you or allow; those four things worked with simplicity, perseverance, and above all, *with love, and love,* AND LOVE: these will, Blessing, bring you to an unshakeable, because creaturely strength, a deep joy, and a steady homely heroism, a gently flowing love and service of your fellow-creatures in, with and for God, the Infinite, our Home.

God bless you, darling spiritual daughter,

Your loving fatherly friend.

My last three Holy Communions have been specially for you.

LIST OF ABBREVIATIONS

BM Add. MS – British Museum Additional Manuscript.

CE – 'Du Christ éternel et de nos christologies successives', *La Quinzaine*, Paris, June 1904, pp. 285–312.

CFA – 'Caterina Fiesca Adorna, the Saint of Genoa', *Hampstead Annual*, 1898, pp. 70–85.

EA1 – *Essays and Addresses on the Philosophy of Religion*, First Series, London, 1921, 1963.

EA2 – *Essays and Addresses on the Philosophy of Religion*, Second Series, London, 1926, 1963.

EL – *Eternal Life*, Edinburgh, 1912.

ET – 'Experience and Transcendence', *Dublin Review*, April 1906, pp. 357–79.

EU – *Evelyn Underhill*, by Margaret Cropper, London, 1958.

GS – *The German Soul*, London, 1916.

LN – *Letters from Baron Friedrich von Hügel to a Niece*, edited with an introduction by Gwendolen Plunket Greene, London, 1928, 1965.

ME1, ME2 – *The Mystical Element of Religion as Studied in Saint Catherine of Genoa and Her Friends*, 2 vols., London, 1908; 2nd edition, 1923, 1961 (unchanged except for new preface, and the edition used in this study).

MK – 'Der Mystiker und die Kirche', *Hochland*, December 1924, pp. 320–30.

PC – 'Petite consultation sur les difficultés concernant Dieu' (1912), in Pietro Scoppola, *Crisi modernista e rinnovamento cattolico in Italia*, Bologna, 1961, pp. 368–92.

RG – *The Reality of God and Religion and Agnosticism*, edited by Edmund G. Gardner, London, 1931.

RGM – 'The Relations Between God and Man in "The New Theology" of Rev. R. J. Campbell', *Albany Review*, September 1907, pp. 650–68.

RP – 'The Religious Philosophy of Rudolf Eucken', *Hibbert Journal*, April 1912, pp. 660–77.

SL – *Baron Friedrich von Hügel: Selected Letters, 1896–1924*, edited with memoir by Bernard Holland, London, 1927.

LIST OF ABBREVIATIONS

St Andrews MS – Von Hügel Manuscript Collection, St Andrews University Library.

VH & T – *Von Hügel and Tyrrell: The Story of a Friendship*, by Maude Petre, London, 1937.

NOTES

CHAPTER ONE

1. In Michael de la Bedoyère, *The Life of Baron von Hügel*, London, 1951, p. xi.
2. Jean Steinmann, *Friedrich von Hügel, sa vie, son oeuvre et ses amitiés*, Paris, 1962, pp. 41–2.
3. *The Mystical Element of Religion as Studied in Saint Catherine of Genoa and Her Friends*, 2 vols., London, 1908; 2nd edition, 1923, 1961 (unchanged except for new preface, and the edition used in this study).
4. Edinburgh, 1912, 1913.
5. In de la Bedoyère, op. cit., pp. xi, 223. Archbishop Temple made his remark after von Hügel's death in 1925.
6. *Les Modernistes*, Paris, 1909; English translation, London, 1908, pp. 40–4.
7. *The Letters of Evelyn Underhill*, edited by Charles Williams, London, 1943, p. 129; *EU*, p. 68.
8. Cited by Bernard Holland in his introductory memoir in *SL*, p. 52. See also Alfred Loisy, *Mémoires pour servir à l'histoire religieuse de notre temps*, 3 vols., Paris, 1930–1, Vol. II, p. 462.
9. Quoted in *SL*, p. 49. Jesuit historian James Brodrick remembered for me an identical impression of his own from von Hügel's visit to the chapel at Campion Hall, Oxford.
10. Ibid., p. 53.
11. Henri Bremond discusses a similar necessary precision of materials and questions in his monumental *Histoire Littéraire du Sentiment Religieux en France*, Paris, 1916; English translation of Vol. I, London, 1928, p. xii.
12. Except where noted, all biographical information here is taken from de la Bedoyère, op. cit., or from Holland's memoir in *SL*.
13. Letters to Clement Webb, 1 October 1909 and 26 September 1912, in *SL*, pp. 170–1, 196–8.

14. E.g., the letter to Webb just cited, ibid., p. 171, and another of 15 August 1919, ibid., pp. 282–4; letter to Edmund Bishop, 29 September 1905, in 'Friedrich von Hügel's Letters to Edmund Bishop', edited by Nigel Abercrombie, *Dublin Review*, 1953, pp. 184–8. Also, *LN*, pp. 187–8.
15. A. L. Lilley in Preface to *VH& T*, p. viii.
16. Letter to J. M. Connell, 31 December 1913, in *SL*, pp. 203–5; letter to Juliet Mansel, 23 March 1910, ibid., pp. 175–6; and *LN*, p. 45.
17. For the tenuous character of von Hügel's religion and Catholicism before 'conversion' at the age of 18, see letter to Edmund Bishop, 23 May 1906, in Abercrombie, op. cit., pp. 288–93, esp. pp. 288–9.
18. The more or less Jesuit influence, I should think (and perhaps not thereby necessarily altogether Ignatian: see, e.g., François Roustang, *Une initiation à la vie spirituelle*, Paris, 1963; English translation, *Growth in the Spirit: An Initiation into the Spiritual Life on the Lines of the Spiritual Exercises*, London, 1966. Roustang runs remarkably parallel to von Hügel on many questions.).
19. To any reader finding this smug, I can only say: read on.
20. *EA2*, p. 234.
21. *ME1*, p. vii; *EA1*, p. 286; *Times Literary Supplement* (obituary of Louis Duchesne), 25 May 1922, cited in de la Bedoyère, op. cit., pp. 47–8.
22. Letter to von Hügel, 1904, *St Andrews MS* 2702. *SL*, pp. 57–63, contains the original French of von Hügel's notes on advice given to him by Huvelin in 1886.
23. For a description and evaluation of von Hügel's textual work on the '*opus catharinianum*', see da Genova in *Dictionnaire de spiritualité*, Paris, Vol. II, cols. 290 ff.
24. Our study should sufficiently reveal the breadth of von Hügel's reading in religious and philosophical areas. The education of his niece indicates the size of his reading in classical and medieval literature, in history, poetry and the novel (see, e.g., *LN*, pp. xii–xiii). And see, for example, Diaries for 28 May 1921, which indicate that a fifth reading of Jane Austen's *Mansfield Park* is in progress. Von Hügel's personal library, now at St Andrews, Fife, in addition to large collections on other subjects, contains more than 85 volumes on numismatics, 20 on geology and 15 on the morality of war. Of interest too are the many books with personal dedications to von Hügel from their authors, e.g. Miguel de Unamuno.
25. For von Hügel's activities in these groups, see Lilley, in Preface to *VH& T*, p. ix, and de la Bedoyère, op. cit., pp. 89–90; also letters to Edmund Bishop, 7 May, 27 May, 10 June, 16 September, 1904, and 29 September 1905, in Abercrombie, op. cit., pp. 71–8, 179–82, 184–8.

Diaries for 2 June 1914 and 3 May 1921 give current membership lists of the L.S.S.R.

26. For the rarely discussed question of Newman's relation to and influence on von Hügel, see John Heaney, *The Modernist Crisis: von Hügel*, Washington, D.C., 1968, pp. 22–5; R. K. Browne, 'Newman and von Hügel: A Record of an Early Meeting', *The Month*, July 1961, pp. 24–33.
27. Diaries for 21 May 1921, for example, list a card from Rudolf Otto among the day's mail. Heaney, op. cit., pp. 15–16, discusses von Hügel's lifelong familiarity with famous ecclesiastics. He is thus never the 'small boy addressing the clergy'.
28. See the letters to Juliet Mansel ('J.M.') and to the young Henri Garceau in *SL*. There are illuminating remarks on the dynamics and difficulties of this catechizing in a letter to Clement Webb, 13 October 1916, ibid., pp. 236–7.
29. Quoted in de la Bedoyère, op. cit., p. 323.
30. The record of this direction is in *EU* and *LN*.
31. Holland provides a large sampling from the obituary notices and letters of condolence in *SL*, pp. 52–7.
32. Ibid.
33. Von Hügel's strong tendency toward novelty and his changing enthusiasms, apparently very different from Tyrrell's, are recorded by Wilfrid Ward in Maisie Ward, *The Wilfrid Wards and the Transition*, London, 1934, pp. 308–9, 318 ff. Father Martin D'Arcy confirms this trait for me from his own experience of von Hügel.
34. I have found René Marlé's *Au Coeur de la Crise Moderniste*, Paris, 1960, the most useful and moving account of von Hügel's role in the 'modernist' crisis. The book builds on a massive citation of the correspondence with Blondel. John Heaney, op. cit., gives a particularly careful and complete account and analysis, especially of the major themes of exegesis, authority, and the nature of the Church. He also has a useful appendix, pp. 219–34, 'A Short Sketch of Modernism'. Nédoncelle, *Baron Friedrich von Hügel*, London, 1937 (translated from the French edition, Paris, 1935), is also extremely valuable; de la Bedoyère, op. cit., and Steinmann, op. cit., perhaps less so, on this particular question. The most recent account of the whole movement and question is Emile Poulat, *Histoire, Dogme et Critique dans la Crise Moderniste*, Paris, 1962 (Poulat, pp. 40–1, 513, questions the entire reliability of Marlé's work).
35. P. 20.
36. For the two meanings of 'modernism', see letter to Maude Petre,

13 March 1918, in *SL*, pp. 247–9; letter to René Guiran, 11 July 1921, ibid., pp. 333–7.

37. Letter to Tyrrell, 18 June 1899, ibid., pp. 76–7.

38. 'Father Tyrrell: some memorials of the last twelve years of his life', *Hibbert Journal*, January 1910, p. 234. Brief reference to von Hügel's relationship to Loisy's thought will occur further on.

39. *VH & T*, p. 203; 'Friedrich von Hügel, Personal Thoughts and Reminiscences', *Hibbert Journal*, October 1925, p. 85; de la Bedoyère, op. cit., p. 172. Von Hügel's conduct in face of the proposed suppression of the journal *Rinnovamento* is one of the main questions here (see *VH & T*, pp. 165 ff.). There is a good deal about *Rinnovamento* in the letter to Edmund Bishop, 16 June 1908, in Abercrombie, op. cit., pp. 422–7.

40. Cock, *A Critical Examination of von Hügel's Philosophy of Religion*, London, undated, pp. vii, 151; Nédoncelle, *von Hügel*, gives his own views, pp. vii–viii, 35–6 (pp. 31–4 describe and assess the contrary views of Jean Rivière's *Le Modernisme dans l'Eglise*, Paris, 1929); de la Bedoyère, loc. cit. Martin Green, apropos of Petre's judgment, has interesting and very valuable things to say about sanctity, martyrdom and heroism, and about von Hügel's performance and personality generally, *Yeats's Blessings on von Hügel*, London, 1967, pp. 6–8 *et passim*.

41. Sabatier, op. cit., pp. 40–4, substantively given, from Gallarati-Scotti's account, in Nédoncelle, op. cit., p. 30; and de la Bedoyère, op. cit., pp. 195–8.

42. Letter to Gallarati-Scotti, undated original or autograph copy, *St Andrews MS* 2649; *ME1*, pp. xxi–xxii.

43. Letter to Henri Bremond, 15 July 1900, *St Andrews MS* 30284.

44. It is a careful phrase. Marlé, op. cit., p. 342, n. 1, believes it indicates von Hügel's growing disagreement with Loisy.

45. Letter of 11 December 1908, cited with comments, ibid., pp. 341–2: 'Je me suis fort consciencieusement absorbé ici en des questions autres que les points qui en premier lieu occupent l'abbé Loisy, voire même, me semble-t-il, Edouard Le Roy. Je n'ai nullement pensé à me différencier, en ces temps, de mes amis qui souffrent tant pour des convictions qui ne peuvent pas être rien que de pures erreurs; mais aussi ai-je été plein de problèmes dont j'ai été épris, comme de matière d'importance spirituelle pour mon âme et sa vie religieuse, il y a déjà trente ans, bien avant que je sache même l'existence de mes amis critiques, voire même de l'abbé Laberthonnière et de vous.'

46. Nédoncelle, *von Hügel*, p. viii; Douglas Steere, *Spiritual Counsels and*

Letters of Baron Friedrich von Hügel, London, 1964, p. 5. See also *LN*, pp. viii–ix.

47. Letter to Leslie Johnston, 9 October 1914, in *SL*, pp. 213–15; *TLS* for 22 December 1921.
48. *EA1*, pp. xviii, 107–8.
49. *RG*, pp. 36, 42; *EA1*, p. 104. See also A. H. Dakin, *Von Hügel and the Supernatural*, London, 1934, p. 16, and letter to Tyrrell, 26 September 1898, in *SL*, pp. 71–4: apprehension occurs 'more through the purification of the heart than through the exercise of the reason . . .'
50. Munich, 1918; English translation, *Prayer*, Oxford, 1932, New York, 1958, pp. 98, 362. Peter Baelz cites Heiler in his fine discussion of this and other questions, *Prayer and Providence*, London, 1968.
51. *ME1*, pp. xxii–xxiv, xxxiii; *LN*, pp. 165–6. These hopes and goals are not far from those advanced in *Gaudium et Spes*, Vatican II's Pastoral Constitution on the Church in the Modern World (*The Documents of Vatican II*, edited by Walter Abbott, New York, 1966, no. 62, pp. 268–9).
52. *RG*, p. 33; *ME1*, p. xvii.
53. In *SL*, p. 62.
54. *GS*, pp. 208–9. My italics.
55. See Algar Thorold, *Readings from Friedrich von Hügel*, London, 1928, p. xi; also *ME1*, p. 71, for the quality of 'unconditional surrender' in the distinctively 'religious' act.
56. See Nédoncelle, 'Un texte peu connu de F. von Hügel sur le problème de Dieu', *Rev. des Sciences religieuses*, April 1962; English translation as 'A Recently Discovered Study of von Hügel on God', *International Philosophical Quarterly*, February 1962, pp. 19–20.
57. See Nédoncelle, *von Hügel*, pp. 46–7. See also above, p. 25. Von Hügel's hopes are well expressed in Léon-Joseph, Cardinal Suenens, *Coresponsibility in the Church*, London, 1968, esp. pp. 136–51, 'The Coresponsibility of Theologians'.
58. Quoted in de la Bedoyère, op. cit., pp. 266–7.
59. 'An Emotional Unity', *The Dial*, February 1928, pp. 111–12.
60. Undated letter (probably before 1905) to Wilfrid Ward, cited in Maisie Ward, *The Wilfrid Wards*, Vol. 1, pp. 301–2. A fine and similar statement made to Algar Thorold in 1921 is cited in de la Bedoyère, op. cit., p. 330.
61. *EA1*, pp. 100–5, 145; *ME2*, pp. 134, 139. See also *LN*, pp. xvi–xvii; and Gwendolen Greene, 'Thoughts from Baron von Hügel', *Dublin Review*, 1931, pp. 254–5.

62. *ME1*, pp. 45, 65; *EA1*, pp. 11, 68, 70; *EL*, pp. 134, 222; Evelyn Underhill, *Mixed Pasture*, London, 1933, p. 215.
63. Cited in *EL*, p. 376.
64. *LN*, p. 134. And see Nédoncelle, *von Hügel*, p. vii.
65. *EA2*, p. 131.
66. *Religion and Agnosticism*, in *RG*, p. 187.
67. *LN*, pp. xiii–xiv.
68. In *SL*, p. 58.
69. *ME1*, p. xviii. And see *ME2*, pp. 262, 270.
70. *ME1*, pp. 46–7; *RP*, p. 666.
71. See, for example, *EA1*, pp. 22–3.
72. *ME2*, p. 367.
73. *EA1*, p. 95.
74. *EA2*, p. 272. Suenens, op. cit., has said this finely, pp. 54–6: 'Evangelisation and Humanisation'.
75. *ME1*, p. 368.
76. See de la Bedoyère, op. cit., pp. xi–xii; and especially Martin Green, op. cit., pp. 24, 47, 57, 65–7.
77. L. Lester-Garland, *The Religious Philosophy of Baron F. von Hügel*, London, 1933, p. 4. And see de la Bedoyère, op. cit., pp. 328–30, and Nédoncelle, *von Hügel*, pp. 28–9, and esp. pp. 35–6.

CHAPTER TWO

1. Letter to Blondel, 25 March 1905, *St Andrews MS* B3280.H8: 'Le Christianisme est essentiellement religion d'Incarnation: il est bien réellement Dieu incarné en le temps et l'espace.'
2. *LN*, p. viii.
3. Cock, op. cit., p. 135.
4. What Cock, ibid., p. 6, says of von Hügel's major work, *The Mystical Element of Religion*, as regards Christ, could be said of his writings as a whole: 'She [St Catherine] is, as it were the finite centre of the circle whose circumference is nowhere and whose real centre is the Incarnate Logos.' Maurice Nédoncelle also believes Christ to be the framework of von Hügel's thought: 'It is the idea of the Incarnation which serves as Ariadne's thread', *von Hügel*, pp. 170–3. Also, Heaney, op. cit., p. 141: 'First, his thought is theocentric, but without heavy Trinitarian emphasis; second, it is incarnational, but with a stronger emphasis on Christ in glory than on the Incarnate in history; third, it is ecclesiological, but with more attention to the Church as a reli-

gious philosophy than as an organic mystery.' The difference here is perhaps more apparent than real (as our own remarks on Christocentrism may show). The sheer preponderance of von Hügel's preoccupation with the problem of God and his exegetical conclusions on the Church and on Christ (especially in the *Quinzaine* controversy with Blondel) lend strong initial support to Heaney's view. The reader may judge as we go along. Finally, Evelyn Underhill's assessment of von Hügel's governing idea and experience, though differently formulated, is, I believe, in basic agreement with the position taken by Cock, Nédoncelle and this study. For Underhill see the discussion on monism, pp. 65–6.

5. The reader is alerted to this circumstance. A frequent return to this text may serve at once to unify the present study and to test its validity.
6. *ME1*, pp. 26–7.
7. In Christology, a preoccupation with the integral humanity of Christ (its danger will be Nestorianism, a term taken to mean denial of the eternal Logos as the only personal subject of Christ's humanity, resulting in a moral and not a hypostatic union); as opposed to Alexandrian, which emphasizes the divinity and unity of Christ (its danger will be monophysitism, in which the humanity is absorbed by the divinity, or at least where the integrity of Jesus' human intellect and will is endangered). See Karl Rahner and Herbert Vorgrimler, *Theological Dictionary*, New York, 1965.
8. *EA2*, p. 223.
9. Ibid., pp. 195–7, 223. For von Hügel's attitude on the biblical evidence, see his disapproval of Loisy's judgment on Christ's divinity 'comme étrangère à l'object d'un enseignement scientifique sur l'histoire de Jésus', quoted in Alfred Loisy, *Mémoires*, III, p. 156.
10. See p. 33. My italics.
11. *RP*, pp. 670–1. My italics.
12. *EA2*, pp. 248–9. We thus abruptly encounter, in its central, incarnational context, von Hügel's critical realism. It is just here that Kant's general position is judged hostile to incarnation. See *EL*, pp. 158–66.
13. *EA2*, pp. 107–8. Some italics are mine.
14. *EA1*, p. 125. And see *CE*, p. 296.
15. *LN*, p. xxxi.
16. *EA2*, pp. 264–5.
17. Ibid.; and see *LN*, p. 154.
18. *LN*, p. 55.
19. Ibid., p. 113. We shall consider the Church later in this study. It may be said now, however, that the Church *is* part of Christ's mystery, as

the earlier of the two statements makes clear. And see letter to Tyrrell, 7 December 1908, *BM Add. MS* 44931: 'What is occasioned in history by His Spirit is part of His larger biography.'

20. *RG*, p. 36.
21. *EA1*, pp. 134–5. This view, well stated here, lays the foundation for von Hügel's extraordinary breadth of ecumenical, and especially of other-than-Christian and other-than-religious interests. The position is nuanced and yet somehow seems to suffer from insufficient consideration of the pre-existence of Christ and of the Church, the role of Christ in creation, and of all grace as the grace of Christ and therefore as, in some sense, ecclesial. The position does avoid, however, the provoking aspect of the 'anonymous Christian' concept.
22. *LN*, p. xxxvi. The same point is powerfully made, *EA1*, pp. 293–4, in the context of the supernatural as God's real, yet *incomplete*, presence, even to the humanity of Jesus.
23. *EA2*, pp. 217–18.
24. Ibid., and see *ME2*, pp. 263–7, esp. p. 267.
25. Nédoncelle, *von Hügel*, p. 100, commenting on *EL*, p. 198.
26. Jungmann, Joseph, S.J., *The Place of Christ in Liturgical Prayer*, 2nd revised edition, London, 1965, esp. pp. 105–23, 144–90. Also relevant is a discussion of the question within the context of the New Testament itself, pp. 127–43.
27. See *CE*, p. 308 *et passim* for remarks about the celestial Christ. I have found this essay of little use in this section, despite its subject-matter, which concerns the Jesus of history and Christ of faith controversy, where von Hügel largely sides with Loisy against Blondel. The concern is exegetical and historical, and much of the tone is polemical. The earthly Jesus is seen as mainly Synoptic, while the celestial Christ, mostly Pauline and Johannine, tends to become a spiritual force, largely without biography. Individual statements correct this impression (e.g., p. 301: 'Là, au contraire . . .'), but the atmosphere on the whole is divisive and little resembles *ME1*, pp. 26–7, and other texts we have cited. The approach is never wholly abandoned (see *EA1*, p. 142, where the results are even more complicated).
28. The Holy Spirit is rarely individualized in von Hügel. But see *ME1*, p. 26. The explanation for this may lie in his understanding of St Paul: *ME2*, pp. 84, 320–2, and *EL*, pp. 67–72.
29. It is within this framework, I believe, of Jesus *vis-à-vis* the Father, that we must locate and understand von Hügel's major preoccupation with the problem of God, which we shall consider in Chapter 3.
30. Patrick Burke similarly asks for a 'patrocentric' Christology in 'Man

without Christ: An Approach to Hereditary Sin', *Theological Studies*, March 1968, p. 12.

31. *EA1*, p. 84: These needs are not appearances, not 'sheer condescensions', but are 'real for the human soul of Jesus', as we have him in the Synoptics.
32. *EA2*, pp. 196–7, 220–1; *LN*, pp. 124–5.
33. *EU*, pp. 79–80. Von Hügel was Underhill's spiritual director from 1921 until his death in 1925.
34. See below, on monism; and Chapter 4, on personality. Our central text, *ME1*, pp. 26–7, makes the point massively.
35. See, for example, *CE*, pp. 299–303; *EA1*, pp. 81–4; and *RG*, p. 14, where Aquinas is praised for giving us a 'joyous and active' Jesus and not just a suffering and redemptive one. Von Hügel can be unintentionally comic too: see *EU*, p. 82, on cats.
36. I.e. Blondel's position on Christ's human knowledge.
37. Letter to Blondel, 12 February 1903, *St Andrews MS* B3280.H8: '. . . c'est une assez grande absence, dans son ton et son tempérament moral et spirituel, de cette noble faim et soif de l'absolu, de l'Ultime, que j'aime si éperdument chez Platon et Plotin, chez St Augustin. . . . Vous avez tant vous-même de ce ton, mon cher Ami.'

    'A votre thèse, je ne vois vraiment pas comment, votre science qui n'a rien et rien d'implicite et d'instinctif, reste véritablement humaine, du moins humaine *in statu viatoris*, et en un sens le moins du monde touchant, modèle, et partant pénétrant en son attrait rédemptif. Et cependant, je suppose bien que c'est pour cela, ou pour cela aussi, que nous avons reçu l'Emmanuel. Pas, je crois, pour ne nous être qu'une vision . . . mais pour nous être la manifestation, touchante même en sa perfection, de l'exercise ineffablement parfait de toutes nos fonctions fondamentales. . . . De cette façon seulement nous serait-il réellement, *non seulement le modèle de ce qu'il faut être; mais encore le modèle de la manière de le devenir*. De cette façon aussi la doctrine que la vertu nait du contact avec les choses, des luttes, des conflits, et jamais, au grand jamais, en sa grande plénitude possible à l'humanité, de leur simple esquivage, ou simplement en planant par dessus, même où cela est possible, serait non nié mais exemplifié dans le Chef des Saints. Car enfin, mon cher Ami, quel aide réel, en ce point de nos *luttes*, de mon contact douloureux, mais innocent et fructifiant . . ., quel aide-modèle en ceci me fournira une vie intérieure . . ., qui ne connaît *rien* de l'implicite, de mes obscurités, de mes tâtonnements; de mes pauvres héroïsmes *humains*, en tant que ceux-ci dépendent de ceux-là: et, je vous le demande, lequel de mes petits héroïsmes n'en dépend pas en très grande partie?

'Je sais bien que les théologiens ont la plus grande répugnance de s'apprivoiser à des faits pareils. . . . N'est-ce pas qu'ici encore nous retrouvons trop le *concept grec* de la perfection humaine? Perfection si abstraite, tellement au dessus et en dehors des choses et des occasions, toute statique, et de pure lumière et harmonie ininterrompue. Notre Maître, mon Ami, c'est plus, ce n'est pas cela: Nazareth, Capharnaum, Gethsemani, Golgotha, c'est plus, c'est autre que l'Académie, la Stoa Poecile. . . . Le naturalisme réel est bien plutôt du côté d'un Christ à la vertu facile, que d'un Christ à l'immolation coûteuse. Contact, contact pur et sanctifiant, avec les états essentiels de l'homme, je vous prie, et non le contraire; et cela aussi pour notre Modèle et notre Mesure, ou bien il cesse d'être l'un et l'autre.'

38. *RG*, p. 30. And see *LN*, p. 109; and Martin Green, op. cit., pp. 79–81. Green's discussion of von Hügel is endlessly stimulating if somewhat categorical. It may be well to notice at this point Green's view, ibid., p. 92, that 'von Hügel probably could be convicted of telling us not of a risen and triumphant Christ, but of a suffering and dying one'. The issue is central, and we will return to it, pp. 61–4. On the question of Christian and Devout humanism the reader may wish to refer to the classical treatment in Henri Bremond, op. cit., esp. pp. 3–15, 397–405.
39. *EU*, p. 75.
40. Ibid., p. 98; and see pp. 71, 77, 80, for examples of von Hügel's direction of Underhill on the subject of Christ and Holy Communion.

There are many passages in von Hügel's writings which directly touch on Christ or the Incarnation in connection with a specific issue. Some of these texts will appear later in this study. But see esp. *CFA*, pp. 81–2; and letter to Gallarati-Scotti, undated, *St Andrews MS* 2649: von Hügel has mentioned frequentation of Mass and sacraments, 'daily visits and spiritual reading', and the rosary: 'For thus the very activities of one's daily life, keep one, thank God, well in touch with, completely under the great vitalizing shadow of, the great incarnational doctrine and practice of the Church, according to which man reaches God through the God-man; and God gives himself to us in and through Christ, specially present and energizing in and through his visible representatives and followers, and those sensible means and veils, the sacraments, so profoundly in keeping with the mysterious double-sidedness, the spirit and matter of our human nature. The widest universalism and most profound spirituality are thus ever resought in the divine homeliness of the apparently local and contingent.'

41. See pp. 30 ff.
42. *EA2*, p. 246; and see *GS*, p. 205.
43. *EA1*, pp. xv–xvi.
44. See *EA1*, pp. xv–xvii, 140–2; and *RG*, pp. 27–30, for remarks on methodology, especially the genetic and analytic methods.
45. We have looked ahead here somewhat, as well as back. See Chapter 4 for a discussion of the individual and the personal. For Jesus as both successive and simultaneous (in the Synoptic and Johannine portraits), see *ME1*, pp. 36–7.
46. For John of the Cross and Darwin, see indexes of *ME2*, *EL* and *EA1*.
47. *EL*, pp. 1–3. Notice that the first statement is already qualified, with man's likeness and unlikeness to God thus early in view.

    Von Hügel digs deep. *Eternal Life* and major portions of several essays are the result. We mention below only the highlights of his search. The reader is further warned that he will find here no judgment of von Hügel as scholar in the history of religions and philosophy. This is neither our purpose nor our competence. Throughout this study we are concerned with von Hügel's spiritual doctrine as found in his writings. Our one concern with his reading is its effect upon that doctrine.
48. *EL*, pp. 23–7; *ME2*, pp. 192–3, 197–9. The last citation places and answers objections to belief in immortality, the most interesting being that belief in an individual future life fosters a selfish, ungenerous type of religion, and that it is plausible to say that denial of such a belief fosters heroic concentration on earthly aspiration and endeavour.
49. *EL*, pp. 8–10; *EA1*, p. 89; *RG*, pp. 215–17.
50. *EL*, pp. 286, 292–302; *EA1*, p. 132, and p. 49: Evolution is 'modal', and gives us at most 'not the ultimate *why*, but the intermediate *how*'.
51. *EL*, pp. 32–42; *EA2*, pp. 50–1, 161; *PC*, p. 384.
52. *EL*, pp. 66–78 (notice, p. 76, in the comment on John 6:40, eternal life means indissolubility and is thus not a consequence, but the 'presupposition of the Resurrection'); *ME1*, pp. 32–9. We omit the Synoptic teaching because it will occupy us fully in the next section. Enough here to notice that von Hügel rates the Synoptic teaching above that of Paul, John, the Areopagite writings, and Catherine of Genoa. As *ME2*, p. 110, makes clear, his reasons are incarnational.
53. St Augustine, as quoted and commented on in *EL*, pp. 87–94. See also *EA1*, pp. 86–7.
54. *EL*, pp. 342, 368–9, 378; and see pp. 159–61, where von Hügel gives Kant his due on the necessity of human freedom and becoming, while

yet stressing eternal life as adoration, the 'affirmation of, and joy in, what already *is*'.

55. Ibid., p. 357; and see pp. 315–19.
56. See ibid., pp. 364–71, for von Hügel's summary and pp. 383–4 for the point we are about to make.
57. Ibid., p. 1, already cited; and see pp. 383–4.
58. Letter to Tyrrell, 7 July 1900, in *SL*, pp. 85–7.
59. *EA2*, p. 139; *EL*, p. 297; *PC*, p. 372.
60. *EL*, p. 231.
61. *EA1*, p. 215.
62. Ibid.; *EL*, p. 231. Von Hügel, as we saw in Chapter 1, is wary of 'clarity', both in life and in thought. It is probably the main cause of his early animus towards the scholastics.
63. *EL*, p. 302, quoting Bosanquet's estimate of Bergson.
64. *EA2*, pp. 139–40, quoting James Ward and William James. And see *EL*, pp. 105–6, where von Hügel compares Aquinas' *aevum* with Bergson's *durée*.
65. *EA2*, p. 50, where he cites H. J. Holtzmann.
66. *EA1*, pp. 69–70; *EL*, p. 231.
67. *EL*, p. 231. My italics. And see ibid., pp. 383–4. For other texts on Bergsonian time: *ME1*, pp. xvii–xviii; *ME2*, p. 247; *PC*, pp. 383–4. Many of these passages offer severe criticism as well as appreciation. Von Hügel is working from the *Essai sur les Données Immédiates de la Conscience* and *l'Evolution Créatrice*. Nédoncelle, *von Hügel*, pp. 149–50, remarks that the criticisms lose 'a good deal of their force' in the light of Bergson's later writings.
68. *ME2*, p. 248, again utilizing Holtzmann.
69. The essay, 'Suffering and God', *EA2*, pp. 167–213, is a discussion in depth of this question. And see *RG*, pp. 244–5; and *EL*, p. 286, where, with some of the other passages just cited, the doctrine of Creation is treated in its relation to time and/or epigenesis. The positions taken here, I believe, explain why, when von Hügel discusses prayer, questions about its causality and efficacy do not arise. C. S. Lewis works out the position in *Letters to Malcolm: Chiefly on Prayer*, London, 1964, esp. pp. 69 ff., 141–2.
70. *EA2*, pp. 49–51.
71. Ibid., pp. 51, 53. It is duration, not time, which captures 'the very notion of worth'. And see *EL*, p. 298: 'Duration is . . . at its highest, not in its element of change, but . . . of permanence.'
72. And as human, his becoming is 'twice-born', for as man Jesus too is subject to the twofold gift and task: to become human: spirit, and to

be sanctified: openness to Spirit. Von Hügel holds firmly, if not always clearly, the reality and distinction of nature and grace, the natural and the supernatural. For the notion of the two-step or twice-born, see *ME2*, p. 342, where he quotes William James; also *EA1*, p. 233; and *RG*, pp. 213–14.

73. Chapter 3, on God, and Chapters 4 and 5, on personality and science, will work out some of the consequences of this dualistic position. Pages 64 ff. of this chapter treat the question of dualism as such.

74. Letter to Tyrrell, 31 December 1898, in *VH & T*, pp. 56–68, insists on time as not just 'the preface or prelude to eternity', but 'as already environing . . . eternity'. Nédoncelle makes the same point in a thumbnail sketch of *EL* in 'von Hügel on God', p. 7.

75. *EA2*, p. 52. My italics.

76. Review of Friedrich Heiler's *Das Gebet*, *International Review of Missions*, April 1921, p. 267.

77. *RG*, pp. 117–18.

78. Ibid.

79. Letter of 1 September 1919, in *LN*, pp. 58–60.

80. Ibid., letter of 10 August 1920, pp. 93–5; and also pp. xi–xii.

81. For asceticism and involvement, *EL*, pp. 315–17; monasticism and Coventry Patmore's Christian sexualism, letter to Tyrrell, 20 December 1900, *BM Add. MS* 44927, and more fully in letter to Maude Petre, 20 April 1902, *BM Add. MS* 45361.

82. *CE*, p. 287.

83. *EA2*, pp. 53–5; *ME2*, pp. 285–6.

84. For von Hügel's appreciations and criticisms of St Catherine, especially on the question of time, see *ME1*, pp. ix, 105–7, 237–9; *ME2*, pp. 90, 211–13, and a comparative estimate, p. 110, already cited; also a long letter to Tyrrell on mysticism, 26 September 1898, in *SL*, pp. 71–4.

85. *EL*, p. 94, already cited.

86. Letter to Tyrrell, 28 November 1902, in *VH & T*, pp. 108–10; for 1912: *EL*, pp. viii–x, 56–66; 1916: *EA1*, pp. 81–4; 1919: *EA1*, pp. 119–43. There is also relevant material in the 1916 study on morality and war, *GS*, esp. pp. 39–41. The book's thesis is argued largely in terms of Kingdom and Church. The result is a dualist ethic (see pp. 107–17).

87. *EL*, pp. viii–ix; *EA1*, pp. x–xi, 119–20.

88. *EL*, p. ix. Ibid., pp. 258–9, analogously formulates philosophy as either 'civilized' or 'wild'.

89. *EA1*, p. 120.

90. Letter of 31 December 1921–3 January 1922, *St Andrews MS* 30420.

Von Hügel is quoted to the same effect in Gwendolen Greene, 'Thoughts from Baron von Hügel', *Dublin Review*, 1931, pp. 257–8.

91. *EL*, p. ix; *EA1*, p. 120.
92. *EL*, pp. ix–x, 62, footnote; *EA1*, p. 121.
93. *EA1*, p. 81. My italics.
94. Ibid., p. 82; *EL*, p. 59.
95. *EA1*, p. 120.
96. *EL*, pp. 59–61.
97. *EA1*, p. 82; *EL*, pp. 56–9.
98. *EA1*, p. 82.
99. Ibid., p. 121.
100. *EA1*, p. 81.
101. Ibid., pp. 82–3, 121–3; *EA2*, p. 81; Gwendolen Greene, *Dublin Review*, 1931, pp. 257–9. Greene's quotations from von Hügel are from conversations that began in 1919 and lasted until his death in 1925 (see *LN*, p. xi).
102. *EA1*, pp. 123–4; Greene, op. cit., pp. 258–9. Von Hügel is well aware that exegetical and dogmatic questions arise here with regard to Christ's divinity, knowledge and inerrancy. In addition to texts cited, see *EA1*, pp. 124–6; letter to Blondel, 12 February 1903, *St Andrews MS* B3280.H8, previously cited; *CE*, p. 302; and letter to Clement Webb, 20 March 1909, in *SL*, pp. 157–60.
103. See letter to Tyrrell already cited on p. 52.
104. Greene, op. cit., pp. 258–9.
105. See p. 52.
106. *EA1*, p. 123.
107. Ibid., pp. 81–3, 124. My italics. The *Sitz im Leben Jesu* application of the Isaian title to Jesus, disputed by von Hügel's contemporaries, is allowed today. See John L. McKenzie, *Dictionary of the Bible*, Milwaukee, 1965, pp. 791–4; and the same author, *The Power and the Wisdom*, Milwaukee, 1965, pp. 58 ff., 90 ff. In the light of the central conception just enunciated, it is not surprising that suffering and joy are frequent themes in von Hügel's writings.
108. See p. 52.
109. *RGM*, pp. 659–60.
110. *EA1*, pp. 126, 130–2. Page 130: 'There certainly lurks here far more than a merely racial category of thought'.
111. Ibid., pp. 126–7. My italics.
112. *LN*, p. 73: 'that tenderness in austerity, and that austerity in tenderness, which is the very genius of Christianity.'
113. *EA1*, p. 160, quoting Ernst Troeltsch.

114. Ibid., p. 127; *LN*, pp. xix, 109.
115. *EA2*, p. 82; and see p. 81.
116. *EL*, p. 62. To this extent at least, the Church, as product of the prophetical movement 'essential to the physiognomy of Our Lord' (*EA1*, p. 81), is of divine institution. We will return to this in Chapter 5.
117. Ibid.
118. Ibid., pp. 63–4; and see pp. 316–17, for the social and ascetical force of both movements. The context is von Hügel's discussion of Marx and secularism, which begins on p. 304; also *EA2*, p. 274, where the incarnational implications of our present point are stressed.
119. *EL*, p. 65. My italics.
120. Ibid., pp. 64–5.
121. *EA1*, p. 129, where he adds that this synthesis is 'the most original and the most divinely true of all the discoveries and powers of Christianity'.
122. Ibid., p. 130.
123. Ibid. The final point made here is repeated, with regard to pantheism, p. 132; and more generally, p. 134. The two movements are related to the essence of religion: *God is*, in *GS*, p. 73. This latter points the present discussion towards our next chapter.
124. *EA1*, p. 138.
125. *EA2*, p. 273.
126. *EA1*, p. 139.
127. Ibid., pp. 139–40; *EA2*, p. 273.
128. Ibid., pp. 273–4; and *EA1*, pp. 139–40, just cited; also *EL*, pp. 312–23, esp. pp. 318–19. A very real, but really limited, doctrine of divinization is thus in view.
129. Letter to Kemp Smith, 19 April 1919, *St Andrews MS* 30420. On social idealisms and utopias see *EL*, pp. 58–9; *EA1*, pp. 191–4, 201.
130. Martin Green, op. cit., p. 92.
131. *LN*, pp. xxxi–xxxii.
132. It is not my intention to badger Mr Green, whose treatment of von Hügel is often persuasive and largely favourable. And indeed it is precisely von Hügel as humanist which attracts Mr Green. His remark rather gives me an occasion. I do, however, question whether he has thoroughly considered what is the necessary ground for a Christian, and not just a theistic, humanism, and what such a humanism will look like where it allows the Cross as well as the Resurrection full and freely willed effect in the continuing history of the corporate Christ.

It should be said too that Mr Green is evaluating biographical as well as literary evidence.

133. Gwendolen Greene, *Two Witnesses*, London, 1930, pp. 94, 101, 140–1; and the same author, 'Baron Friedrich von Hügel', *Pax*, September 1932, p. 131. But see *RG*, p. 95: 'We can also see that beauty and the sense of beauty come from God, by noticing how narrow and hard, or vague and empty, remains the specifically religious sense in souls greatly lacking in the aesthetic capacity.'

134. De la Bedoyère, op. cit. See for example Chapter 1, 'The Faultless Young Man', pp. 3–22. There is often an atmosphere dominated by suffering and struggle. And this in addition to von Hügel's growing concern about immanentism, which in so far as Christian at all, would mean for him, in our present context, a *too* realized eschatology. For further remarks on von Hügel's temperament, see his own vivid pen sketches in *LN*, pp. xxv–xxvi, 101–2; and a letter to his daughter Hildegarde quoted in de la Bedoyère, pp. 117–18.

135. In *SL*, pp. 60–2.

136. *LN*, p. xvi.

137. E.g., *EA1*, p. 18; *EA2*, pp. 242, 247.

138. Letter to Tyrrell, 4 June 1902, in *VH& T*, pp. 107–8.

139. *LN*, p. xix; and see ibid., p. 84: 'Good Friday *and* Easter . . . only this twin fact gives us Christianity.' *RG*, p. 14, asks for a Jesus Christ who is 'joyous and active' as well as 'suffering and redemptive'.

140. Ibid., p. xliii. Von Hügel's central positions in this whole section on the Kingdom and Parousia are substantively maintained in Rudolf Schnackenburg's masterly *God's Rule and Kingdom*, London, 2nd edition, 1968.

141. *EA1*, dedication.

142. See p. 40; and *CE*, p. 288.

143. See p. 41.

144. *ME1*, p. xvi.

145. *PC*, p. 379: 'L'amour éffectif de nos ennemis, le pardon réel . . ., l'humilité vraie, profonde, le sens du pêché, l'experience de la conversion, la conviction du Donné, de la Grâce, la soif si noble du non-contingent et du non-successif, de la Réalité Parfaite, Simultanée: tout cela . . . perd rapidément sa couleur native, sa poignance virile et libératrice, sous l'influence de n'importe quel Monisme.'

146. *RG*, p. v.

147. Ibid., pp. 3–5, 36, *et passim* in the introductory first chapter.

148. Ibid., p. 30.

149. Evelyn Underhill, *Mixed Pasture*, pp. 218–21. Von Hügel writes of the

priority of 'creatureliness of mind' in connection with his daughter Gertrude's crisis of faith, in letter to Tyrrell, 26 January 1898, in *VH & T*, pp. 20–5. See also *RG*, pp. 19–20: the 'creaturely mind' of 'the young Carpenter, the lover of the individual lilies and sparrows'.

150. Underhill, op. cit., p. 211. See *RG*, pp. 48–9, for the consequences in epistemology, and the humility required; also *ME1*, pp. xxxi–xxxii, for a description of a spirituality of the finite and the infinite 'across the centuries'.

151. *EL*, pp. 197 (Schleiermacher), 304–12 (Marxist secularism), 233–44; and *EA1*, pp. 29–41 (Feuerbach).

152. *EL*, pp. 110–11 (Eckhart); *ME2*, p. 328, for the general tendency of mystics towards pantheism and monism; *EA1*, p. 220, for the results of monism for the doctrine of 'Abiding Consequences' (Hell).

153. *EL*, p. 111. This passage also touches on *preliminary* monism, of which von Hügel forcefully approves. It will provide a central element in our discussion of the place of science and of things in von Hügel's spiritual doctrine. See Chapter 5.

154. *EA1*, p. 132. And see *EL*, pp. 280–3.

155. *RG*, p. 32.

156. Ibid., and also p. 3; *ME1*, pp. xv–xvi and 231–3, where the *practice* of the mystics (here Catherine) with respect to humility – often as opposed to their *doctrine* – prevents pantheism and monism. Chapter 3, p. 99, also touches briefly on Hegel.

157. *ME1*, pp. 65–6.

158. Ibid., p. 68. My italics. And see *ME2*, p. 134, for a definition of 'living simplicity'.

159. *ME1*, pp. 66–7. And see main text, ibid., pp. 26–7, already cited, pp. 34–5, above.

160. *ME2*, p. 249.

161. Ibid., pp. 250–5. Much of this is developed from an earlier article, *ET*, pp. 369–71.

162. Letter of 26 September 1900, in *SL*, pp. 88–96, esp. pp. 93–4. For the same point twenty-one years later, see *EA1*, p. xii, where von Hügel writes of his 'conviction . . . as to the necessity, for all fruitful human life, and especially for all powerful religious life, amongst men here below, of friction, tension, rivalry . . ., between this religious life and men's other . . . tasks; and . . . the persistent danger . . . of working religion in such a way as to remove from its path, as far as ever possible, any and all of these frictions which in reality are essentially necessary to its own force and fruitfulness'. He calls it 'a tendency to self-starvation' and a 'grave . . . antinomy for the

practical life'. See also Chapter 1, pp. 30–1, and Chapter 5, on Science; and *ME1*, p. 54, where religion itself is seen as a tension: 'I believe because I am told, because it is true, because it answers to my deepest interior experiences and needs.' This is a paraphrase of the famous three elements of religion: the institutional, intellectual and mystical (see Chapter 4).

163. *LN*, pp. xi, 61–2, 80.

164. Quoted in *EU*, p. 82.

165. Underhill, *Mixed Pasture*, p. 231; and see letter quoted in *EU*, p. 71, where von Hügel asks her to develop 'some non-religious interest'.

166. Undated letter, 1921, cited in *EU*, p. 75. In his exegetical labours and especially in his lifelong interest in geology, we see von Hügel as good as his own advice. There is a pleasant, if by hindsight sad, picture in his last letter to Tyrrell, 6 May 1909, cited in Maude Petre, *Autobiography and Life of George Tyrrell*, London, 1912, 2 vols., II, p. 97: 'I am fifty-seven yesterday and am giving myself a set of newer geological books, a geological hammer and a set of geological specimens. So expect to tramp about with me to gravel-pits and quarries, please.' Tyrrell died in July. This preoccupation with the poor, as urged on Underhill, by the way, was apparently a staple of von Hügel's spiritual direction (Gwendolen Greene, *Two Witnesses*, p. 154).

167. The major discussions of Troeltsch may be found in *ME2*, pp. 273, 358–62; *EL*, pp. 199–200; *EA1*, pp. 144–94 (esp., for our purpose here, pp. 165–9); and Ernst Troeltsch, *Christian Thought*, London, 1923, edited with introduction by von Hügel, pp. xi–xxxi, where von Hügel points out the differences between his own outlook and that of Troeltsch.

168. See Chapter 6. The citations in this present section are all from *EA1*, pp. 165–9; and *ME2*, pp. 358–62, and see p. 366. Both von Hügel and Troeltsch see in this whole conception of doubleness a metaphysical structure, whose definitive resolution can only be metaphysical: life after death (*EA1*, p. 169). They also find in it the doctrine of the natural-supernatural: 'a tension, a friction, a one thing at work in distinctly another thing – like yeast in meal, like salt in meat' (*EA2*, p. 219).

169. *ME2*, p. 297.

170. Ibid., pp. 126–9.

171. *LN*, pp. 175–7, shows von Hügel's awareness of excessive tension in the spiritual direction of his daughter Gertrude. *CE*, pp. 296–7, shows a tendency to friction for its own sake. The context is somewhat

polemical, as the contemporary correspondence with Blondel indicates. Von Hügel is most rightly defending here the principle of the independence of history and biblical criticism as intellectual disciplines, a principle valiantly fought for by Loisy. Loisy's application of that principle and von Hügel's partial but very real defence of that application is another and very vast subject. For the distinction between principle and application of principle, see, e.g., letter to Clement Webb, 9 March 1908, in *SL*, pp. 145–7. Von Hügel's ardent defence of the principle of secular autonomy is strongly prophetic of *Gaudium et Spes*, no. 36 (Abbott, op. cit., pp. 233–4). Finally, and also pertinent to *CE*: to the extent that von Hügel there calls for any *excessive* separation of the Jesus of history and the Christ of faith, he is imperilling both dualism itself and the fruitful 'interaction' and 'friction' he would wish to demand. Nédoncelle, *von Hügel*, p. 188, perceptively suggests that 'such a dichotomy is in direct opposition to the Baron's "incarnational" method', and is 'a very unHügelian idea'.

172. Letter to Emelia Fogelklou Norlind, 11 January 1911, cited in de la Bedoyère, op. cit., p. 254. My italics.
173. See p. 33; and *EL*, p. 317.
174. *CE*, pp. 286–8: 'l'unité prematurée . . . Il faut accepter la lutte . . ., la guerre . . ., il faut se crucifier . . . La victoire . . . c'est une unité organique, et elle ne s'atteint que par une lente harmonisation.'
175. *LN*, p. xxi; *ME1*, p. xxvi; *ME2*, pp. 138–9; undated letter to Wilfrid Ward, in Maisie Ward, *The Wilfrid Wards*, pp. 323–5; and letter to Maude Petre in *SL*, p. 95, already cited. Von Hügel's writings are crowded with expressions of tension, paradox and antinomy. Many have appeared already in this study, and we shall see others. P. Franklin Chambers, *Friedrich von Hügel*, London, 1945, paperback edition, 1964, pp. 36–8, has collected a large number of such sayings. *EL*, pp. 386–7, gives particularly rich, synthetic statement to this view of reality as organic harmony through tension. And again, here at the end, I would refer the reader to *ME1*, pp. 26–7.
176. Letter to Auguste Valensin, 31 December 1926, cited in Christopher F. Mooney, S.J., *Teilhard de Chardin and the Mystery of Christ*, London, 1966, p. 263, n. 54. A 1955 statement, ibid., pp. 209–10, expresses a similar view in language more characteristically Teilhardian.
177. See p. 53.
178. See p. 38.
179. *RP*, pp. 670–1; letter to Kemp Smith, 20 December 1922, *St Andrews MS* 30420.

180. Letter to Loisy, March 1910, cited in Alfred Loisy, *Mémoires*, III, pp. 155–7: '. . . je crois que cela (la divinité de Jésus) peut avoir ou ne peut pas avoir de sens acceptable pour l'homme moderne, selon que l'on maintient ou l'on abandonne la foi dans le transcendant, l'ontologique, Dieu.'

CHAPTER THREE

1. *EA2*, p. 246.
2. See Chapter 2, p. 73.
3. Letter to Tyrrell, 12 June 1905, in *SL*, pp. 129–32. My italics.
4. *EA1*, p. 46. The historical-institutional and intellectual elements of religion, together with non-religious, especially scientific, values, are treated in Chapters 4 and 5.
5. *ME2*, pp. 394–5. My italics.
6. *ME1*, pp. xv–xvi.
7. Ibid., p. v.
8. *RG*, pp. 80–1. And see ibid., pp. 3–4, where von Hügel describes his early attempts to formulate 'these deepest things' with an 'Idealistic philosophy of an Hegelian type'. It is the *formulation* of religious experience just here, and not the experience, which develops and alters as von Hügel becomes clear on the '*transcendence* present in all our knowledge, so that knowledge is never primarily simply a knowledge of our states, but a knowledge' of objects. 'Realism is in possession', and it was the study of geology 'which made the notion that the human mind creates reality a preposterous one'. Such subjectivism is never really in evidence in von Hügel's writings. His major work rather displays a subjectivity apparently heavily influenced by Blondel. The next section of this chapter illustrates this strand of his thought, which Nédoncelle, quoting Sciacca, calls 'objective interiority'. It is an approach that is with von Hügel to the end (see, e.g., *RG*, pp. 60, 62–4). In later life, however, through the mounting influence of one line of Troeltsch's thought, von Hügel comes to admire Aquinas, and we get examples of objective 'exteriority' in the hints of a cosmological approach, ibid., p. 40 (chaos-cosmos), which becomes a full-blown argument, pp. 55–8. Von Hügel himself gives a rather stern judgment of his intellectual odyssey on this whole question in a letter to René Guiran, 11 July 1921, in *SL*, pp. 333–7. But de la Bedoyère, op. cit., pp. 328–31, suggests, and I think correctly, that the change was more apparent than real. Some of the early texts we

have used in Chapter 2, and others we will cite in this chapter, may indicate this. For Nédoncelle, cited above, see 'von Hügel on God', pp. 19–20. Nédoncelle notices that von Hügel's basic insistence is upon the objectivity of cognition and the degrees of the real. 'His proof of God proceeds by way of anthropology but transcends it; it is interior to us but leaves us within the cosmos.' It is seen to be 'a proof by disengagement: a certain inevitability of God is vitally experienced before being thought'.

The distinction (not separation) met in this passage between religion and ethics ('what is' and what 'ought to be') is fundamental in von Hügel's experience and doctrine. It will come up again in our study. Among many texts, see *ME2*, pp. 272 ff.; *EA1*, pp. 22–3; and letter to Martin D'Arcy, 9 January 1919, in 'Friedrich von Hügel's Letters to Martin D'Arcy', edited by Joseph Whelan, *The Month*, July–August 1969, pp. 24–7.

9. *EL*, pp. xi–xii. In a letter to Tyrrell, 12 June 1905, in *SL*, pp. 129–32, von Hügel speaks of the necessity of transcendence and of his fear that his forthcoming book (*ME*) will have to create in its readers the need it is trying to satisfy. See also letter to Newsom, 21 September 1911, ibid., p. 192, which speaks of 'this (depend upon it now dominant) subjectivist direction'.
10. *RG*, p. 5.
11. *LN*, pp. xviii–xix. And see letter to Maude Petre, 2 January 1914, in *SL*, pp. 205–6: 'God *is* overflowingly; and there is an end of that point. . . . it is we who are necessarily in movement and in becoming. Yet even we not altogether; even we not in the very best of what we are.'
12. *LN*, p. xxxiv. It is important to see that this judgment on humanitarianism comes as high praise. It is the most subtle enemy precisely because it is the most beautiful, and the truest, substitute for the fuller truth into which von Hügel seeks to incorporate it.
13. *PC*, p. 378: 'du reste il est clair que si la prière, surtout si l'adoration, sont l'âme de la réligion, la conviction ontologique, qui est la base de telle prière et adoration, doit pareillement appartenir à l'âme même de la réligion.'
14. The remark is paraphrased from *EL*, pp. 186–8, where von Hügel discusses Schleiermacher's *Reden über die Religion.*
15. *EA2*, p. 59; and *RG*, p. 71. This surely is the foundation of von Hügel's devotion to the adoration of the Holy Eucharist. The Diaries (see de la Bedoyère, op. cit., p. 23) show him habitually receiving Communion two or more times a week long before Pius X advocated frequent

Communion. But the diaries also show a habit of very frequent visits before the Blessed Sacrament, as does another testimony from von Hügel recorded in Greene, *Two Witnesses*, pp. 139–40. See *EA2*, pp. 248–9 (already cited, Chapter 2, p. 35), where after speaking of the presence, the isness, the reality of God, he remarks: 'The doctrine of, and the devotion to, Jesus Christ, truly present, God and man, body and soul, in the Holy Eucharist, thus forms, most characteristically, the very heart of the Catholic worship.' This double attitude towards the Eucharist, as meal *and* as the God of his adoration, is a striking instance of the '*et-et*' over the '*aut-aut*'. For an amusing anecdote on the 'arch-modernist' von Hügel and devotion to the Blessed Sacrament, see de la Bedoyère, op. cit., pp. 214–15; also *LN*, p. xx, for the proper place of awe and reverence and fear, and their relation to love and adoration. Finally *EA2*, pp. 157–8, where, on the basis of history, von Hügel justifies his use and restriction of the term religion.

It is clear, I take it, that von Hügel's central use of the term religion to indicate the fact of God as primarily constitutive of man's humanity and as indicating man's elementary response of adoration, while in no way arguing against a genuine, legitimate and broadly understood secularity, cannot finally adjust to the *vocabulary*, at least, of a 'religionless Christianity'. As von Hügel understands the term, man would not be fully human and would not be Christian at all without religion. Nor is all religion systematically to be seen as idolatry (see letter to Maude Petre, 8 June 1922, in *SL*, pp. 355–8; we will return to this letter again below). Bonhoeffer's programme for a Christian existence lived '*etsi deus non daretur*': 'God is teaching us that we must live as men who can get along very well without him', is susceptible of many interpretations (see the symposium *World Come of Age*, edited with Introduction by Ronald Gregor Smith, London, 1967, esp. p. 149, from which our citation of Bonhoeffer is taken). The extent to which von Hügel could endorse this, and what he would intend by doing so, ought to be clear in Chapter 5, where his approbation and understanding of 'preliminary pantheism' is considered.

16. *ME2*, pp. 46–7. This is also the criterion of Teresa of Avila and of John of the Cross (see ibid., pp. 48–52; and *LN*, p. 83). In intensely contemplative mystics, where these phenomena sometimes occur as valid, they represent the heavy price paid. *ME2*, pp. 57–61, has a fine discussion of whether 'the fruits of that life are worth that cost'. Von Hügel's ardent humanism is sternly probed, surely, in the remark, p. 57, that 'physical health [and this would include psycho-

logical health] is not the true end of human life, but only one of its most important means and conditions'. There is but one goal finally worthy of man: 'spiritual personality'. For von Hügel's profound disinterest in spiritualism, see letter in de la Bedoyère, op. cit., p. 304.

17. *ME1*, p. xii.
18. 'John, Gospel of St.', *Encyclopedia Britannica*, 11th edition, XV, p. 455. Von Hügel is extremely wary of that central and self-destructive defect of mysticism which involves the disregard or perversion of the other elements of religion, especially the historical-institutional element, with its incarnational and social dynamisms. He refers to such deficient mysticism as 'pure' or 'exclusive'. Mysticism that is properly located as just one factor of life, and one factor too of *religious* life, is called 'inclusive' or 'partial' mysticism. We will return to this question in the next two chapters. See *CFA*, pp. 79–82, for a list of the strengths and weaknesses of mysticism as seen in history; also *ME2*, p. 338, where the essential mystical experience which alone here concerns us is importantly argued as a product of the '*normal* consciousness of mankind' (my italics). This last point (surely crucial) is confirmed in letters to Maude Petre, 5 December 1899, in *SL*, pp. 82–5, esp. p. 84, no. 2, and to Mrs Lillie, 29 November 1922, ibid., pp. 360–6, esp. pp. 363–4.

Von Hügel is well aware that his view of mysticism as a *normal* state and as a consciousness of a *distinct*, *personal* Spirit is controversial (see *ME1*, pp. xi–xii). His positions are substantively reflected in a series of articles on mysticism by Rufus Jones and Abbot John Chapman in Hastings' *Encyclopedia of Religion and Ethics*, 1917, Vol. 9, pp. 83–4, 89–103 (though he would maintain against Jones that the mystical consciousness of Presence is not wholly 'undifferentiated' (p. 84), but is shot through with a concomitant consciousness of contingency. Nor would he accept as descriptive of orthodox Christian mysticism any idea of 'something in the human soul which is unsundered from the absolute, something which essentially is that reality' (ibid., where 'in' does not seem to name the indwelling of *distinct* Spirit). And he would find Chapman's article too little incarnational). I have also found helpful and generally congenial to von Hügel's thinking on mysticism Dakin, op. cit., pp. 164–7; Dom Cuthbert Butler, *Western Mysticism*, London, 1922, esp. pp. 3–4, 179–92, 307, 313; R. C. Zaehner, *Mysticism Sacred and Profane*, Oxford, 1957, esp. pp. xvii–xviii, 198–207; William Johnston, *The Mysticism of the Cloud of Unknowing*, New York, 1967, esp. pp. 257–84.

Finally, Abbot Chapman is enormously sensible and clear in 'What *Is* Mysticism?', an appendix in *The Spiritual Letters of Dom John Chapman*, London, 2nd edition, 1935, pp. 297–321, which in conscious regard of von Hügel (p. 313) nevertheless finds mysticism 'unusual', however 'ordinary' and 'natural' where it *does* occur. But this is not a real disagreement. 'Normal' for von Hügel does not mean frequent, as our present chapter, pp. 85–8, 113–16 (with their references), makes clear.

19. *RG*, pp. 135–6.
20. *EL*, pp. 15–23. This last point is fundamental with von Hügel (though not our subject just here) and the point ought not to seem subtle: preoccupation with God does not mean flight from the world or from the needs and love of other men. To deny this is certainly almost entirely to disagree with, if it is not to misunderstand, von Hügel's spirituality.
21. *EA1*, pp. 79–80. It is the inscription on von Hügel's tombstone (see Holland's memoir in *SL*, p. 52).
22. *EA2*, p. 264, already cited, Chapter 2, p. 37; *EA1*, p. 134.
23. The ethical equivalent of the prophetic, as opposed to this apocalyptic, movement would be the Golden Rule morality of Matt. 6:12. See *GS*, p. 71; also *ME2*, p. 274: 'We can perceive the difference between the two forces most clearly in Our Lord's life and teaching – say, the Sermon on the Mount; in the intolerableness of every exegesis which attempts to reduce the ultimate meaning and worth of this world-renewing religious document to what it has of literal applicability in the field of morality proper.'
24. *GS*, pp. 70–3. *ME2*, p. 269, supports Holtzmann's view that none of the New Testament writings – not even the Synoptic literature – is without 'metaphysical factors'.
25. See Chapter 2, p. 55.
26. *EA1*, pp. 133–4. It is a 'real' or 'inclusive' mysticism because it is neither static and essentialist nor simply relativist, but historical, incarnational, durational. The simultaneous is, of course, our point just here. The successive character of inclusive mysticism and spirituality will be a central implication of the following two chapters. Chapter 2 has already initiated our description of von Hügel's total spirituality under the rubrics of simultaneity and succession – with their perfect union in the incarnation of Christ – and of duration: the human Jesus' and all men's historically appropriated quasi-eternity.
27. *EL*, pp. 70–2. *EA1*, pp. 276–7, makes a similar point about the priority of God in relation both to the Church and to the eschatological

Kingdom: 'The root, the centre and the crown of all this social joy will be God.'

28. *EL*, p. 80.
29. *EA1*, pp. xiii, 39–40.
30. *EA2*, p. 59; *LN*, p. 54; *ME1*, pp. xvi–xvii.
31. *EA2*, pp. 130–1.
32. *LN*, p. 72. Dakin, op. cit., pp. 81–3, seems to accuse von Hügel of what he would wish most readily to admit. His thought *begins* and ends with the religious experience of God. There are no 'proofs'. *EA1*, pp. 43–4, gives an entirely clear statement of the basic method and procedure: The data of religious experience are given, not constructed. Life supplies the data, and critical reflection aims at showing the data to be 'what they themselves claim to be'.
33. *RG*, p. 36.
34. From a conversation recorded by Mrs Cecil Chapman and cited by Holland in *SL*, p. 51.
35. Letter to Juliet Mansel, 13 October 1911, in *SL*, pp. 193–4.
36. *LN*, p. xxx; *EA1*, p. 12; letter to Tyrrell, 12 June 1905, in *SL*, pp. 129–32; letter to Juliet Mansel, 24 May 1911, ibid., pp. 188–9; and letter to Mrs Lillie, 29 November 1922, ibid., pp. 360–4, esp. pp. 363–4.
37. Letter to Clement Webb, 15 February 1924, quoted in de la Bedoyère, op. cit., p. 311.
38. *EA1*, pp. 27–8. And see *ME2*, pp. 271–2.
39. Perhaps this was Loisy's option. See n. 140, below. Ethics is a large subject in von Hügel. The question is basically twofold: the dualist character of ethics; and the distinction of ethics from, and its relation to, religion. Some useful texts: *ME2*, pp. 259–60, 263–8, 272–4; *EA2*, pp. 157–64. Lester-Garland, op. cit., pp. 54–5, clearly states the central position.
40. See Chapter 2, p. 65.
41. *LN*, pp. xxxi, xxxvi. Von Hügel also thought that man's self-centredness had occasion for humility in the strong possibility of other intelligent worlds. See ibid., p. xxxi; *EL*, p. 277; and *EA1*, p. 136.
42. *EL*, p. 207.
43. Ibid., pp. 207, 216–18, 221–3; *EA1*, p. 136. Paul Tillich, *Perspectives on Nineteenth and Twentieth Century Protestant Theology*, London, 1967, pp. 115–18, treats this element of 'hybris' in Hegel's system. Here, as with von Hügel, the judgment of pride is passed on Hegel's system, not on his person.

    It may be helpful here to notice once again (see Chapter 2, n. 47) that the value for this study of von Hügel's use of the thought of other philosophers as a foil for the statement and understanding of his own spiritual doctrine – the value of this does not depend upon the accuracy of his reading of those other philosophers.

44. *EA1*, pp. 12–13.
45. Op. cit., pp. 6–7.
46. See *EA2*, pp. 217–26. The second half of the essay, 'The Facts and Truths Concerning the Soul Which Are of Most Importance in the Life of Prayer', pp. 226–42, will occupy us elsewhere. The entire essay is separately printed as *The Life of Prayer*, London, 1927, 1960.
47. *RP*, p. 676.
48. *EA1*, pp. 62–3.
49. Ibid., p. 63; and see pp. viii–ix. Also, letter to Tyrrell, 31 December 1898, in *VH & T*, pp. 56–68, esp. p. 59, where the remainder in this 'difference' is seen as the mystical element so neglected by 'scientific' theology.
50. *EA1*, p. 190. For von Hügel's theory of knowledge, see, e.g., *ME2*, pp. 275–84; *EL*, pp. 153–4; *EA1*, p. 189.
51. *PC*, p. 378: 'une affirmation ontologique'.
52. This point is absolutely clear in von Hügel, as texts just cited in n. 50, and others yet to be mentioned, indicate. Nédoncelle, *von Hügel*, pp. 86, 173, confirms this interpretation. I have found but two instances, in similar statements about man's experience of God, suggestive of the contrary: *PC*, p. 377, '*indirectement*', and there the term probably means that the experience is not *in vacuo*, but occurs in and on the occasion of the experience of the self and other, trans-subjective, finite realities; and *ME1*, p. 57, where von Hügel is talking about the indirect element in *all* cognitive experience, whether of God, a rose, or anything at all.
53. *ET*, pp. 357–62, esp. p. 362.
54. *ME2*, pp. 283, 308; *ET*, pp. 376–8.
55. *LN*, pp. 8–16. We shall cite and comment on pp. 11–16.
56. Von Hügel's youngest daughter, born March 1886, entered the London Carmel in 1907. See de la Bedoyère, op. cit., pp. 25, 187–8.
57. *EA1*, p. 56.
58. Letter to Clement Webb, 3 October 1910, in *SL*, pp. 181–2; letter to René Guiran, 11 July 1921, ibid., pp. 333–8; letters to Tyrrell, 4 March 1900, in *VH & T*, pp. 123–8, esp. p. 127, and 20 April 1906, in *SL*, pp. 135–6; and letter to Edmund Bishop, 16 June 1908, Abercrombie, op. cit., pp. 422–7, esp. p. 425.
59. Compare with *LN*, pp. 54–5.
60. For Feuerbach, *EL*, pp. 236–43; *EA1*, pp. 29–41. For Descartes, *RG*,

p. 188. For von Hügel's own opinion on the datum of experience as 'subject *and* object', *EA1*, p. 51.

61. *LN*, p. 150. And see *ME2*, p. 3, which follows up a statement on the fundamental, yet subordinate, importance of psychology with a searching examination of psychological factors in Catherine of Genoa. It is an unfortunate and disappointing surprise just here, however, to discover that von Hügel, often called the most learned man of his time in England, and widely read in contemporary Continental thinkers, gives no evidence I can find that he had even heard of Freud. However, there is perhaps indirect evidence in his definite (and very unfavourable) mention of Jung in a letter to Martin D'Arcy, 7 November 1921, Whelan, op. cit., pp. 33–4. For von Hügel's views on the wide area of *legitimate* subjective response in religion, see *ME2*, pp. 112–20. Here, under title of 'Interpretative Religion', he discusses the value and difficulties of subject-object interaction in religion. The point is exemplified by reference to John and Paul (deep, but 'partial developments of the full Gospel ideal') as compared with the more balanced but less articulated Synoptic statement. Much as von Hügel admires Paul and John, he more than once complains of John's 'thin' and 'abstractive' quality and of Paul's 'antithetical' character and strident, 'convert' tone.

62. See *EL*, pp. 156–67, for the results of Kant's position for grace, worship and history, and von Hügel's reactions to these positions. Von Hügel quotes Kant there, pp. 157–8: ' "All that man thinks he can do, outside of a good life, towards pleasing God, is sheer religious illusion and false worship of God." "A disposition to execute all our actions *as though* they took place in the service of God is the spirit of praying 'without ceasing'. But to incorporate this wish, even interiorly, in words can, at most, only have the value of a means for the repeated awakening of that disposition within us." . . . any "devout but still, as regards pure religious conceptions, backward man, whom another would surprise even simply in the attitude indicative of praying aloud" would be expected "at once to become confused, as over a condition of which he has to be ashamed." ' And von Hügel replies, p. 160: 'Religion, indeed, has ever been, at its fullest and deepest, *Adoration*, hence apprehension and affirmation of, and joy in, what already *is*.' Clearly, whatever the merits of the case, epistemology has its consequences for spirituality. But we have already seen von Hügel say (Chapter 2, p. 50) it is 'simply moonshine' to suggest that it does not.

63. One in a series of much-loved dogs.

64. *EA1*, p. 56.

65. We shall not have the space to give it due attention, but at least three times in this chapter (pp. 77–8, citing *ME2*, p. 395; p. 98: ibid., p. 240: Tiele; and p. 112: ibid., p. 336) and in other places (e.g., *ME2*, p. 86: John and Catherine of Genoa; ibid., pp. 337–8: Aquinas; *EL*, p. 79: John) there occurs something very akin to Rahner's supernatural existential: 'an ontological modification of man, added indeed to his nature by God's grace and therefore supernatural, but in fact never lacking in the real order' (*Theological Dictionary*, with Vorgrimler, New York, 1965).

The supernatural is a major subject in von Hügel. We indicate here some lines of development, with references: The supernatural is, in itself, neither preternatural nor miraculous (*EA1*, pp. 197, 279), and while distinct from all evil and all simply natural goodness, always has its situation and occasion 'amongst the specific qualities and ends of nature' (*EA1*, pp. xi, 198). The distinction occurs, then, between good and good (*EA1*, pp. xi, 283; *EA2*, p. 219), which is the basis for a dualist ethic (*GS*, pp. 71–3); and it is *this* distinction that is fundamental in Christian existence, whose *basic* polarity is weakness and strength, and not sin and redemption, the former distinction being Synoptic and Thomist, the latter (which is properly located *within* the former) being more Pauline and Augustinian (*ME2*, p. 69; *EL*, pp. 391–2; *EA1*, pp. 279–80; *GS*, pp. 160–72 (a history of the supernatural); *LN*, pp. xxviii, 48–9 (stressing the reality of sin and thus justifying the Augustinian 'moment')). *Both* nature and supernature, though different in kind and degree, are *given*, and to that extent, grace (*EA1*, p. xiv), and both must be *gained* (*SL*, p. 233). Nature always has and does exist at least potentially mingled with grace (*EA1*, p. xiv; *ME2*, p. 218). 'Wheresoever there are acts, experiences, necessities of sheer self-surrender, in the deepest search and work within the visible and temporal, the contingent and relative, to the invisible, the eternal, and the unconditional: wheresoever such self-surrender is from these temporalities, apprehended as such, to these eternities, accepted, adored as such: there is the supernatural. . . . So long as either movement and conviction [preoccupation with the specifically human, *or* with other-than-human finite realities] is primarily busy with the beauty, the truth or the goodness simply in their particular forms, and only vaguely or derivatively assumes or implies their unconditional claim upon the soul, you have nature. So soon as either movement and conviction attains to a central occupation with the abidingness, the non-contingency, of the beauty, the truth or the goodness thus partially revealed and to a recognition of their right to the unlimited service of the observer, you have supernature' (*EA1*, p. 198). Supernature does not require 'explicit reference to Christ, or even to God' (*EA1*, p. 280); it does require more than a hypothetical horizon (*SL*, p. 233). Again, supernature is 'a self-love in God, which loves not the natural self, but the self united to God; and a brotherly love in God, which loves not the natural fellow-man, but the brother in God' (*EA1*, pp. 175–7). Nature and supernature are inter-related parts of one great whole (*LN*, pp. 61–3), easily though not certainly distinguished into the homely and the heroic, more normally and hiddenly met in the heroic *within* the homely (*EA1*, p. 284). Supernature and nature are the *raison d'être* of the Church-State distinction, the former being superfluous unless, the latter being fanatical if and when, it insists on unconditional love and self-surrender (*EA1*, pp. 96, 283). The supernatural does not annihilate the natural, but like Monica's love, enables Augustine to become Augustine (*PC*, p. 389). The supernatural is the story of the martyrs, who, unlike Shakespeare's great men, look *forward* (*LN*, pp. 36–7, tempered on p. 68). It is decency become devotedness and may be expected to occur outside Catholicism and Christianity (*EA1*, p. 281). It is witnessed with particular power by consecrated chastity (see Dakin, op. cit., p. 232), and All Saints' Day is its feast (*EA1*, p. 200; *LN*, pp. 72 ('the feast of . . . every heroic act inspired by God since man began on earth'), 106, 196). The supernatural life is the life of prayer (*LN*, p. xxiv). See also Nédoncelle, *von Hügel*, pp. 92 ff.; also Martin Green, op. cit., pp. 76 ff., where von Hügel's humanism, already clearly distinguished from such as Yeats', is vividly and usefully marked off from another and Catholic sensibility, represented by such as Bernanos, T. S. Eliot, Waugh, Graham Greene and J. F. Powers. Von Hügel's whole doctrine here is incarnational: Man responds to the real, both infinite and finite. His direct response to the infinite – always in and on the occasion of the finite – is supernatural. His response to the finite may be either natural or supernatural, according to whether the response is to the thing or person as conditioned, as loved in itself, or as unconditioned, as loved in God. In either case, man's journey to God is through the definite, and in the world.

66. E.g., *ME2*, p. 278; *EL*, pp. 139–41.
67. *EL*, pp. 150–1.
68. *EA1*, pp. 187–8.
69. See *EL*, pp. 165–6, for von Hügel's assessment of Christ in Kant's philosophy.

70. *ET*, p. 378.
71. See *ME2*, p. 279, where von Hügel cites James Ward.
72. Letter to Tyrrell, 31 December 1898, in *VH & T*, p. 64; *ET*, p. 364.
73. See letter to Tyrrell, 26 September 1898, in *SL*, pp. 71–4, esp. pp. 71–2, nos. 1 and 2; also letter to Clement Webb, 13 October 1916, ibid., pp. 236–7. Nédoncelle, *von Hügel*, pp. 60–1, believes that one of von Hügel's main contributions as a theologian is his insistence on 'the insertion of religion in a definite and durational environment. . . . He observes the slow evolution of a humanity disquieted by its restless search for God.' Such a view leads to a theory of dogmatic development seen 'not so much as the germination of a seed, but rather as the refining of an ore'. It is a conservative view, but very sensitive to abuses and the need for purification. 'It holds that evolution and novelty do certainly exist, but belong solely to the human side of the picture, their function being to reveal the immutable presence of an absolute to which they add nothing.' Nédoncelle is correct here, I believe. I would wish only to emphasize the profound significance of that very real novelty which is human sanctity and the building of the material world. A permanent, an eternal achievement is in question here, one intrinsically effected by man's graced freedom in history. For remarks by von Hügel on dogma, see letter to Thorold, 15 August 1921, in de la Bedoyère, op. cit., p. 338, where von Hügel rejects the 'pragmatizing of dogma'. Religion is evidential, metaphysical, and if dogma is 'one remove from the Realities apprehended by faith', it is yet connected with these realities. 'Some objective relation' is insisted on. The alternative is 'sheer humanism'. See also *ET*, p. 369, where von Hügel cites with approval Deschamp's view of dogma as a divine response to man's aspirations (aspirations which are finally God himself prevenient to man and constituting him as man). It is clear in von Hügel that reformulation as well as progress in the content and understanding of dogma is not only allowed, but looked for; and equally clear that any total cultural relativizing of dogma is excluded. In a much annotated book now in the St Andrews collection, William Scott Palmer, *The Diary of a Modernist*, London, 1910, p. 295, von Hügel writes in the margin that dogmas 'are not as far from life' as Tyrrell and Palmer pretend. Nédoncelle, op. cit., p. 190, sounds a cautionary note on some of von Hügel's early and very liberal applications of his principles for the purification of dogmatic 'imagery'. Just how lively that application can be may be gathered, for example, from the 1908–09 *Rinnovamento* articles on Loisy's

Evangiles Synoptiques as analysed in Heaney, op. cit., pp. 134–7 (but see the important note 38, p. 266).

74. *EA2*, pp. 63–4.
75. *ET*, pp. 362–3.
76. *ME2*, p. 286. My italics.
77. Ibid., pp. 286–7.
78. Letter to Henri Bremond, 24 May 1915, *St Andrews MS* 30284, 2299–2354: von Hügel is discussing Bremond's *Histoire*: 'You are sure to be able to give us many a fine, all but forgotten, doctrine, spirit, life. That you should there especially put forward Jesuit figures and Jesuit convictions is as wise as it is natural [Bremond, a diocesan priest, had been a Jesuit]. But two limitations, learnt from G. Ward, who was at least as strong a Molinist as yourself: 1. The "Jansenist" trend (if we are quite fair and fully historical, and if we take the term quite generally), goes right back from Pascal (so great, with all his limitations), over Luther and especially Calvin, to St Augustine, and finally to St Paul. It is a current so broad and persistent, and (upon the whole) so illustrious, that its very exaggerations and errors somehow enclose and hide a precious constituent of the full truth. It is surely plain what this constituent is – the givenness, the prevenience, the over-and-aboveness of religion. I know well that every religious act and disposition involves also man's liberty and cooperation; also that man's nature is essentially not bad but good, and that this nature, tho' weak and of itself incapable of supernature, is, in its turn, necessary to supernature itself – as the latter has to operate in man. Still, I believe it is the "Jansenist" list of underlinings which is the more especially religious element of religion; just as the molinist list of underlinings is the element central, not in religion but in ethics. The Synoptic Gospels, and, across the centuries, some of the largest-and-deepest of the Catholic saints give, I am confident, the full truth in this matter.' The second point von Hügel announced goes on to contend that all but two of 'the spiritually greatest of the SJs of the XVIIth and XVIIIth centuries known to me at all, are all, I think, in their temper and tone, really "Jansenist," not Molinist, however they may speak if brought to book'.
79. *EL*, p. 302. My italics.
80. As far as I can find, von Hügel unfortunately does not consistently differentiate the meaning of this term from what he intends by subjectivism and immanentism.
81. *ME2*, pp. 338–40. Some italics are mine. Von Hügel makes a great deal of this theme of man's sense of oppression at the experience of the

finite. There is also frequent and often stern support for anthropomorphism. See *RG*, p. 73: 'Where is the wisdom of laughing at every kind of anthropomorphism as if it had no other roots than our foolish self-centredness?' Purification of conception is always required. But man *knows* he is anthropomorphic, and this awareness is the foundation of anthropomorphism's own, and more than pictorial, truth, containing, as it does, at once the judgments of both negation and affirmation. For other texts on this question of anthropomorphism and on the frustrating experience of the contingent as not arising from the contingent alone, see *ME2*, pp. 281–2; *EL*, pp. 236–43; and *ET*, pp. 360–2.

82. The word *human* in the last phrase here, I believe, gives the passage its point. It takes the fact of God and the sense of God to make our worldly enterprise the human thing it is and ought to be. At least twice von Hügel speaks sympathetically of Nietzsche. He interprets the idea of the superman, 'that pathetically hopeless misapplication of our instinctive need of adoration', as springing 'largely from a thirst and search for what religion alone can give'. See *EL*, pp. 263–4; *ME2*, p. 274.
83. See pp. 87–8.
84. *ME2*, p. 341. And see Chapter 5, pp. 191 ff.
85. *CFA*, p. 79; *ME2*, p. 277. And see above, p. 96.
86. *LN*, pp. xliii, xlv. And see *RG*, p. 42.
87. Letter to Norman Kemp Smith, 30–31 July 1920, *St Andrews MS* 30420.
88. See *EL*, pp. 188–9, for a good description of this religious experience of God as an immanent transcendence.
89. Letter to Clement Webb, 3 March 1909, in de la Bedoyère, op. cit., p. 228.
90. *ET*, p. 367.
91. *EA1*, p. 57. Von Hügel is well aware, in the same context, of 1 John 4:10, 19: 'He loved us first.' See *EL*, pp. 78–9.
92. *LN*, p. xvii.
93. Ibid., pp. 85–7.
94. 'Clearly' here, as the accompanying 'concretely' suggests, connotes vividness, immediacy, and not Cartesian or abstract clarity. The Incarnation further spells out, it does not attenuate, God's mystery.
95. *ME2*, p. 121, finds Catherine of Genoa close to the danger point here. With any less of the 'factual, historical, and institutional . . . her religion would be a simple, even though deep religiosity, a general aspiration, not a definite finding, an explicit religion'.

96. *EA1*, pp. 134–5; and see p. 63. This theme of ecumenism is prominent in von Hügel's writings, as it was in his life. See, e.g., *EL*, p. 393; *EA1*, pp. 234–5, 252. Neither Evelyn Underhill nor Gwendolen Greene (while von Hügel was alive and giving her spiritual direction) were Roman Catholic.

97. *ET*, pp. 365–6. And see ibid., p. 363, for a discussion of the movement from religiosity or sense of the infinite, to a personal God, to Jesus Christ. A difficult formulation of this same point, which at times seems to threaten von Hügel's own incarnational method, is given in *CE*, pp. 288–92. A more self-consistent statement occurs in *Encyclopedia Britannica*, 11th edition, 'John, Gospel of St.', XV, p. 455: 'Man's spirit . . . can respond actively to the historic Jesus, because already touched and made hungry by the all-actual Spirit-God who made that soul akin unto himself.'

98. *ME2*, pp. 279–80; *EA2*, pp. 142–4.

99. *LN*, p. 25.

100. It ought to be emphasized here that von Hügel views nature and grace as indeed really distinct, but not as separable realities. In *ET*, pp. 367–8, he reproduces Ruysbroeck's formulation of the traditional 'difference between man's "natural" and necessary, and his free and supernatural union with God', and where 'both the image and the likeness are held to be Christ'. But von Hügel would prefer that the image and the likeness 'were not distributed among nature and grace respectively, but were both taken as, in various degrees and ways, the work of grace in and with nature'.

101. *ME2*, pp. 312–13, 316; *EL*, pp. 82–7, 119–20.

102. *EA1*, p. 50; *RGM*, p. 656.

103. Letter to Tyrrell, 26 September 1898, in *SL*, pp. 71–4, esp. p. 73. And see *PC*, pp. 378–9.

104. *EA2*, p. 217. And see *RG*, pp. 65–6.

105. *EA1*, pp. 49–50. And see 'Professor Eucken on the Struggle for Spiritual Life', *Spectator*, 14 November 1896, p. 681; *CFA*, pp. 82–4; *ET*, pp. 364–5; *ME2*, p. 257; letter to Blondel, 14 March 1900, *St Andrews MS* B3280.H8 (the contents of this letter are reported in Steinmann, op. cit., pp. 129–30); Loisy, *Mémoires*, III, pp. 20–5 (for Loisy's own views on personality in God, together with a statement of some of von Hügel's views and Loisy's opinion of them); and letter to Marcel Hébert, 17 July 1901, in *SL*, pp. 100–2. Remembering a brochure of Hébert's, von Hügel writes: '. . . je me rappelle très nettement que je ne pouvais accepter le troisième point, qui semblait certes vouloir écarter l'idée de personnalité de celle de

Dieu. Or sur ce point, je sais bien que mes convictions sont de l'autre côté: épurer, élargir, spiritualiser notre propre caractère et, surtout par là, notre conception de personnalité humaine; éveiller et tenir de plus en plus en éveille, notre sens de l'inadequat nécessaire de toute idée que nous puissons former à Dieu, l'esprit absolu; mais enfin l'appliquer avec ces deux conditions continuelles, comme étant ce que nous connaissons le mieux, et de mieux, et ce que, à un degré et d'une façon pour nous inconcevable, Dieu ne peut manquer d'être. Les autres conceptes de loi, tendance, etc. me semblent être démonstrablement que des abstractions, et comme au dessous et non au dessus de la personnalité haute et spirituelle.'

106. *ME1*, p. 26.

107. *EA1*, p. 55.

108. *RGM*, p. 658.

109. *LN*, p. xxxi.

110. *ME2*, pp. 256–8; *RGM*, p. 360. This is wisdom, the *docta ignorantia* of the Fathers and the scholastics.

111. *EA2*, p. 136, where von Hügel lists four systems or tendencies rival to theism. The other two are materialism, and pluralism (ultimate reality is dual and finite).

112. *EL*, p. 260; *ME2*, pp. 287–8, 345–6; *ET*, pp. 372–3.

113. *EL*, p. 261, citing *Final Unscientific Postscript*.

114. Ibid., p. 262.

115. *ME2*, p. 288. In *ET*, p. 373, von Hügel notices that, much as with Kant, Kierkegaard's position is not finally agnostic, since it claims to *know* God is qualitatively Other.

116. *ET*, p. 374. Von Hügel frequently cites both Pseudo-Dionysius (in the positive of his two strains) and Aquinas for the position that negative theology is based on a positive affirmation, an *experience* (Aquinas's 'confused knowledge') of *what*, as well as the fact *that*, God is. See *ET*, pp. 368, 375–6. *LN*, pp. 135–6 suggests the powers, limits and dangers of analogy. Of special interest is the insistence there on the religious experience of the joy of God as a solid *fact* not to be dismissed by *problems* concerning how it is that God can be significantly said to sympathize if he does not suffer (and see ibid., pp. 50–1, for remarks on care and respect in assessing the achievements of dogmatic language).

Von Hügel's firm dissociation of himself from Kierkegaard on this whole question has caused several commentators to point out that he is similarly unlike Karl Barth. See Underhill, *Mixed Pasture*, pp. 227–8; Nédoncelle, *von Hügel*, pp. 150–1, 172, where, in a footnote, p. 151, Nédoncelle notices that von Hügel's incarnationalism cannot sustain itself by otherness alone, but requires 'otherness in likeness'; and Steere, op. cit., p. 5, who quotes Canon Streeter's remark on Britain's good fortune in having received the accent on transcendence from von Hügel instead of Barth: 'We shall one day have so much less to unlearn.' It should be remembered, however, that these judgments on Barth are not recent and antedate his 1956 essay, 'The Humanity of God'.

117. Letter to Clement Webb, 24 April 1907, in *SL*, pp. 137–8.

118. Von Hügel sees a suggestion of Kant here: agnosticism about the trans-subjective real, except its almost certain heterogeneity to our impression of it.

119. Letter to Maude Petre, 8 June 1922, in *SL*, pp. 355–8. The two understandings of agnosticism discussed in this section are developed in *RG*, pp. 181–7.

120. *ET*, p. 374.

121. *ME2*, p. 326.

122. *LN*, pp. 166–7.

123. *RGM*, pp. 656–7. Von Hügel is suggesting that it is the *profoundly*, it is the greatly and *successfully*, human which is *most* humbling (which may be why humility and joy so often co-exist). Only a *superficial* experience of man can long sustain the human both as man's only necessary means and as his final and worthy end. Man would be much less than man, if man – even at his most ideal – were God enough for him.

124. Ibid., pp. 663–4. Von Hügel is well aware that mystical literature, including the writings of orthodox Catholic mystics, is crowded with such 'identity' formulations. In addition to Plotinus and Spinoza, he comments on a number of Christian mystics. See *ME2*, pp. 319–28; *EL*, pp. 110–20, 125–32. Von Hügel also discusses some philosophical reasons for pantheism. Among them would be: the mistake of taking union for unity and of conceiving all oneness as empty and beyond richness and multiplicity; a materialist view of substance (correct enough in its own context) applied to consciousness, whereby spirit is impenetrable by Spirit, with the result that their intimate *presence to* one another is explained as their *identification*. (The alternative would be a deist alongsidedness, with distinction becoming separation.) For these and other reasons for pantheism, see references above, and *RGM*, pp. 653–6.

125. *EA2*, pp. 150–4. Von Hügel is referring here to Pringle-Pattison's understanding of the metaphysical Trinitarian creeds as 'sheer unity's

own self-unfolding, determination, differentiation – as though all this were a historical account of successive happenings'. For von Hügel, the root of the 'great Trinitarian movement' is not such Hegelian thought, nor is it philosophy at all, but 'two utterly concrete realities': the God both of the Jewish people and of Jesus, *and* this same Jesus; *and* 'the need somehow to co-relate them . . . and to protect this richness of the life of God against all absolute co-ordination with the world'. Pringle-Pattison's notion that 'although the individual may not make himself his own end, the world of finite individuals may constitute the end of the absolute' is deeply repugnant to von Hügel and drives him grudgingly to admire the scholastic doctrine of God's essential and accidental glory. This doctrine may be 'clumsy, wooden, what not'. But at least it is bent on 'explaining, not explaining away'. And see *LN*, pp. xvii–xviii, for another riposte on God and man as unqualified 'mutualities'.

126. See Chapter 2, pp. 38, 66.
127. *ME2*, pp. 329–30.
128. Ibid., pp. 331–2.
129. And see 'Notes for remarks at LSSR Meeting, May 1, 1917', *St Andrews MS* 2655, p. 14: Pantheism has 'its great nobility and deep function . . . against the "my God", the "God and my own soul" type'. But it must not be taken as simply ultimate. It is a means, a purification of what was previous, and of what will be subsequent to it.
130. A statement on the Holy Eucharist echoes this incarnationally structured movement in and through the narrow, the definite, the material, to spiritual enlargement. See text cited in Greene, *Two Witnesses*, p. 127: 'I go up as though I were all bent down, drawn down; I am drawn down as though I were about to enter a tunnel; I am all crouched down to receive the Blessed Sacrament; and afterwards I feel expanded – I breathe freely in a great deliverance.'
131. *ME2*, pp. 330–1. This large subject, only broached here, if at length, will be our direct concern in Chapter 5.
132. Ibid., pp. 334–5. On God as not only love, but lover, see *RG*, pp. 99–100.
133. *ME2*, pp. 320–2.
134. Ibid., pp. 324–5; *ET*, p. 368; *RGM*, pp. 364–5.
135. For panentheism and its distinction from pantheism, see *ET*, pp. 374–5; *RGM*, pp. 364–5; *ME2*, pp. 325, 336–7. The text cited is from the last reference given here. For the immanence of Christ in the Christian and the Christian in Christ, see *ME1*, pp. 32, 35, 39.
136. Letter to Wilfrid Ward, 18 February 1900, in de la Bedoyère, op. cit., p. 115.

137. Letter to Blondel, 30 July 1899, *St Andrews MS* B3280.H8: 'par moyen d'une sortie de chez Lui et d'une entrée permanente de chez nous, par une immanence éternelle en les profondeurs de l'humanité . . ., un point fort délicat, mais de la dernière importance.' The point becomes increasingly delicate. In a letter to Tyrrell, 4 December 1902, in *SL*, pp. 113–14, von Hügel asks for a balance between the 'Wernle-Troeltsch-Loisy contention as to the large element of Hereafter' and 'this Blondel-Munsterberg-Fichte line', which emphasizes the 'interiority and presence of the Kingdom'. But in a letter twenty-two years later to René Guiran, 11 July 1921, in *SL*, pp. 333–7 (already cited, n. 8, above), von Hügel dissociates himself from Blondel (see n. 8). Yet Nédoncelle, who remains von Hügel's best commentator, believes that the repudiation 'de toute conception purement immanentiste de la Realité Ultime' at the beginning of the 1912 monograph *PC*, intends by 'purement' explicitly to exclude 'a Maurice Blondel' from its strictures. See Nédoncelle, 'von Hügel on God', p. 9.

138. *EA1*, pp. 35–8.

139. Letter to Tyrrell, 30 May 1903, in *SL*, pp. 124–5.

140. Letter to Tyrrell, 14 May 1907, ibid., pp. 138–9. A letter of 6 August 1910, cited in de la Bedoyère, op. cit., p. 247, tells Clement Webb of 'two forces which certainly each is *the* stimulant and producer of the other – a tyrannous transcendentalism and a sceptical immanentism'. Loisy, and Maude Petre with him, thought von Hügel's concern about immanentism an 'obsession', and his transcendent God a 'gendarme métaphysique'. See Petre, *Alfred Loisy*, Cambridge, 1944, p. 36; also Loisy, *Mémoires*, III, pp. 106–7, 153–70, for both von Hügel's and Loisy's views. There is no doubt the point becomes central for von Hügel. However, the reader may judge whether it is so that 'le cas du bon baron relevait de la psychiatrie plutôt que de la psychologie normale' (Loisy, p. 164). Loisy also declares his mind on the issue itself, ibid., p. 107 (translation taken from Petre, op. cit., p. 87): 'I certainly cannot lodge his transcendent in my mind as an indispensable guest; it is equally true I do not imagine the human ideal to be founded on nothing. First of all, this common ideal of humanity is transcendent in relation to each separate individual; furthermore, it corresponds to the profound law or reality of the universe, which makes it transcend humanity. But is it consequently necessary to conceive this profound reality as the metaphysical object of religion, . . . *as a reality superior and exterior to the universe itself?* . . . I do not know this, I do not see it, I do not understand it.' My italics.

Von Hügel is aware of this in Loisy at least as early as 1908 (see letter to Tyrrell, 16 April 1908, in *SL*, pp. 148–51, esp. p. 149, as well as remarks to Blondel in 1903, only partially cited in Chapter 2, p. 41). For an additional text from Loisy himself, see citation from *Choses passées*, 1912, p. 314, in Steinmann, op. cit., p. 410: 'Dieu est . . . un moi supérieur . . . et . . . la personnification transcendente de la société, de l'humanité.'

Tyrrell reaches other conclusions of his own in letters to von Hügel, 9 April 1909, and to A. Fawkes, 3 June 1909, the year he died: 'I feel that my past work has been dominated by the Liberal-Protestant Christ and doubt whether I am not bankrupt. . . . If we cannot save huge chunks of transcendentalism, Christianity must go. Civilization can do (and has done) all that the purely immanental Christ of Matthew Arnold is credited with. The other-world emphasis, the doctrine of immortality, was what gave Christianity its original impulse and sent martyrs to the lions. If that is accidental, we only owe to Jesus in a great measure what we owe to all good men in some measure.' 'As to "development", we all want to claim Jesus. But I fear he belongs to the obscurantists. . . . His ethic was not his own . . . Eternal Life, which was the substance of his Gospel, was *not* the moral life, but the super-moral. Morality was but its condition – like the Faith which shall be done away. . . . His two discoveries were that the end was near and that he was the Messias. The first we know was a mistake; the second may have been. Liberal Protestantism is the development of the ethic . . .; but not of his Gospel, his message. Of that, Catholicism is the development.' If one concentrates exclusively on the ethic, then Jesus is merely 'a convenient symbol of the enlightened conscience of mankind'. Both letters are cited in Maude Petre, *Autobiography and Life of George Tyrrell*, II, pp. 398–400.

141. *RP*, pp. 670–1, already partially cited, Chapter 2, p. 74.
142. *RGM*, p. 659.
143. Ibid.
144. Ibid., pp. 660–1.
145. The following pages, including all direct citations, are drawn from *EL*, pp. 303–23. The immediate context there is a discussion of Marxist philosophy and economics in their relation to eternal life.
146. For a similar statement, see *GS*, pp. 205–7: The obsessive race for wealth and material power dulls man's sense of himself as amphibious. Writing in 1916, von Hügel was optimistic that this obsession was 'too near mania to last permanently anywhere'. However,

he perhaps more accurately suggests that the alternative to this obsession would not be necessarily 'a real God, a real soul, a life of each in the other, begun here and completed beyond the grave – but in some form of pure immanence – or, at most, in some variety of Fichteism – belief in the more than human, quite ultimate, reality of certain laws of the ethical life'.

147. My italics. I omit the term 'Immanentism' which occurs in this passage – conjunctive to 'Incarnational doctrine' – because it is distracting. Von Hügel almost always reserves it for pejorative use. We would expect 'immanence', which is clearly what he means, both from the immediate context and from the whole thesis of *Eternal Life*.

148. There are some splendid texts on *God* as the root of man's necessarily agapeistic service of his fellow-men and the world. Perhaps especially moving is the comparison of Socrates and Jesus in their attitude towards prostitutes, in *PC*, pp. 285–7: 'amour prophétique et createur'; 'l'amour *ecstatique*, la sortie de nous même'.

149. Von Hügel insists on the balance: 'Man is to do his utmost to improve his fellow-man's earthly lot; but that lot, whilst greatly improvable with time and care, is deliberately held to find its completion in another life alone.' Man thus avoids 'utopian fanaticism' and the inevitable reaction into cynicism and despair. He thus too protects the sense of mystery, his belief in sin, and a proper pessimism about man when left to himself. Von Hügel agrees with Georges Sorel that where these values, together with a respect for chastity, disappear, so too does Christianity.

150. Jean Daniélou, *Prayer as a Political Problem*, London, 1967, pp. 23–42 (I refer to these pages only), takes a stand markedly similar to von Hügel's position in this whole section. Of course, Daniélou's purview is rendered vastly more complex by contemporary technology, by the accelerated disappearance of the sacral and by totalitarianism.

151. See Chapter 2, p. 63.

152. *EA2*, p. 179.

153. Ibid., pp. 167–213.

154. Ibid., pp. 168–97. See also *RG*, pp. 97–100.

155. Ibid., p. 188. Some italics are mine.

156. Ibid., pp. 206–7. There is no slightest suggestion here, however, that man's being 'busy' with God in himself can or ought to occur other than in and through creation and, pre-eminently, in and through the created humanity of the risen Christ. The sacramentality of Christ's humanity is not pressed by von Hügel at this point, but this sacramentality is certainly not excluded nor, I think, is its function

weakened, by this part of his spiritual doctrine. Indeed, the contrary seems rather the case. Von Hügel is asking here about the God-ness of God and about man's experience of God and reception of him precisely in his *un*-created reality. Christ remains the uniquely adequate Way to and Sacrament of that experience and reception. He *is* man's entrance into the uncreated Trinity. Von Hügel's point seems to be that man is called – also – to adoration of God in this his 'uneconomic' triune joy. Surely, then, something very powerful and truly demanding, but also something deep in the tradition and hardly esoteric or extraordinary, is here being said.

157. Ibid., pp. 208–9.

158. Here von Hügel alludes to, among other things, his previous insistence on understanding God's freedom as Augustinian in conception and not at all as a liberty of choice (the latter being a real, characteristically human, but less perfect, freedom). And he agrees with Aquinas on the greater propriety of speaking 'of things that cannot be done, than of God as incapable of doing certain things'. See ibid., pp. 202–3, 206.

159. Ibid., pp. 209–10. Evil is another large subject in von Hügel. See, e.g., in addition to this the essay on suffering in God, *ME2*, pp. 221–5, 290–308. Von Hügel claims no explanation for evil. Especially in this question are deduction and inference very dangerous and very common. One must begin and end with *facts*, facts of experience, which witness both to the reality of evident and widespread evil *and* to the reality of an all-joyful God. Christianity has not solved this mystery, but in Jesus, in its creed and in its saints, Christianity alone has fully and fruitfully faced both facts and *lived* both facts. See *ME1*, pp. 26–7, already cited so often in Chapter 2.

160. *EA1*, p. 96. My italics.

161. *LN*, p. 75.

162. *EA1*, pp. 18–19; and see *RG*, pp. 94–5. There is nothing antinomian here, as the context makes massively clear. The creature's appropriation of this Godlike spontaneity is a gift, and it is never such as to exclude 'a chaste fear and filial reverence'.

163. *LN*, pp. 161–2.

164. *EA2*, p. 247. And see *LN*, pp. xix–xx ('Christ teaches a great austerity'), xxiii–xxiv (celibacy and mortification), xliii ('Our Lord is full of a great tenderness – tenderness and austerity'). Von Hügel tells Gwendolen Greene that the 'astringency' of the martyrs is essential to the Christian outlook (p. 137). He condemns 'worldliness' as 'thoroughly vulgar', yet it is 'a less dangerous foe of the spiritual life than is

brooding and self-occupation' (pp. 42–3). He will not give her Newman's *Parochial and Plain Sermons*, 'certainly classics', because they 'are rigorist – how they have depressed me' (p. 114). Jesus is not a rigorist. And so von Hügel, ibid., p. 146, prays to be a very demanding, but thoroughly human and gentle spiritual director: 'Blessing, the cry of my old heart is to be – to become – a not all unworthy follower of him who broke not the bruised reed and quenched not the burning flax!'

165. The same God-centred approach has splendid results in von Hügel's attitude towards immortality. The position is wholly devoid of any suggestion of that security-consciousness or escape mentality so often charged against those who show strong interest in the after-life. See *EA1*, p. 197: 'The specifically religious desire of immortality begins, not with immortality, but with God; it rests upon God; and it ends in God.' And *LN*, pp. xxxii–xxxiii: 'The central fact of religion is not survival, but God. . . . Survival must mean God, or it means nothing. There are people who try to prove God only as a means to immortality; they have got it all upside down. How secondary is immortality to God!' For von Hügel, the *religious* belief in immortality grows out of the *this-life* experience of the joy of God, an experience *expressed* in the ethical life (see *EL*, pp. 22–3; *EA1*, p. 296). From this experience of God as self-*communicated*, *eternal* joy, arises the need for and the belief in immortality. And in *this* context, disbelief or disinterest in immortality would indicate, not courage, or responsible independence and involvement in the world, but a shallow spirituality.

166. *EA2*, pp. 211–13. My italics.

167. Ibid., pp. 217–26.

168. See Chapter 2, p. 38.

169. *EA2*, p. 224.

CHAPTER FOUR

1. The word 'production' is von Hügel's own. See 'Professor Eucken on the Struggle for Spiritual Life', *Spectator*, 14 November 1896, p. 680.
2. Nédoncelle, *von Hügel*, p. 160.
3. Pp. 3–82, to which should be added the related and synthetic passages, ibid., pp. 367–70, and *ME2*, pp. 387–96. I place these last references here for the reader's convenience. This study considers them at the end of Chapter 5. Discussion of *ME1*, pp. 41–8, is also deferred to the next chapter.

4. *ME1*, p. 3. We shall be giving a summary now of pp. 3–82, with the exception mentioned in n. 3, above. References to the text will be limited to direct citations.
5. Ibid. My italics.
6. Ibid., p. 7.
7. For lack of space, I can only refer the reader to the wealth of historical corroboration, both cultural and religious, that von Hügel supplies for the bare statements I make. See ibid., pp. 6–10.
8. Ibid., pp. 10–11.
9. Ibid., pp. 24–5. Pp. 10–25 sufficiently show von Hügel's generalizations to be born of a close study of, and an admiring awareness of the complexity involved in, the thought of the pre-Socratics, Plato, Aristotle, Plotinus and Proclus. For example, he finds in Plato (p. 25) 'at times strikingly incarnational conceptions'.
10. Ibid. Once again the reader is urgently referred to Chapter 2, pp. 34–5, for von Hügel's classic portrait of the person, Jesus Christ. This text remains the focus of our entire study.
11. Ibid.
12. These last statements, surely a climactic issue, are anticipating this and the next chapter's repeated suggestion of a Christology at once descending and ascending. Connected too is von Hügel's emphasis on God as *creans*. The participle here, perhaps better than the substantive *creator*, suggests the dynamic, present and immanent quality of God's action in the world, as von Hügel understands it – an action *directly* proportioned to man's both religious and secular independence. The position perhaps accounts for von Hügel's strong and untroubled acceptance of evolution and for his enthusiasm for the secular as a category *within* Christian spirituality. It is well to have this clear here. In von Hügel's thought, the religious and the secular describe legitimate and very different human activities. They do not enunciate a distinction between human dependence and independence. Within a Christian doctrine of creation and redemption, human dependence and independence increase and decrease together. So too of human and divine-human love.
13. Ibid., pp. 29–30. And see B. C. Butler, *Spirit and Institution in the New Testament*, London, 1961.
14. Ibid., p. 39.
15. Ibid.
16. Ibid., p. 40.
17. Ibid. Von Hügel describes here, surely, the exact sciences. His own mature understanding of history, at least where not momentarily

pressured polemically to over-insist on history's independence from religion, would not answer to this description. See Chapter 5, n. 101.

18. Ibid., p. 48.
19. Ibid.
20. Ibid., pp. 48–9.
21. Ibid.
22. Ibid.
23. Ibid., p. 51.
24. Ibid., p. 52.
25. Ibid.
26. Ibid., pp. 52–3.
27. Ibid., p. 54. And see ibid., p. xxiii, where the tendencies to which the three elements answer are argued as intrinsic to man.
28. See Chapter 2, n. 162.
29. *ME1*, pp. 54–5.
30. Ibid.
31. Ibid.
32. Ibid.
33. Ibid., p. 58. My italics.
34. Ibid., pp. 58–65 give this historical survey and analysis. Only as generalization culled from careful research can and does von Hügel's thesis avoid caricature and woodenness. This chapter of *ME* has been perhaps the most admired of anything von Hügel wrote (see, e.g., ibid., p. viii).
35. See Chapter 2, pp. 67 ff.
36. *ME1*, p. 70.
37. Ibid., pp. 71–2.
38. Ibid., pp. 72–3.
39. Ibid., pp. 73–4.
40. Ibid., p. 76.
41. Ibid., pp. 76–7. My italics.
42. Ibid., p. 78.
43. Ibid., pp. 79–80.
44. Ibid., pp. 81–2.
45. Ibid., p. 85.
46. Ibid., pp. 47, 72–3.
47. Ibid., p. 86: Religion 'begins with an at least incipient person and ends in the fullest self-expression of personality, the determination of the will'; ibid., p. 334: '. . . that faithful and heroic use of free-will and that spirit and grace of God in which the whole substance of sanctity consists . . .'

48. Von Hügel's description of personality is not, in its larger outlines, original to himself, though he surely leaves his personal stamp upon the materials he uses and organizes. He claims originality only for the purificatory function he assigns to science (see Chapter 5). We have seen his debt to Augustine and to Bergson in his analysis of man and personality as *durée* (Chapter 2). Acknowledgement is made to Hermann Lotze (*EA1*, p. 50), but the massive influence here seems to be Rudolf Eucken (see *Spectator*, 14 November 1896, pp. 679–81; and *Hibbert Journal*, April 1912, pp. 660–77 (*RP*)). Eucken's idealism is richly modified and supplemented by Maurice Blondel's philosophy of incarnation (*CFA*, p. 84; and *SL*, p. 96). And von Hügel declares to Gwendolen Greene the peremptory importance for himself of the classical Christian tradition, as enunciated in Augustine, on the question of moral 'seriousness' and sin (though he will *locate* this central concern within Aquinas's larger framework: see n. 65 in Chapter 3). Von Hügel's whole doctrine of spirituality and personality depends on a traditional view of sin: 'The average, conventional, latter-day, enlightened, etc., outlook as to moral responsibility, purity, humility, sin, is just so much childishness compared to the spirit that breathes in those deathless pages [the *Confessions*]. That entire way of recording one's own or other lives, as though they were just so many crystals, or at most so many plants; as though they could not, in the given circumstances, have been other than in fact they were: all that sorry naturalism and determinism, with its cheap self-exculpation and its shallow praise (because also shallow blame) of others: all this is nobly outsoared, is obviously nowhere, in that deep manly world of St Augustine' (*LN*, pp. 48–9). Finally, we may note von Hügel's importantly qualified but frequent reference to F. R. Tennant's view of sin and original sin as an atavism, and therefore an anachronism of the moral personality (e.g., *ME2*, pp. 299–300).
49. Letter to Maude Petre, 26 September 1900, in *SL*, pp. 88–96. Here, pp. 88–9.
50. Ibid.
51. Ibid., pp. 90–1.
52. Ibid., p. 90.
53. Ibid., p. 92.
54. *ME1*, p. 242.
55. See Chapter 3, p. 113.
56. *ME1*, p. 242.
57. Ibid., pp. 242–3. For other formulations, see *EA2*, pp. 65–6.
58. *ME2*, pp. 228–9. The concluding citation is from 2 Cor. 4:16.

59. Ibid.
60. Ibid., pp. 229–30; *EL*, pp. 390–1. Some italics are mine. For further texts on personality and time, see *EL*, p. 294 (the 'I' or personality as permanence and change); ibid., p. 298 (personality as a 'mysterious union' of these 'opposites', i.e. as duration). *EA1*, pp. 130–2, contains a good discussion of the Neoplatonist dangers *and* the Christian truths contained in simultaneity and presence as mystical categories.
61. *ME1*, p. 220.
62. Ibid. My italics.
63. Ibid., p. 179.
64. *RP*, pp. 666–7.
65. *ME1*, p. 243.
66. See also Chapter 3, p. 82 and its n. 16, where something of this present point is made.
67. *ME2*, p. 3.
68. For psycho-physical factors as *conditions* of sanctity, see ibid., p. 41; for the same as *means*, see p. 57; and on the neural conditions for contemplation, *ME1*, p. 336.
69. *ME2*, p. 60. A clear statement of method is given on p. 8. Von Hügel's basic position here gets well stated in Roustang, op. cit., pp. 199–204, esp. p. 199, note: 'When it [psychology] is successful, it restores health, but it is incapable of suggesting to the patient when cured what he should do and why he should do it.'
70. *ME2*, p. 5; and see p. 16 for this same point (the relation of spiritual realities to psycho-physical phenomena) as analysed in the spiritually fruitful and the '*maladif*' experiences of Catherine of Genoa.
71. Ibid., pp. 46–7.
72. For the possible cost of spiritual personality, see *ME1*, p. ix; *ME2*, p. 57; for humility and charity as principle and test, *ME2*, pp. 19–34, 46–51 (and Chapter 3 as mentioned in n. 66, just above). *ME1*, pp. 222–3, gives a fine analysis and portrait of Catherine of Genoa (and of von Hügel himself?) which illustrates the essential points of our present discussion. Catherine is not presented as typical, yet the general truths and intentions of von Hügel's spiritual doctrine may be discerned here and are indeed applicable to calmer, more sensual, or more extrovert temperaments. His shrewd assessment of Catherine's greatness and of the severity of her problem ('her immensely sensitive, absolute, and claimful self') issues in a splendid compliment: '. . . she became a saint because she had to . . ., to save . . . the fruitful life of reason and of love . . . ' (ibid.)

73. Letter to Maude Petre, 5 December 1899, in *SL*, pp. 82–5: 'Fight self constantly, and you need never think of the devil.'
74. *ME2*, p. 336; letter to Maude Petre, 6 June 1914, in *SL*, pp. 208–9.
75. Letter to Juliet Mansel, Epiphany, 1921, ibid., pp. 321–3.
76. Letter to the same, 23 March 1910, ibid., pp. 175–6.
77. Letter to a girl (on her Confirmation, Anglican), 11 April 1922, ibid., pp. 351–2.
78. *ME1*, pp. 106, 190; letter to Maude Petre, 26 September 1900, in *SL*, pp. 88–96, esp. p. 91. Von Hügel's few comments on the grace controversy are anti-Molinist rather than Banezian. See also Chapter 3, p. 97, n. 78, for remarks to Henri Bremond on God and human freedom. Finally, see *PC*, p. 389, for an excellent formulation of disinterested love as a force productive of *another's* true self in freedom. (For the unacquainted reader, the *de auxiliis* controversy may be briefly described as a late and unresolved, somewhat acrimonious dispute about the 'coexistence of God's absolute sovereignty with man's genuine freedom' (Rahner, *Theological Dictionary*, pp. 196–7).)
79. *ME2*, pp. 173–4. David Knowles gives admirable precision to this 'great theological truth' in *The English Mystical Tradition*, London, 1961, p. 165.
80. *CFA*, p. 82. And see letter to Maurice Blondel, 30 July 1899, *St Andrews MS* B3280.H8: '. . . l'action de Dieu et de l'homme montent et descendent ensemble, de façon que partout où il y a plus d'action divine il y en a plus d'humaine.' The contrary view is called 'egotistical', 'anti-supernaturalist', 'not Christian at all'.
81. *EL*, pp. 58–9.
82. *ME1*, pp. 233–4.
83. Ibid., pp. 69–70, citing the *Tractatus de Gratia et Libero Arbitrio*. For von Hügel's own formulation, see ibid., p. 370.
84. See Chapter 3, pp. 104–13. For human freedom as divine self-restraint, see, e.g., *EL*, p. 160, and esp. the letter to Maude Petre, 26 September 1900, in *SL*, p. 93 (the relevant passage of which is given above, Chapter 2, p. 69).
85. *EL*, pp. 387–8. *PC*, pp. 372, 382–3, offers a further, more penetrating and technical analysis of the needs, including the need for purification, of religious intelligence and devotion based on a notion of the vertical and horizontal (spatialization) as developed from Bergsonian time and space. Maurice Nédoncelle, in the already cited article, 'von Hügel on God', pp. 21–2, sees here a deeply sympathetic but critical anticipation of Bultmannian demythologizing, where myth is defined as a 'spatialization of things divine'.

86. Letter to Juliet Mansel, 24 May 1911, in *SL*, pp. 188–9.
87. See Chapter 2, pp. 45, 57, 68, 72–3; also *ME2*, pp. 201–3. In *ME1*, p. 223, von Hügel, while praising Catherine of Genoa for the absence of 'moral vulgarity of any kind', indicts her lack of that 'normal sensuousness, which appears to form a necessary element of the complete human personality'. Years later he tells Norman Kemp Smith that the sex instinct is so essential to human life that we must attribute it to Mary and to Jesus, 'unless we would be docetists' (letter of 8 January 1921, *St Andrews MS* 30420).
88. See Chapter 3, pp. 76–7, 89.
89. *EA1*, pp. 168, 190–1, citing Troeltsch. The image 'succession of steps' could be misleading. The priority is ontological and qualitative, not temporal, let alone spatial. Nature and supernature are present at the beginning and at the end and throughout the process which is man as we historically have him. It is a matter of deepening, exalting and actuating the former through its permeation by the latter. Nature is not destroyed or replaced, but undergoes, and is a partner to, a transformation which yet involves a difference of kind and not of degree only. See Chapter 3, p. 94, n. 65.
90. Mainly in *ME2*, pp. 152–81. Nédoncelle, *von Hügel*, p. 155, says that it is from von Hügel that Henri Bremond derived his classical statement and solution of this question, including even the vocabulary employed. *ME1*, pp. 140–1, 160–1, 266–80, presents the issue as analysed in Catherine of Genoa.
91. *ME2*, p. 153.
92. *ME1*, p. 280; *ME2*, pp. 157, 162.
93. *ME2*, pp. 158–9.
94. *ME1*, p. 280; *ME2*, pp. 170, 176 (citing Spinoza).
95. *ME2*, pp. 173–4, citing Fénelon. The context here is 'passive' contemplation. But the necessity and presence of freedom, affirmed in this most difficult case, applies generally.
96. The reader may notice how this multiplicity or polarity-in-unity, with its accompanying tension and friction, exactly parallels von Hügel's understanding of Jesus. See especially Chapter 2, pp. 53 ff.
97. *ME2*, p. 172.
98. For von Hügel's New Testament survey of the question, see ibid., pp. 153–60.
99. *ME1*, pp. 67–8; *RG*, pp. 140–1.
100. *ME2*, pp. 157, 301.
101. *ME1*, p. 68; *ME2*, pp. 169–70.
102. *ME2*, pp. 252–4. Also *RG*, p. 19; and *ME1*, p. 30. For this important

question of a *direct* relationship and love of both God and other creatures, see Chapter 2 above, pp. 49–50; also letter to Tyrrell, 20 December 1900, *BM Add. MS* 44927, and letter to Maude Petre, 20 April 1902, *BM Add. MS* 45361.

103. *ME2*, pp. 237–9, 249–51.

104. Ibid., pp. 251–2; letter to Maude Petre, 5 December 1899, in *SL*, pp. 82–5.

105. *LN*, pp. 92–3; *EU*, pp. 75, 124.

106. *ME2*, pp. 34–5; *LN*, pp. xx-xxi. This position has received important and much admired articulation as an incarnational theory of the creative imagination in William F. Lynch, *Christ and Apollo*, New York, 1960.

107. *ME2*, pp. 220–1. Von Hügel's doctrine here does not disturb the Catholic doctrine of objective and subjective sin. Rather, it finely enunciates that distinction's real magnitude and necessity. See also ibid., pp. 245–56.

108. *ME1*, p. 107, already cited above, Chapter 2, p. 51.

109. For the most complete treatment of quietism, see *ME2*, pp. 129–52. Historically, quietism, as *exclusive* mysticism, has brought mysticism itself into disrepute, by substituting unity for harmony. Pp. 148–52 seek to separate the wheat from the chaff, according to the 'Incarnational action of God'.

110. Von Hügel is not talking here about psycho-physical phenomena, such as trance, but about the *spiritual* experience of the great mystics as they report it.

111. For this paragraph, see *ME2*, pp. 130–4. See also ibid., pp. 285–6; *RGM*, pp. 663–4; *EA1*, p. 216; and *EA2*, p. 51.

112. In this connection, von Hügel comments on: the body, *ME2*, p. 135; vocal prayer and the institutional Church, pp. 136–7; secular, or non-religious interests, pp. 137–8; social morality and the objective element (the '*body* of an action') in ethics, pp. 138–9. It is organic religion, von Hügel concludes, of 'the incarnational type, which is the only fully true, the only genuinely Christian one' (p. 139). We have here, in a short space, von Hügel's doctrine of personality issuing in those positions on prayer, Church, science, etc., which will be the subject of our next chapter. The whole position has its early and clear synthesis in *CFA*, pp. 80–2. For a relevant discussion of the strengths and weaknesses of mysticism, see *ME2*, pp. 284 ff.

113. 'The Spiritual Writings of Father Grou, S.J.', *Tablet*, 28 December 1889, p. 1031.

114. *LN*, pp. xx-xxi, 96; letter to Mrs Henry Drew (*née* Gladstone), 23 May 1898, in *SL*, p. 70. For Fénelon's understanding of passivity,

action and activity, see *ME2*, pp. 141–2. Finally, *LN*, pp. 155–6: 'Holy suffering is the very crown of holy action' (confirmed in *ME1*, p. 27).

115. *ME2*, p. 228.

116. *RGM*, p. 665: 'For how can what is, at bottom, a veritable constituent of God himself, remain abidingly in severance from and conflict with him . . . ?'

117. *EA1*, p. 220; *LN*, p. 49. A doctrine of final option is neither precluded by, nor would it circumvent, von Hügel's position here, provided the proposed option is located *within* history. Further, the position does not contradict Catherine of Genoa's doctrine of the purgatorial 'plunge' (*ME2*, p. 220), nor does it prevent von Hügel's own vigorous effort to purify or remove the vindictive and pictorial trimmings of traditional purgatorial doctrine (e.g., *ME2*, pp. 203–18). For von Hügel's sympathetic but wary response to Julian of Norwich and the doctrine of apocatastasis ('the final restitution of all things and souls'), see *ME2*, pp. 218–19; and *RGM*, pp. 665–6.

Von Hügel's position here does not conflict with his view of freedom of choice as an imperfect freedom. Within *man*, choice is a perfection: man as *homo viator* would not be man without it (*EA1*, pp. 220–1). For the scriptural basis of heaven and hell, see ibid., pp. 209–12; and *LN*, pp. xxxiv–xxxv: 'If Christianity is true, there must be abiding consequences. We can't get rid of it, it's in all the Gospels. Our Lord speaks of it several times. His message is an immense warning to us here and now, a terrific alternative. You must see that. If you read the Gospels and give that up, I don't know *what* you see.' For von Hügel, Christianity is the childlike: the 'little-seeming doings . . . matter truly, because immensely, because abidingly'. He is appalled at any position which logically must conclude that it would not matter, finally, whether one freely lived and died as Nero or as Francis (*RGM*, p. 668).

118. *EA1*, p. 207.

119. Von Hügel elsewhere remarks, in connection with this idea of man as the necessary effect of his own freedom: 'A determinism of consequences . . . does not prevent the liberty of causes' (*ME2*, p. 205).

120. Ibid., pp. 38–9. My italics.

121. Ibid.

122. Ibid., pp. 212, 215.

123. Ibid., p. 212.

124. Ibid.

125. See above in this chapter, p. 125.

126. Letter to Tyrrell, 7 December 1908, *BM Add. MS* 44931, already cited more fully in Chapter 2, p. 38, n. 19.

CHAPTER FIVE

1. *EA1*, p. 181, citing Troeltsch.
2. Letter to Tyrrell, 4 March 1900, cited in *VH & T*, pp. 123–8. Here, p. 126.
3. *ME2*, pp. 194–5; letter to Emelia Fogelklou Norlind, 11 January 1911, cited in de la Bedoyère, op. cit., pp. 253–4.
4. *EL*, pp. xiv–xv; *ME2*, pp. 283–4; *EA1*, pp. xii, 13–16; *RG*, pp. 89–93, 138 ff.
5. *LN*, pp. 69–70.
6. It is far more just to von Hügel, I believe, to see his epistemology and psychology, not as *a prioristically* dictating incarnation and the Church, but rather as extrapolated from and descriptive of the incarnational quality of his *religious experience*.
7. *ME2*, pp. 286, 353.
8. *RG*, pp. 142–3.
9. See *MK*, p. 325: '... "Fortsetzung der Inkarnation", als welche ein Heiliger nach dem andern die Kirche so treffend bezeichnete und empfand.' I am told that this formulation of the Church, almost polemically Catholic, and deeply Hügelian, derives from Bossuet. It is perhaps an unprotestant, and certainly a most unmodernist view, as von Hügel was well aware.
10. *RG*, p. 139. For the dangers and abuses of institutional religion, and the terrible price and great worth of fully lived Roman Catholicism, see Chapter 3, pp. 86–7, and also *EA1*, pp. 59–61, 257–9; *MK*, p. 330. If evil as such surprised von Hügel, evil in the Church did not surprise. In a letter of 30 July 1877, Newman had remarked to him apropos of evil and the existence of a personal God: '*there* is the field of battle.' But *given* these two *facts*, evil in the Church is unsurprising and is indeed 'presupposed in Scripture' (cited in Wilfrid Ward, *John Henry Cardinal Newman*, London, 1912, Vol. II, pp. 417–18).
11. *EA2*, pp. 66–8; *RG*, pp. 143–4; letters to Clement Webb, 7 March and May, 1921, in *SL*, pp. 325–9. Admittedly, the priest and the professor have all too often been virtually identified in medieval and Tridentine Roman Catholicism.
12. Letter to Bishop Edward Talbot, 20 March 1915, in *SL*, pp. 217–20, esp. p. 220. Von Hügel is complaining to his Anglican friend that this theme was so little stressed in William Temple, whom he much admired.

13. As the reader will recognize, these paragraphs synthesize within an ecclesial perspective much of the material of the previous chapters on Christ, God and personality. In addition, the following materials have been directly cited or used: on *opus operatum*, *EA1*, pp. 164, 180; *EA2*, p. 84; and see *LN*, pp. 54–5; on the Eucharist, *ME1*, p. 59; *LN*, p. 187; *EU*, p. 94; and esp. *EA2*, pp. 248–9, which is cited above, Chapter 2, p. 35; on the dangers of mechanical sacramentalism, of superstition and magic, yet the propriety of a preliminary 'thing' or *dinglich* quality with respect to God and the sacraments, *EL*, pp. 328–9; *EA1*, pp. 165, 251; *EA2*, pp. 83–4, 86, 126–9; letter to Maude Petre, 18 May 1901, *BM Add. MS* 45361; *ME1*, pp. 245–7; *ME2*, pp. 374, 387; letter to Friedrich Heiler, March 1921, in *SL*, pp. 318–21. And see *EA1*, pp. 276–7; and *EA2*, p. 233, for God, in himself and as Trinity, as source and goal of the mystical and the social. The last direct citation in the text occurs in a letter to Tyrrell, given without date, in Petre, *Autobiography and Life of George Tyrrell*, Vol. II, p. 69.
14. Troeltsch, *Christian Thought*, in the introduction by von Hügel, pp. xxvi–xxvii. In *RG*, a distinction is made between 'actual, constructive original religion . . ., always full of the here and now; and . . . the attempts to rationalize religion and get it well within the limits of the human mind, to have it something which we hold rather than something which holds us; here the fear is lest we should be run away with it, lest it should master us, lest it should be beyond our mastering of it.' Rationalized religion is 'a thing made to measure', 'devoid of dependence, of *creatureliness*, of *givenness* '(pp. 138–9).
15. *RG*, p. 18.
16. *ME2*, pp. 285–6.
17. *EL*, pp. vii-viii, 132, 162–3, 389; *EA1*, p. 70; *EA2*, pp. 67, 246; letter to Norman Kemp Smith, 31 December 1921 – 3 January 1922, *St Andrews MS* 30420.
18. Letter to E. A. Sonnenschein, 18 April 1916, in *SL*, pp. 232–5, esp. p. 235.
19. I emphasize 'pure' to remind the reader that von Hügel, both by temperament and conviction, strongly endorses the prophetic, the mystical, the non-institutional. He would give much room to the 'protestant principle', but always as part of an organic whole. Indeed, purification and reform largely depend on the 'prophetic' or 'charismatic' gift.
20. *EA2*, pp. 75–6, 84 ff.
21. *LN*, pp. 9–11, 28–31.

22. Letter to Friedrich Heiler, March 1921, in *SL*, pp. 318–21. My italics. For the New Testament witness on the whole question, see *ME1*, pp. 30–8. The second edition of *ME1*, p. xiii, suggests that Heiler later modified his views.
23. *EA1*, pp. 268–9. This reference's faith appeal to the one God of *both* faith (revelation, Church) and reason (scientific history and exegesis) is powerfully confirmed in a letter to Martin D'Arcy, S.J., 5 November 1919, in Whelan, op. cit., pp. 28–32.
24. *EA1*, pp. 260–2. The reference is to a 1918 statement, which of course differs widely – but not in the point essential to us here – from the early and conservative views of *Some Notes on the Petrine Claims*, 1893 (published London, 1930). For a view from von Hügel's more radical period, 1904, see *EA2*, pp. 18–19. Von Hügel's positions here are all comfortably inside the understanding of divine institution given in much recent Catholic ecclesiology. See, e.g., Hans Küng, *The Church*, London, 1967, pp. 70–9.
25. *CE*, pp. 290–1: 'l'éternel manifesté dans le temps. . . . et cela en un sens unique et nettement historique – l'incarnation de Dieu en une âme et un corps determinés, en Jésus de Nazareth.'
26. *EA1*, p. 261. Written in 1918.
27. *EA2*, p. 105. Written in 1914.
28. Ibid., p. 106.
29. *EL*, pp. 342–4.
30. *EU*, p. 78. Clearly, a whole nested hierarchy of questions arises from this position, a position which constitutes an imperative appeal *by* the *institutional to* the *intellectual* element of religion continually to discover, delimit, organize and verbalize for successive cultures the kind, degree and extent of this historical factualness which, through tradition, is the medium *for* the *mystical* element, man's incarnationally and institutionally located, but fully personal response of faith. Von Hügel makes a clear distinction between facts, faith and theology, and between Christianity's need for a nucleus of facts and what (as a matter of fact) are the facts which make up that nucleus. On these and other related questions, see *EL*, pp. 164–5, 342–7; *EA2*, pp. 105–11. We have already touched on the problem of faith and history (Chapter 2, p. 39, n. 27). In addition, see Nédoncelle, *von Hügel*, pp. 67–9, 184–92; and the fine study of von Hügel by John Heaney, op. cit. Von Hügel's own late reservations about some of Loisy's exegesis are expressed in a letter to Norman Kemp Smith, 20 September 1920, *St Andrews MS* 30420.
31. See references to Schnackenburg, in Chapter 2, p. 64, n. 140.

32. As mentioned already in Chapter 2, p. 38, n. 21, I cannot find that von Hügel alludes to the role that the Johannine and Pauline theologies assign to Christ in creation, a vital conception that would have smoothed his ecumenical path here in terms still properly Christological.
33. *EA1*, pp. 234–5; *LN*, pp. 8–9. My italics.
34. See letter to Edmund Bishop, 16 June 1908, Abercrombie, op. cit., pp. 422–7, esp. no. 6, pp. 425–6.
35. Letter to Mrs Henry Drew, 4 June 1904, in *SL*, pp. 125–7.
36. The ecumenical theme ranges wide in von Hügel's spirituality. Some major texts on which this discussion has been directly based: *ME2*, pp. 266–7, 331–3, 344–5; *EA1*, pp. 63, 92, 222–3, 234–5, 252–3, 269; *RG*, pp. 148–51; *LN*, pp. xxxii, xxxiv, 54–8. The anonymous Christian concept is adumbrated in a letter to E. A. Sonnenschein, 18 April 1916, in *SL*, pp. 232–5. For von Hügel's corollary doctrine on conversion, see, e.g., *EU*, pp. 68–9. The point is especially clear in letter to Mrs Lillie, 13 March 1920, in *SL*, pp. 300–2.
37. *ME2*, p. 362. And see *EA2*, pp. 67–8.
38. *EA2*, pp. 112–14, 246, 266–7, 274–5; *EL*, pp. 395–6; *CE*, p. 291; *EA1*, p. 260; *RG*, p. 99.
39. *ME2*, pp. 355–6 and 202. For other texts on the Pauline image of body see ibid., pp. 65–6; and *EL*, pp. 47–8 (its source in stoicism). For the general New Testament witness on Christianity as social, see *EL*, pp. 62–4, 71, 78.
40. *LN*, pp. xxv, 25, 72; *ME1*, p. 59.
41. *ME2*, p. 137; *LN*, pp. x, xxix–xxx, 82–3, 147–8.
42. Letter to Mrs Lillie, 21–23 September 1921, in *SL*, pp. 341–4. Teilhard de Chardin wrote with similar point in a letter to his parents, 16 June 1912, following a visit to the Carthusian charterhouse at Parkminster in Sussex. He was struck by ' "the forceful affirmation of the supernatural represented by the life of these men"; those who refuse to see anything but human progress will say that this life "is no use at all; and it is not a bad thing that it should be possible for this to be said, in this sense, about some people, in the Church: in that way, there can be no possible misapprehension" ' (cited in Henri de Lubac, *The Religion of Teilhard de Chardin*, London, 1967, pp. 359–60).
43. *LN*, pp. x, 3, 23–4; *EU*, pp. 74–5, 80–1; *EA1*, pp. 98–9.
44. *EA1*, p. 293; *LN*, pp. ix, xiv, 111; *ME2*, pp. 362–5; *EL*, pp. 375–6, citing Francis of Sales; review of Heiler's *Das Gebet*, p. 268. See also the letter to Gallarati-Scotti, cited at length above, Chapter 2, p. 43, n. 40.

45. *EA2*, pp. 86–8; *ME1*, p. 315; *LN*, pp. 26–8. At least twice von Hügel, in his daughter Gertrude and in Tyrrell, had the deeply painful experience of damaging someone's *attrait* by rushing, contradicting or distorting it. For the events, and his later reflections on them, see *LN*, pp. 122–3; letters to Tyrrell, 9 October 1897, 26 January 1898, 4 December 1902, 25 March 1908, 27 June 1908, in *VH & T*, pp. 13–15, 20–5, and in *SL*, pp. 113–15, 147–8, 152–3. Von Hügel tells Gwendolen Greene: 'The golden rule is, to help those we love to escape from us; and never try to begin to help people, or influence them, till they ask, but wait for them' (*LN*, p. xxix).
46. *LN*, pp. 82–3, 147–8; but esp. *MK*, pp. 321, 328–9.
47. *EA2*, pp. 17–18; letter to Blondel, 30 July 1899, *St Andrews MS* B3280. H8: the institutional Church is *absolutely* necessary, and yet a *means:* it is for the sake of personality; letter to Maude Petre, 27 November 1902, *BM Add. MS* 45361 (on the priest as mediator and minister).
48. Letter to Tyrrell, 18 December 1906, in *SL*, pp. 136–7.
49. Letter to Malcolm Quin, 17 November 1909, in *SL*, pp. 172–5.
50. Letter of June 1912, cited without name of recipient in de la Bedoyère, op. cit., pp. 263–5; letter to Canon Newsom, 7 December 1912, in *SL*, pp. 200–1.
51. *EA2*, pp. 20–3. Nédoncelle, *von Hügel*, p. 102, n. 1, observes that this generally legitimate approach to Jesus must yet take account of 'the spiritual perfection which belongs to Our Lord from the beginning'. And see ibid., p. 139, n. 2, for von Hügel's understanding of infallibility.
52. In addition to most of the literature already cited in connection with the issue of authority, see letter to Tyrrell, 1 October 1907, in *SL*, pp. 141–2; and the important letter to von Hügel's daughter Hildegarde, 1899, cited at length in de la Bedoyère, op. cit., pp. 117–19.
53. From a 'reminiscence' by Ward, written sometime before his death in 1916 and cited in Maisie Ward, *The Wilfrid Wards*, p. 300. For examples of von Hügel's unbuttoned, even violent responses to authority, see, e.g., letter to Tyrrell, 20 November 1907, in *VH & T*, pp. 166–7; letter to the same, 25 November 1907, *BM Add. MS* 44930. Of the highly charged pages 357–64 in *EL*, he writes to Maude Petre, 12 October 1912, *BM Add. MS* 45362, that the strong ripostes on institutionalism in those pages 'will not be liked, are calmly, not nervously written, and are an inevitable part of the book's central argument'. Quite true, too. But see also the late, definitely qualified, yet substantive acceptance of *Pascendi* in a letter to Petre, 13 March 1918, in *SL*, pp. 247–9.

54. *EA2*, p. 276; letter to Tyrrell, 18 December 1901, in *VH& T*, pp. 80–100, esp. p. 99.
55. *EA1*, pp. 275–7; letter to Mrs Lillie, 13 October 1920, in *SL*, pp. 312–13.
56. *RG*, p. 113.
57. See Chapter 3, pp. 77–8, 80–2, 88–9, 117–18; and Chapter 4, pp. 138 ff; esp. pp. 153–4, 160.
58. This view – surely classical – of prayer as primarily man *en face du donné* and of God as the *donné* is the basis of Marcel Domergue's *L'oraison au-delà des méthodes*, Toulouse, 1967.
59. See Chapter 2, p. 40.
60. *ME2*, pp. 259–60.
61. See Chapter 3, pp. 122–3.
62. Letter to Wilfrid Ward, 6 March 1916, in *SL*, pp. 228–30. For von Hügel's similar view of a retreat as prayer-and-reformation rather than as speculation-discussion, see *LN*, pp. 117–18.
63. Letter to J. M. Connell, 31 December 1913, in *SL*, pp. 203–5.
64. *EA2*, p. 227; letter to Wilfrid Ward, 28 February 1916, in *SL*, pp. 227–8.
65. *SL*, p. 58.
66. *LN*, pp. 43–4. And see letter to Maude Petre, 26 March 1909, in *SL*, pp. 161–2.
67. *LN*, p. 46.
68. *ME1*, p. 74; *LN*, p. 44. Also, ibid., pp. xxxviii–xxxix, 94–5. And see *EA2*, pp. 226–42, where von Hügel discusses this point and a whole range of other incarnational presuppositions, conditions and effects of prayer, e.g., the fact of sexuality; the nature of temptation; the necessity of non-religious, of secular interests for the sake of prayer itself. This essay is von Hügel's one lengthy treatment of prayer. It gathers together much, but by no means all, of his thought and advice on the subject.
69. *LN*, pp. 185–6. And see *EL*, pp. 325–7.
70. Letter to Y. Brilioth, 12 April 1920, in *SL*, pp. 303–4.
71. Letter to Bernard Holland, 22 March 1919, ibid., p. 269.
72. *LN*, p. 44.
73. Ibid., pp. 140–1.
74. Letter to Tyrrell, 31 December 1898, in *VH& T*, pp. 56–68, esp. pp. 62–3.
75. *LN*, p. 25; and *EL*, pp. 286–7.
76. *EU*, pp. 91, 95, 107, 111.
77. Ibid., p. 77. And see *LN*, pp. 66–7.
78. *EU*, p. 95.
79. *LN*, p. 72.

80. Ibid., p. 196.
81. *ME1*, p. 336; and *LN*, p. 116. The context makes the meaning of 'action' here sufficiently clear. The meaning is not identical with the term as used in the 'action-activity' distinction (see Chapter 4, p. 158). In *that* usage, genuine contemplation *is* action. But this is obvious.
82. *LN*, p. 4. The prayer is by Ignatius Loyola.
83. *EA1*, p. 192, interpreting a text from Troeltsch.
84. *ME2*, p. 342, citing *The Varieties of Religious Experience*, p. 364.
85. *EL*, pp. 255–6, 321; *ME2*, pp. 358–60; and see Chapter 2, pp. 60 ff.
86. *EA2*, pp. 240–2.
87. Letter to Maude Petre, 5 December 1899, in *SL*, pp. 82–5; *EL*, pp. 65, 253–4.
88. *SL*, p. 59.
89. *ME2*, pp. 257–8, 344–7; *EA2*, p. 218.
90. See Chapter 2, p. 52. My italics.
91. *ME1*, pp. 248–9; *EA1*, pp. 167–8 (citing Troeltsch), 285–6; letter to Clement Webb, May 1921, in *SL*, pp. 327–9; letter to Bernard Holland, 27 February 1922, ibid., p. 350; letter to Tyrrell, 10–12 November 1903, *BM Add. MS* 44928; letter to Maude Petre, 15 December 1910, ibid., 45362; *MK*, pp. 323–4, 326, 330. We get a rare, untypical, fiercely negative example from life, concerning von Hügel's treatment of his daughter Hildegarde, in de la Bedoyère, op. cit., p. 150.
92. *ME1*, p. xxiii. And see the dangers posed, and the ascetical friction called for, among the elements of religion, ibid., pp. 70–7 (briefly treated in Chapter 4, pp. 135 ff.).
93. Letter to Maude Petre, 26 September 1900, in *SL*, pp. 88–96, esp. p. 95. Some italics are mine. And see letter to Tyrrell, 26 September 1898, ibid., pp. 71–4, esp. p. 72.
94. And here lies the reason why, for von Hügel, human aspects of religion (institution, worship, sacrament, theology, etc.), while in constant need of prophetic reform, protest, purification, cannot be declared idolatrous on principle.
95. *ME2*, pp. 348–51. And see *ME1*, pp. 24–5.
96. *ME2*, pp. 348–51.
97. Ibid. In *RG*, pp. 31–2, briefly, and in a rather complete statement for Rev. H. Handley, 14 September 1918, in *SL*, pp. 252–3, von Hügel gives a fine appreciation and a trenchant criticism of the *Imitation of Christ* (he read it almost daily) as touching these large issues.
98. See Chapter 4, pp. 154–5, 159–60. Also, *ME1*, pp. 232–3, 238–9, 244–6, 248–9; *ME2*, pp. 124–5.

99. On the institutional as purification, see *EA1*, pp. 264–7; *EA2*, p. 88; letter to Tyrrell, 19 August 1900, in *SL*, pp. 87–8; letter to Canon Newsom, 7 December 1912, ibid., pp. 200–1.
100. *EL*, pp. 332–3.
101. For texts on science and philosophy as intellectual element of religion, on the necessity of this intellectual element, and on the asceticism required, see, e.g., *ME2*, pp. 269–72, 388–90; remarks to the 'Religion in the Army' Committee, 1917, in *SL*, pp. 63–5; letters to Tyrrell, 4 December 1899 and 23 June 1908, ibid., pp. 77–82, esp. p. 81, and pp. 151–2; letter to Mrs Lillie, 20 April 1922, ibid., pp. 352–4 (*of particular value*); *RG*, pp. 30–1 (where the 'philosophy of the insoluble conflict of head and heart' is rejected); *The Papal Commission and the Pentateuch* (with Rev. Charles Briggs), London, 1906, pp. 47, 54–7. Von Hügel's own intellectual history, carefully detailed and analysed in Heaney, op. cit., is often concerned with asserting the legitimate independence of science from religion, especially the sciences of history and biblical exegesis. To secure this end, he only slowly (about 1905, according to Heaney, p. 81) came sufficiently to differentiate as well as to compare, precisely as science, such disciplines as physics and history and to take account of what he always knew: that metaphysical presuppositions are involved in scientific method and judgment. The preface of the first edition (1908) of *ME1*, pp. xxiv–xxv, speaks clearly of the 'deeply different' methods and aims of history and physical science.
102. *CFA*, pp. 82–4. My italics. And see above, Chapter 3, pp. 110–11. The following texts either produce the basic scheme or throw further light on one or more of its several parts: *ME1*, pp. 41–8; *ME2*, pp. 367–86; letters to Tyrrell, 26 September 1898 and 18–20 December 1901, in *SL*, pp. 71–4, 102–3; letter to Maude Petre, 26 September 1900, ibid., pp. 88–96, esp. p. 96; 'The Spiritual Writings of Father Grou, S.J.', *Tablet*, 21 December 1889, p. 991 (showing early influence of Grou); 'Professor Eucken on the Struggle for Spiritual Life', *Spectator*, 14 November 1896, p. 680 (showing massive influence of Eucken).
103. *ME1*, pp. 77–9; *ME2*, pp. 379, 381–2; *LN*, p. 59.
104. *ME1*, p. 43. And see *ME2*, pp. 303–4. For Darwin, see *EL*, p. 281.
105. *ME2*, pp. 377–81; letter to Maude Petre, 26 September 1900, in *SL*, pp. 88–96, esp. pp. 94–5.
106. *SL*, p. 58.
107. Letter to Tyrrell, 26 September 1898, ibid., pp. 71–4, esp. p. 73.
108. *ME2*, pp. 350, 374–9.

109. See Chapter 4, pp. 143–4. The idea of purification as chosen is frequent in von Hügel. For its source in Catherine of Genoa and Newman, see *ME1*, p. xxii.
110. See Chapter 4, p. 160.
111. Letter to Juliet Mansel, 13 October 1911, in *SL*, pp. 193–4.
112. *EL*, pp. 393–4; *ME2*, pp. 378, 383–4.
113. *ME2*, p. 378.
114. Ibid., p. 384. And see *ME1*, pp. 43–7.
115. *LN*, pp. 61–4, 75, 79–80, 121; *EU*, pp. 71, 97; *CE*, p. 296. For the direct citation, see Chapter 4, p. 155.
116. See Chapter 3, p. 77.
117. *ME2*, p. 395. This trilogy of God, Incarnation (Christ, religion, science), and Cross appears at least three times in von Hügel's writings: here, pp. 393–5; *EA1*, pp. 238–9; *LN*, pp. xlii–xliii.
118. *ME2*, p. 395. My italics.
119. Chapter 4, pp. 126–7; and references to *ME1* and *ME2* in n. 3 there.
120. This must and wants to be said, in view of the very real limitations von Hügel and most modern exegetes impose on the historical Jesus' knowledge, temperament, achievement, etc. (see Chapter 2, pp. 36, 40–3), and in view of von Hügel's faith in the Church as 'part of his larger biography' (ibid., p. 38, n. 19). However, no limitation is thereby imposed on the *spiritual* perfection of the earthly Jesus.
121. See *ME1*, pp. 26–8, cited at length (but not completely) in Chapter 2, pp. 34–5; also in *ME1*, pp. 367–70, where spiritually persuasive personality is explicitly considered in relation to God, incarnation and science, thing and person, friction and harmony; *ME2*, pp. 387–96, where von Hügel provides an even larger summary and synthesis of the three great realities: God, man, and the world, and of the three elements of religion. Similar syntheses of his spirituality are given in *EL*, pp. 365–71, 382–93, under the rubric of eternal life, and in *EA1*, pp. 215–19, as the four qualities of supernatural experience. Finally, as noted, von Hügel's description of the three stages of spiritual life is a synthetic statement (Chapter 4, pp. 140–3).
122. *EA1*, pp. 161, 276; *LN*, p. xliii.
123. *EL*, p. 394. But our whole present study ought to be the real verification of this statement.
124. Ibid., p. 395. But see too Tyrrell's complaint to von Hügel: 'In your just revolt against the fallacy of simplification, I sometimes wonder whether you are not driven to value complexity for its own sake'

(letter to von Hügel, 22 June 1908, in *VH & T*, pp. 171–5). Earlier, von Hügel writes to Tyrrell that Bremond seemed 'somewhat puzzled by my doctrine of slowly acquired harmony in and by the resistance and friction of every kind of recalcitrant, apparently desperate material. But what is life, all moral, spiritual rational – and Christian and Catholic life and reform in self and others – but *that?*' (letter of 30 April 1904, ibid., pp. 152–3). It remains a question of fact. What are the actual dimensions of the real? What has God done, what is he continuing to do? The most *objective* answer possible to this question must determine the size and the style of man's response: his *subjectivity* and personality.

125. *LN*, pp. xvi, xix, 104; *EU*, p. 77. *ME1*, p. xii; and *LN*, pp. 46–7, dilate on the dangers of straining, the need of moderation and 'creatureliness', and yet of the rightness of striving greatly, 'unless, indeed, Dante is to disappear before Tennyson, and Beethoven before Sir Arthur Sullivan'.

126. *LN*, p. viii.

127. A whole series of texts treat of spirituality and personality in terms of attachment and detachment. See, e.g., *CFA*, pp. 80–1; *ME1*, pp. 248–9.

128. See Chapter 2, p. 72.

129. *EA1*, p. 270. De Lubac, op. cit., p. 233, finds Teilhard de Chardin's whole thought 'summed up' in a parallel vision and ambition: to 'Christify evolution'. Teilhard's modern-traditional stance in relation to contemporary man's preoccupation with 'the material, the personal and the relative' is sensitively spelled out in Christopher F. Mooney, 'Teilhard de Chardin and Christian Spirituality', *Thought*, Autumn 1967, pp. 383–402. The similarity to von Hügel is striking.

CHAPTER SIX

1. *LN*, p. xliii.
2. Ibid.; and see Chapter 5, pp. 178, 205.
3. See Chapter 2, p. 73.
4. This is a far cry from personality as 'cult' of self-assertion and fulfilment. For von Hügel, self as personality occurs only in consciously seeking the *other*.
5. Von Hügel goes this far. On the making of God, see Chapter 4, p. 139.
6. See previous note.
7. I have treated the doctrines of creation and resurrection as presuppositions because, while certainly interior to and therefore part of

von Hügel's faith experience, they are not so much themes that he explores as ground on which he builds. It is the *consequences* of these truths that mostly occupy his spiritual doctrine.

8. The mystery of Christ as the Father's *ordering* love of the world is also central to the spirituality of St Ignatius. William Peters, S.J., in a recent commentary remarks: 'The text of the *Spiritual Exercises* proves that Ignatius is almost obsessed with the question of order and harmony' (*The Spiritual Exercises of St Ignatius: Exposition and Interpretation*, Jersey City, 1968, p. 5).
9. See Chapter 2, p. 50.
10. There is a recent example of such periodization in Herbert W. Richardson, *Theology for a New World*, London, 1968, esp. pp. 30–49: 'Five Kinds of Faith'. Sociologist Peter Berger discusses the problem with wit and perception in the first two chapters of *A Rumor of Angels: Modern Society and the Rediscovery of the Supernatural*, New York, 1969, pp. 1–60.
11. See Chapter 2, pp. 42–3.
12. See Chapter 3, p. 92.
13. And see below, pp. 227–8, on the aesthetic, and on games and dancing. Furthermore, the Diaries, especially in later years, show a steady diet of theatre, cinema and museums.
14. Martin Green, op. cit., pp. 90–6, makes some very perceptive comments on this whole question.
15. Cock, op. cit., p. 17, suggests that von Hügel's writings are for 'advanced souls'. Yet von Hügel does give much time to teenagers, and even to young children such as Henri Garceau. For correspondence with the latter, see index in *SL*.
16. See below, p. 227.
17. The letter is anonymously published, with autobiographical introduction by the recipient, in *Dublin Review*, Second Quarter, 1951, pp. 1–11.
18. The reader is here made aware that, while von Hügel is immediately about to list *all* the factors and areas of experience that comprise spirituality, the four principles he is going to develop at some length directly deal only with the *religious* aspects of full spiritual life.
19. Those who have made Jesuit retreats – at least until recently – will easily recognize much of this advice. Von Hügel once said to a young man: 'Under God I owe my salvation to the Jesuits, but' and then added after an apparently mighty pause, 'don't *you* ever become a Jesuit' (in Cock, op. cit., p. 4).
20. 1 Cor. 1:23–25.

BIBLIOGRAPHY

This bibliography is confined to materials directly used for this study. The main work on von Hügel bibliography was done by A. H. Dakin in 1934. Substantive additions were made by Maurice Nédoncelle in 1935 and by John J. Heaney, S.J., in 1963.

I. WORKS OF FRIEDRICH VON HÜGEL

A. *Published Material*

1. *Books, Articles and Addresses*

'The Spiritual Writings of Father Grou', *Tablet*, 21 and 28 December 1889, pp. 990–1, 1029–31.

Some Notes on the Petrine Claims, 1893. Published London, 1930, 103 pp.

Letter to *Tablet*, 2 June 1894, pp. 857–8, replying to review, 24 February 1894, of a new English edition of Fénelon's *Spiritual Letters*.

'Professor Eucken on the Struggle for Spiritual Life', *Spectator*, 14 November 1896, pp. 679–81.

'The Historical Method and the Documents of the Hexateuch', *Catholic University Bulletin*, April 1898, pp. 198–226, as revised and translated from 'La Méthode historique et son application à l'étude des documents de l'Hexateuque', Paris, 1898, 35 pp.

'Caterina Fiesca Adorna, the Saint of Genoa', *Hampstead Annual*, 1898, pp. 70–85. Cited as *CFA*.

Notes on Wilfrid Ward's 'Authority a Reasonable Ground for Religious Belief', 1899, in *Papers Read Before the Synthetic Society, 1896–1908*, London 1909, pp. 235–9. Manuscript in Archives, St Andrews University Library.

'Experience and Transcendence', *Dublin Review*, April 1906, pp. 357–79. Cited as *ET*.

'Official Authority and Living Religion', 1904, in *Essays and Addresses on the Philosophy of Religion*, Second Series, London, 1926, pp. 3–23. This volume cited as *EA2*.

'Du Christ éternel et de nos christologies successives', *Quinzaine*, June 1904, pp. 285–312. Cited as *CE*. The same journal published a reply by Wehrlé, 15 August, and a second, brief statement by von Hügel, 16 September.

'The Place and Function of the Historical Element in Religion', 1905, included in *EA2*, pp. 27–55.

The Papal Commission and the Pentateuch (with Rev. Charles Briggs), London, 1906, 64 pp.

'The Relations Between God and Man in "The New Theology" of Rev. R. J. Campbell', *Albany Review*, September 1907, pp. 650–68. Cited as *RGM*.

The Mystical Element of Religion as Studied in Saint Catherine of Genoa and Her Friends, 2 vols., London, 1908; 2nd edition, 1923. 888 pp. Cited as *ME1*, *ME2*.

Review of Loisy's *Evangiles Synoptiques*, *Hibbert Journal*, July 1908, pp. 926–30.

'Religion and Illusion' and 'Religion and Reality', Italian original in *Coenobium*, 1909; translated and expanded in *Quest*, April and July 1918, and included in *Essays and Addresses on the Philosophy of Religion*, First Series, London, 1921, pp. 20–6. This volume cited as *EA1*.

'Father Tyrrell: some memorials of the last twelve years of his life', *Hibbert Journal*, January 1910, pp. 233–52.

'John the Apostle' and 'John, Gospel of St', *Encyclopedia Britannica*, 11th edition, XV, pp. 432–3, 452–8.

'The Religious Philosophy of Rudolf Eucken', *Hibbert Journal*, April 1912, pp. 660–77. Cited as *RP*.

Eternal Life: A Study of its Implications and Applications, Edinburgh, 1912, 1913, 443 pp. Cited as *EL*.

'Petite consultation sur les difficultés concernant Dieu', 1912, published as appendix in Pietro Scoppola, *Crisi modernista e rinnovamento cattolico in Italia*, Bologna, 1961, pp. 368–92. Manuscript in possession of Contessa Eugenia Salimei, Via Bertoloni 3, Rome. Cited as *PC*.

'The Essentials of Catholicism', London, *Liddon House Occasional Paper*, 1913, and included in *EA1*, pp. 227–41.

'On the Place and Function, within Religion, of the Body, of History, and of Institutions', 1913, included in *EA2*, pp. 59–88.

'On the Specific Genius and Capacities of Christianity', *Constructive Quarterly*, March and December 1914, and included in *EA1*, pp. 144–94.

'On Certain Central Needs of Religion, and the Difficulties of Liberal Movements in Face of the Needs: as Experienced Within the Roman Catholic Church During the Last Forty Years', 1914, included in *EA2*, pp. 91–131.

'On the Preliminaries to Religious Belief and on the Facts of Suffering, Faith and Love', 1914, included in *EA1*, pp. 98–116.

The German Soul in its Attitude Towards Ethics and Christianity, the State and War, London, 1916, 223 pp. Cited as *GS*.

'Progress and Religion', in *Progress and History*, edited by F. S. Marvin, Oxford, 1916, and included in *EA1*, pp. 242–53.

'The Convictions Common to Catholicism and Protestantism', *Homiletic Review*, 1917, and included in *EA1*, pp. 242–53.

'What Do We Mean by Heaven? And What Do We Mean by Hell?' *Church Quarterly Review*, April 1917, and included in *EA1*, pp. 195–224.

'The Idea of God', 1918, included in *EA2*, pp. 135–54.

'The Apocalyptic Element in the Teaching of Jesus: its Ultimate Significance and its Abiding Function', 1919, included in *EA1*, pp. 119–43.

'Christianity and the Supernatural', *Modern Churchman*, 1920, and included in *EA1*, pp. 278–98.

'Responsibility in Religious Belief', 1920, included in *EA1*, pp. 3–19.

'Morals and Religion', 1920, included in *EA2*, pp. 157–64.

'Suffering and God', 1921, included in *EA2*, pp. 167–213.

Essays and Addresses on the Philosophy of Religion, First Series, London, 1921, 308 pp. Cited as *EA1*. Contents are itemized in this bibliography.

'The Facts and Truths Concerning God and the Soul Which Are of Most Importance in the Life of Prayer', 1921, included in *EA2*, pp. 217–42; published separately as *The Life of Prayer*, London, 1927, 63 pp.

'The Catholic Contribution to Religion', *Student Movement*, 1921, and included in *EA2*, pp. 245–51.

Review of Friedrich Heiler's *Das Gebet*, *International Review of Missions*, April 1921, pp. 266–70.

Letter to *Times Literary Supplement*, 22 December 1921, p. 860, replying to review of *EA1*.

'The Difficulties and Dangers of Nationality', *Challenge*, 4 and 11 August 1922, and included in *EA2*, pp. 255–76.

'Introduction', in Ernst Troeltsch, *Christian Thought*, London, 1923, pp. xi–xxxi.

'Der Mystiker und die Kirche', *Hochland*, December 1924, pp. 320–30. Cited as *MK*.

Essays and Addresses on the Philosophy of Religion, Second Series, London, 1926 (posthumous), 287 pp. Cited as *EA2*. Contents are itemized in this bibliography.

The Reality of God and Religion and Agnosticism, being the literary remains of Baron Friedrich von Hügel, edited by Edmund G. Gardner, London, 1931, 264 pp. Cited as *RG*.

2. *Notes and Letters*

'Talks With Fr. Newman', 14, 16, 18 June 1876, published in R. K. Browne, 'Newman and von Hügel: A Record of an Early Meeting', *The Month*, July 1961, pp. 24–33, from the autograph notebook in the Archives, St Andrews University Library. Browne includes selections from von Hügel's letters to Newman, 13 December 1874, and to Fr. Ryder, 18 August 1890 (both letters in Birmingham Oratory Archives).

Letter (hitherto unpublished) from von Hügel to a young girl, 11 March 1910, *Dublin Review*, April 1951, pp. 1–11 (with introduction by anonymous recipient).

Baron Friedrich von Hügel: Selected Letters, 1896–1924, edited with memoir by Bernard Holland, London, 1927, 376 pp. Cited as *SL*. (This volume also includes 'Some of the Sayings of Abbé Huvelin: Advice given to F.v.H., Paris, May 26–31, 1886', and 'Remarks Made by Baron F. von Hügel at a Meeting of the Committee to Inquire into Religion in the Army, 1917'.)

'Friedrich von Hügel's Letters to Edmund Bishop', edited by Nigel Abercrombie, *Dublin Review*, 1953, pp. 68–78, 179–89, 285–98, 419–38 (22 letters, 1897–1913).

Letters from Baron Friedrich von Hügel to a Niece, edited with introduction by Gwendolen Greene, London, 1928, 201 pp. Cited as *LN*.

'Friedrich von Hügel's Letters to Martin D'Arcy', edited by Joseph P. Whelan, *The Month*, July–August 1969, pp. 23–36 (five letters, 1919–21).

'The Parent as Spiritual Director', letter from von Hügel to Mrs Margaret Clutton, 11 June 1912, edited by Joseph P. Whelan, *The Month*, August 1970, pp. 52–7, September 1970, pp. 84–7 (35-page MS now deposited with von Hügel papers in St Andrews University Library).

(A large number of other letters, as well as citations from the diaries, may be found in several works listed below. Mention will be made where quotation seems of sufficient bulk or interest.)

3. *Anthologies*

Thorold, Algar, *Readings From Friedrich von Hügel*, London, 1928, 359 pp.

Chambers, P. Franklin, *Baron von Hügel: Man of God*, London, 1945; reissued in paperback as *Friedrich von Hügel: Selected Writings*, London, 1964, 192 pp.

Steere, Douglas V., *Spiritual Counsels and Letters of Baron Friedrich von Hügel*, London, 1964, 186 pp.

B. *Unpublished Material*

Von Hügel-Tyrrell Correspondence (almost intact), *British Museum Additional MSS* 44927–44931.

Von Hügel's Letters to Maude Petre, *British Museum Additional MSS* 45361–45362.

Von Hügel's Diaries, 43 vols., 1877–79, 1884–1900, 1902–24, currently c/o L. Barmann.

The following are in the von Hügel Collection, Archives, St Andrews University Library, Fife (to which most of von Hügel's personal library and papers were sent after his death):

Von Hügel-Blondel Correspondence, *St Andrews MS* B3280.H8: autographs of Blondel, typed copies of von Hügel's 43 letters and cards (autographs at Archives blondeliennes, Aix-en-Provence).

Von Hügel-Bremond Correspondence, *St Andrews MS* 30284: autographs of Bremond, photostats of von Hügel's 64 letters and cards (autographs in private archives).

Letters of Abbé Louis-Joseph Huvelin to von Hügel, *St Andrews MSS* 2690–2704: 16 autograph letters; also a six-page essay by von Hügel on the conversion of Paul Emile Littré (autograph, with *marginalia* by Huvelin).

Letter from von Hügel to Sir Alfred (Lyall?), *St Andrews MS* 2650: autograph.

Letter from von Hügel to Gallarati-Scotti, *St Andrews MS* 2649: autograph (perhaps a draft copy).

Von Hügel-Norman Kemp Smith Correspondence, *St Andrews MS* 30420: both sets of autographs; 39 letters and cards from von Hügel.

(In addition to the above, the St Andrews Collection contains a vast number of autograph letters *to* von Hügel from such as Bergson, Duchesne (56 letters), Eucken (93 letters), Gore, Harnack, Laberthonnière (36 letters), Le Roy (10 letters), Newman (20 letters), Sabatier (22 letters), Schweitzer, Troeltsch (22 letters), W. Ward, C. J. Webb, etc.)

II. WORKS ON THE THOUGHT OF FRIEDRICH VON HÜGEL AND ON RELATED QUESTIONS

Abbott, Walter M., *The Documents of Vatican II*, New York, 1966, 794 pp.

Baelz, Peter, *Prayer and Providence*, London, 1968, 141 pp.

Balthasar, Hans Urs von, 'Closeness to God', *Concilium*, November 1967, pp. 20–7.

——, *Man in History*, London, 1968, 341 pp.

Balthasar, Hans Urs von, 'Joy and the Cross', *Concilium*, Vol. 39, New York, 1968, pp. 83–96.

Bedoyère, Michael de la, *The Life of Baron von Hügel*, London, 1951, 366 pp. (Large use of diaries and of letters to H.'s wife.)

Berger, Peter L., *A Rumor of Angels*, New York, 1969, 129 pp.

Bernard, Charles A., *La prière chrétienne*, Bruges, 1967, 390 pp.

Bernard-Maitre, Henri, 'Un épisode significatif du modernisme. "Histoire et Dogme" de Maurice Blondel d'après les Papiers inédits d'Alfred Loisy (1897–1905)', *Recherches de Science Religieuse*, January–March 1969, pp. 49–74.

Bligh, John, 'Did Jesus Live by Faith?' *Heythrop Journal*, October 1968, pp. 414–19.

——, 'Matching Passages in the Gospels', *The Way*, October 1968, pp. 306–17.

Bourke, Joseph, 'The Historical Jesus and the Kerygmatic Christ', *Concilium*, January 1966, pp. 16–26.

Bourke, Myles, 'Reflections on Church Order in the New Testament', *Catholic Biblical Quarterly*, October 1968, pp. 493–511.

Bremond, Henri, *Histoire Littéraire du Sentiment Religieux en France*, Vol. I, *L'Humanisme Dévot*, Paris, 1916; translated as *A Literary History of Religious Thought in France*, Vol. I, *Devout Humanism*, London, 1928, 423 pp.

Brown, Norman O., *Life Against Death: The Psychoanalytical Meaning of History*, London, 1959, reissued in paperback, London, 1968, 315 pp.

Brown, Raymond E., *Jesus God and Man*, London, 1968, 109 pp.

Burke, Patrick, 'Man Without Christ: An Approach to Hereditary Sin', *Theological Studies*, March 1968, pp. 4–18.

Burnaby, John, 'Christian Prayer', *Soundings: Essays Concerning Christian Understanding*, edited by A. R. Vidler, Cambridge, 1966, pp. 219–37.

Butler, B. C., *Spirit and Institution in the New Testament*, London, 1961, 33 pp.

Butler, Cuthbert, *Western Mysticism*, London, 1922, 344 pp.

Chadwick, Owen, *The Victorian Church*, Part I, London, 1966, 606 pp.

Chapman, John, 'Mysticism (Christian, Roman Catholic)', *Encyclopedia of Religion and Ethics*, edited by J. Hastings, Vol. 9, pp. 90–101.

——, 'What *Is* Mysticism?' *The Spiritual Letters of Dom John Chapman*, edited by Roger Hudleston, London, 2nd edition, 1938, Appendix II, pp. 297–321.

Cock, Albert A., *A Critical Examination of von Hügel's Philosophy of Religion*, London (undated), 161 pp.

Cropper, Margaret, *Evelyn Underhill*, London, 1958, 224 pp. Cited as *EU*. (Letters from von Hügel to Underhill.)

Crowe, F. E., 'Christologies: How Up-to-Date is Yours?' *Theological Studies*, March 1968, pp. 87–101.

Dakin, A. H., *Von Hügel and the Supernatural*, London, 1934, 273 pp.

Daniélou, Jean, *Prayer as a Political Problem*, London, 1967, 123 pp.

Domergue, Marcel, *L'oraison au-delà des méthodes*, Toulouse, 1967, 56 pp.

Dulles, Avery, 'Jesus of History and Christ of Faith', *Jesus: Commonweal Papers: 2*, 24 November 1967, pp. 225–32.

Eliot, T. S., 'An Emotional Unity', *Dial*, February 1928, pp. 109–12.

Fenton, Joseph C., 'Von Hügel and His Spiritual Direction', *American Ecclesiastical Review*, August 1955, pp. 109–27.

Fiorito, Miguel A., 'Ignatius' Own Legislation on Prayer', *Woodstock Letters*, Spring 1968, pp. 149–224.

Galot, Jean, 'The Knowledge and Consciousness of Christ', *Theology Digest*, Spring 1964, pp. 48–52.

Genova, Umile da, 'Catherine de Gènes', *Dictionnaire de spiritualité*, Vol. II, cols. 290 ff.

Goodier, Alban, 'Baron Friedrich von Hügel's Spiritual Outlook', *The Month*, January 1929, pp. 11–21.

Graef, Hilda, *God and Myself: the Spirituality of John Henry Newman*, London, 1967, 206 pp.

Green, Martin, *Yeats's Blessings on von Hügel*, London, 1967, 256 pp.

Greene, Gwendolen Plunket, *Two Witnesses*, London, 1930, 199 pp.

——, 'Thoughts from von Hügel', *Dublin Review*, April-June 1931, pp. 254–60.

——, 'Baron Friedrich von Hügel', *Pax*, September 1932, pp. 128–32.

Gutwengler, Englebert, 'The Problem of Christ's Knowledge', *Concilium*, January 1966, pp. 48–55.

Hanbury, M., 'Baron von Hügel, "Letters to a Niece"', *The Month*, January 1961, pp. 13–22.

Hart, Ray L., *Unfinished Man and the Imagination: Towards an Ontology and a Rhetoric of Revelation*, New York, 1968, 418 pp.

Heaney, John J., *The Modernist Crisis: von Hügel*, Washington, D.C., 1968; English edition, London, 1969, 304 pp. (In thesis form for Institut Catholique, Paris, this work contains large bibliography.)

Heiler, Friedrich, *Das Gebet*, Munich, 1918; translated as *Prayer*, London, 1932, New York, 1958, 376 pp.

Johnson, Humphrey, 'Baron von Hügel and the Catholic Religion', *Studies*, 1950, pp. 373–84.

Johnston, William, *The Mysticism of the Cloud of Unknowing*, New York, 1967, 285 pp.

Jones, Rufus, 'Mysticism (Introductory)', 'Mysticism (Christian, NT)', 'Mysticism (Christian, Protestant)', *Encyclopedia of Religion and Ethics*, edited by J. Hastings, Vol. 9, pp. 83–4, 89–90, 101–3.

Jungmann, Joseph, *The Place of Christ in Liturgical Prayer*, London, 2nd edition, 1965, 300 pp.

Knowles, David, *The English Mystical Tradition*, London, 1961, 197 pp.

Küng, Hans, *The Church*, London, 1967, 515 pp.

Lester-Garland, L. V., *The Religious Philosophy of Baron F. von Hügel*, London, 1933, 115 pp.

Lewis, C. S., *Letters to Malcolm: Chiefly on Prayer*, London, 1964, 159 pp.

Loisy, Alfred, *L'Evangile et L'Eglise*, Paris, 1902, 1903; translated as *The Gospel and the Church*, 2nd edition, with Preface by Tyrrell, London, 1909, 277 pp.

——, *Mémoires pour servir à l'histoire religieuse de notre temps*, 3 vols., Paris, 1930, 1931, 1800 pp. (Contains massive quotation and paraphrase of von Hügel's letters to L.)

Louis-Lefebvre, M.-Th., *Un Prêtre: L'Abbé Huvelin*, Paris, 1956, 327 pp.

Lubac, Henri de, *The Religion of Teilhard de Chardin*, London, 1967, 380 pp.

Lynch, William F., *Christ and Apollo*, New York, 1960, 267 pp.

McKenzie, John, *Dictionary of the Bible*, Milwaukee, 1965, 954 pp. (With maps.)

——, *The Power and the Wisdom: an Interpretation of the New Testament*, Milwaukee, 1965, 300 pp.

MacPherson, Duncan M., *The Three Elements of Religion: A Study in the Thought of Baron Friedrich von Hügel*, thesis submitted in the University of Birmingham, 1967, 228 pp.

——, 'Baron von Hügel on Celibacy', *Tablet*, 2 August 1969, pp. 757–8.

Macquarrie, John, *Twentieth-Century Religious Thought*, London, 1963, 391 pp.

Marlé, René, *Au Coeur de la Crise Moderniste*, Paris, 1960, 366 pp. (Many letters of von Hügel, Blondel, Loisy, Bremond.)

Mooney, Christopher F., 'Teilhard de Chardin and Christian Spirituality', *Thought*, Autumn 1967, pp. 383–402.

——, *Teilhard de Chardin and the Mystery of Christ*, London, 1966, 288 pp.

Mussner, Franz, 'Historical Jesus and Christ of Faith', *Theology Digest*, Spring 1964, pp. 21–6.

Nédoncelle, Maurice, *God's Encounter with Man: A Contemporary Approach to Prayer*, New York, 1964, 183 pp. (Published in England as *The Nature and Use of Prayer*.)

——, *La Pensée religieuse de Friedrich von Hügel, 1852–1925*, Paris, 1935, 224 pp.; translated as *Baron Friedrich von Hügel: A Study of His Life and Thought*, London, 1937, 213 pp.

——, 'Un texte peu connu de F. von Hügel sur le problème de Dieu', *Revue de sciences religieuses*, April 1962; translated as 'A Recently Discovered Study of von Hügel on God', *International Philosophical Quarterly*, February 1962, pp. 5–24.

Orsy, Ladislas M., *Open to the Spirit*, London, 1958, 286 pp.

Palmer, William S., *The Diary of a Modernist*, London, 1910, 317 pp. (Annotated copy in St Andrews von Hügel Collection.)

Peters, William A. M., *The Spiritual Exercises of St Ignatius: Exposition and Interpretation*, Jersey City, 1968, 204 pp.

Petre, Maude, *Autobiography and Life of George Tyrrell*, 2 vols., London, 1912, 792 pp.

——, 'Friedrich von Hügel, Personal Thoughts and Reminiscences', *Hibbert Journal*, October 1925, pp. 77–87.

——, *Von Hügel and Tyrrell: The Story of a Friendship*, London, 1937, 203 pp. Cited as *VH & T*. (Contains many unpublished letters.)

——, *Alfred Loisy: His Religious Significance*, Cambridge, 1944, 129 pp.

Poulat, Emile, *Histoire, Dogme et Critique dans la Crise Moderniste*, Paris, 1962, 696 pp.

Rahner, Karl, 'Ignatian Mysticism of Joy in the World', in *Theological Investigations*, Vol. III: *Theology of the Spiritual Life*, London, 1967, pp. 277–93.

——, *Spiritual Exercises*, New York, 1965, 287 pp.

——, 'The Human Knowledge and Consciousness of Christ', *Theology Digest*, Spring 1964, pp. 53–5.

——, with Herbert Vorgrimler, *Theological Dictionary*, New York, 1965, 493 pp.

Ramsey, Arthur M., *From Gore to Temple*, London, 1960, 192 pp.

——, *God, Christ and the World*, London, 1969, 125 pp.

Ranchetti, Michele, *The Catholic Modernists: A Study of the Religious Reform Movement, 1863–1911*, London, 1969, 223 pp.

Ratté, John, *Three Modernists: Alfred Loisy, George Tyrrell, William L. Sullivan*, New York, 1967, 370 pp.

Richardson, Herbert W., *Theology for a New World*, London, 1968, 170 pp.

Roustang, François, *Growth in the Spirit: An initiation into the spiritual life on the lines of the Spiritual Exercises*, London, 1966, 250 pp.

Sabatier, Paul, *Les Modernistes*, Paris, 1909; translated as *Modernism*, London, 1908, 351 pp.

Schnackenburg, Rudolf, *God's Rule and Kingdom*, London, 2nd edition, 1968, 400 pp.

Siegmund, Georg, 'The Encounter with Buddhism', *Concilium*, November 1967, pp. 63–9.

Smith, Ronald Gregor, ed., *World Come of Age: A Symposium on Dietrich Bonhoeffer*, London, 1967, 288 pp.

Steinmann, Jean, *Friedrich von Hügel: Sa vie, son oeuvre, et ses amitiés*, Paris, 1962, 581 pp.

Suenens, Léon-Joseph, *Coresponsibility in the Church*, London, 1968, 218 pp.

Teilhard de Chardin, Pierre, *Le Milieu Divin*, Paris, 1957; translated as *Le Milieu Divin*, London, 1960, 144 pp. (Published in U.S.A. as *The Divine Milieu.*)

Thornton, Martin, *The Rock and the River*, London, 1965, 158 pp.

Tillich, Paul, *Perspectives on Nineteenth and Twentieth Century Protestant Theology*, London, 1967, 252 pp.

Trevor, Meriol, *Prophets and Guardians: Renewal and Tradition in the Church*, London, 1969, 221 pp.

Tyrrell, George, *George Tyrrell's Letters*, edited by Maude Petre, London, 1920, 301 pp.

Underhill, Evelyn, *Mixed Pasture: Twelve Essays and Addresses*, London, 1933, 233 pp.

——, *The Letters of Evelyn Underhill*, edited by Charles Williams, London, 1943, 343 pp.

Vanhengel, M. C., with J. Peters, 'Jesus of Nazareth and Christ of Faith', *Concilium*, December 1966, pp. 82–7.

Vidler, Alec R., with Wilfrid L. Knox, *The Development of Modern Catholicism*, London, 1933, 336 pp.

——, *The Modernist Movement in the Roman Church*, Cambridge, 1934, 286 pp.

——, *The Church in an Age of Revolution: 1789 to the Present*, London, 1961, 287 pp.

——, *20th Century Defenders of the Faith*, London, 1965, 127 pp.

Ward, Maisie, *The Wilfrid Wards and the Transition*, London, 1934, 428 pp.

——, *Insurrection Versus Resurrection*, London, 1937, 588 pp. (This and preceding entry contain letters from von Hügel to Wilfrid Ward.)

——, *Unfinished Business*, London, 1964, 374 pp.

Ward, Wilfrid, *William George Ward and the Catholic Revival*, London, 1893, 468 pp.

——, *The Life of John Henry Cardinal Newman*, 2 vols., London, 1912, 1281 pp.

Watkin, E. I., *Philosophy of Mysticism*, London, 1920, 412 pp.

Whelan, Joseph P., 'Huegel, Friedrich von', *Dictionnaire de spiritualité*, Vol. VII, cols. 852–8.

——, 'Prayer and Religion', *The Way*, July 1969, pp. 224–33.

Zaehner, R. C., *Mysticism Sacred and Profane*, Oxford, 1957, 256 pp.

ACKNOWLEDGEMENTS

I wish to thank most sincerely the Reverend Professor E. L. Mascall, who directed the doctoral research on which this study is based for King's College in the University of London. I would also like to thank Thomas Corbishley, S.J., and James Walsh, S.J., for reading the manuscript, and Robert Curry, S.J., and John Polk, S.J., for their immense assistance in reading the page proofs.

Grateful acknowledgement for their help is due also to the librarians and staffs of the Reading Room and the Department of Manuscripts, the British Museum; St Andrews University Library, Scotland; Dr William's Library, Gordon Square, London; the King's College and Senate House Libraries, London University; and the Jesuit Writers' Library, Mount Street, London.

Finally, acknowledgement is made for permission to quote from the following copyright sources: *Baron Friedrich von Hügel: Selected Letters, 1896–1924*, edited and with a memoir by Bernard Holland, published by J. M. Dent, London, and E. P. Dutton & Co., Inc., New York, and used with their permission; *Essays and Addresses on the Philosophy of Religion*, First and Second Series, by Baron Friedrich von Hügel, published by J. M. Dent, London, and E. P. Dutton, New York, 1921 and 1926; *Eternal Life: A Study of its Implications and Applications*, by Baron Friedrich von Hügel, published by T. & T. Clark, Edinburgh, 1912; *The German Soul in its Attitude Towards Ethics and Christianity, the State and War*, by Baron Friedrich von Hügel, published by J. M. Dent, London, and E. P. Dutton, New York, 1916; 'A Letter from Baron von Hügel', in *The Dublin Review*, Second Quarter 1951, Burns Oates, London; *Letters from Baron Friedrich von Hügel to a Niece*, edited and with an introduction by Gwendolen Greene, published by J. M. Dent, London, and E. P. Dutton & Co., Inc., New York, and used with their permission; *The Mystical Element of Religion as Studied in Saint Catherine of Genoa and Her Friends*, Volumes 1 & 2, by Baron Friedrich von Hügel, published by J. M. Dent, London, and E. P. Dutton, New York, 1908, 1923; *The Reality of God and Religion and Agnosticism*, being the literary remains of Baron Friedrich von Hügel, published by J. M. Dent, London, and E. P. Dutton, New York, 1931;

ACKNOWLEDGEMENTS

The Life of Baron von Hügel, by Michael de la Bedoyère, published by J. M. Dent, London, 1951; *Evelyn Underhill*, by Margaret Cropper, published by Longmans, Green, London, 1958; 'Theology in its New Context', by Bernard Lonergan, in *Theology of Renewal*, Volume I, edited by L. K. Shook, published by Palm Publishers, Montreal, 1968; *Baron Friedrich von Hügel: A Study of His Life and Thought*, by Maurice Nédoncelle, published by Longmans, Green, London, 1937; *Alfred Loisy: His Religious Significance*, by Maude Petre, published by Cambridge University Press, Cambridge, 1944; *Von Hügel and Tyrrell: The Story of a Friendship*, by Maude Petre, published by J. M. Dent, London, 1937; *Christian Thought*, by Ernst Troeltsch, published by the University of London Press, London, 1923; *The Wilfred Wards and the Transition*, Volume 1, by Maisie Ward, published by Sheed & Ward, London, 1934.

INDEX